PERSIAN PAINTINGS
in the John Rylands Library

B.W. Robinson MA, B Litt, FSA

PERSIAN PAINTINGS
in the John Rylands Library

A Descriptive Catalogue

Sotheby Parke Bernet

© B. W. Robinson 1980

First published 1980 for
Sotheby Parke Bernet Publications by
Philip Wilson Publishers Ltd
Russell Chambers
Covent Garden
London WC2 8AA

Edition for the USA available from
Sotheby Parke Bernet Publications
c/o Biblio Distribution Centre
81 Adams Drive
Totowa
New Jersey 07512

ISBN 0 85667 072 3

Designed by Pauline Key
Printed in Great Britain by
BAS Printers Limited, Over Wallop, Hampshire,
and bound by the University Press, Cambridge

Preface

This catalogue completes a trilogy which began over twenty years ago with the publication of *A Descriptive Catalogue of the Persian Paintings in the Bodleian Library* (Oxford, 1958), and continued with *Persian Paintings in the India Office Library* (London, 1976). With its publication, all the major public collections of Persian painting in the British Isles are now fully enumerated and described. The Chester Beatty Library in Dublin was covered in three large volumes in 1959-62 under the direction of the late J. V. S. Wilkinson and Professor Arberry, and recently Miss Norah Titley's comprehensive and invaluable catalogue of the holdings of the British Library and the British Museum has put all students of the subject under a very great debt of gratitude to her. The only considerable collection still not covered by a separate publication is that of the Royal Asiatic Society, but its most important manuscripts have been fully published in monographs and articles, and most of the rest have been on public exhibition at one time or another. Much the same might be said of the two or three important manuscripts at Edinburgh University and in the Selly Oak Colleges Library, Birmingham. From the artistic point of view, the Persian manuscripts in Cambridge University Library are not of sufficient number or importance to warrant a separate publication, though there are some interesting volumes in the college libraries and the Fitzwilliam Museum.

I first became aware of the John Rylands Library's collection when I was preparing a small loan exhibition at the Victoria and Albert Museum which was held in the Indian Section in 1951-52; and on my first visit to Manchester I was astonished, not only at its quality and richness, but also at the fact that it seemed to be completely unknown. The Library was at that time debarred by its constitution from lending material to outside exhibitions, so none of its treasures were to be seen outside Manchester until 1967, when the rules were relaxed, and seven of the best volumes were shown in the rather more ambitious loan exhibition of that year at the Victoria and Albert Museum and described in the catalogue (*VAM* 1967, Nos 27, 36, 72, 77, 122, 124, 143). After my first visit, at the request of Professor Robertson, who was then Librarian, I contributed a general description of the miniatures in the collection to the Library's *Bulletin* (*BJRL* xxxiv, pp 69-80). A few years later I wrote an article, also for the *Bulletin*, on the fifth volume of the *Khamsa* of Nawa'i (the other four are in the Bodleian) of 1485, which I was delighted to find in the Library (*BJRL* xxxvii, pp 263-270). Apart from a few mentions in the late Dr Stchoukine's *Les Peintures des Manuscrits*

Timurides, that is the sum of the existing literature on this important body of material; and in completing this catalogue I have realized an ambition of more than twenty-five years' standing.

I must express my warmest gratitude to the staff of the Library for making my spells of work there so pleasant; and more particularly to Dr Taylor, who guided my steps on my first visit, and has been an unfailing source of help and encouragement up to his recent retirement; and to Miss Matheson, his successor in charge of the manuscripts, who has given me a warm welcome and every assistance on my more recent visits. But the catalogue could never have been published without a most generous subvention from the Hakop Kevorkian Fund in New York, for which the most sincere thanks are due both from myself and from the Library. I had the pleasure of knowing Mr Kevorkian, who invited me, as a result of the favourable impression made on him by the little Victoria and Albert exhibition of 1951-52, to catalogue his remarkable collection of oriental manuscripts and miniatures, which were then housed in the basement of the Metropolitan Museum of Art, New York. This was an invaluable experience for which I shall always feel gratitude. I am most grateful also to the British Academy for making a grant towards my expenses incurred in the course of the work. I owe a debt of gratitude to Mrs Josephine Morris who typed the whole thing immaculately from a none-too-easy manuscript. Mr Cary Welch, whose unrivalled expertise in the early Safawid court style is well-known to all students of the subject, has been able to attribute certain miniatures of this type to specific artists. These attributions I was glad to accept and offer him my warmest thanks for his generous help. Last, but not least, I should like to express my deep gratitude and appreciation to my wife Oriel, not only for her skill and patience in carrying out all the necessary photography for the illustrations, but for her constant support – in fact, for just 'being there'. The catalogue is thus a joint effort of ours, and at the same time a celebration of twenty-one years of happy married life.

As in the two previous catalogues already mentioned, my main aim has been usefulness – an aim, which if I may believe a number of friends and correspondents, I was fortunate enough to achieve in them – and I only hope that this 'third and last half of the programme' will be found worthy of its predecessors.

B.W.R. Manchester, 1979

[8]

Contents

Abbreviations

Ars Or	*Ars Orientalis*, the Arts of Islam and the East, Washington (Freer Gallery) and Ann arbor (Univ. of Michigan) 1954-
BJRL	*Bulletin of the John Rylands Library*, Manchester, 1914-
Burlington	*The Burlington Magazine* for Connoisseurs, London, 1903-
BWG	Binyon, Laurence, Wilkinson, J. V. S. and Gray, Basil, *Persian Miniature Painting*. Oxford, 1933.
CB	Wilkinson, J. V. S. and Arberry, A. (ed.), *The Chester Beatty Library: Catalogue of the Persian MSS and Miniatures*, 3 vols. Dublin 1959-62.
Çiğ	Çiğ, Kemal, *Türk ve Islâm Eserleri Müsezi' ndeki Minyatürlü Kitaplarin Kataloğu*, Istanbul, 1959.
Colnaghi 1976	(Robinson, B. W., Falk, Toby and Sims, Eleanor G.), *Persian and Mughal Art*, London (P. & D. Colnaghi & Co. Ltd.), 1976.
Colnaghi 1978	(Falk, Toby, Smart, Ellen S. and Skelton, Robert) *Indian Painting*, London (P. & D. Colnaghi and Co. Ltd.), 1978.
FE	Fraad, Irma L. and Ettinghausen, Richard, 'Sultanate Painting in Persian Style', in *Chhavi*, Benares, 1969.
Jackson & Yohannan	Jackson, A. V. W. and Yohannan, A., *Catalogue of the Persian Manuscripts presented to the Metropolitan Museum of Art . . . by Alexander Smith Cochran*, New York, 1914.
JIS	*Journal of the Iran Society*, London, 1951-
JRAS	*Journal of the Royal Asiatic Society*, London, 1834-
Keir	Robinson, B. W. (ed.), *The Keir Collection: Islamic Painting and the Arts of the Book*, London 1976.
Kühnel	Kühnel, Ernst, *Miniaturmalerei im islamischen Orient*, Berlin, 1922.
Martin	Martin, F. R., *The Miniature Painting and Painters of Persia, India and Turkey*, 2 vols. London, 1912.
Robinson B	Robinson, B. W., *A Descriptive Catalogue of the Persian Paintings in the Bodleian Library*, Oxford, 1958.
Robinson IO	Robinson, B. W., *Persian Paintings in the India Office Library*, London, 1976.
Robinson PD	Robinson, B. W., Persian Drawings (Drawings of the Masters series), New York, 1965.

Spink	*Persian and Islamic Art*, to be exhibited for sale by Spink and Son Ltd. . . . London 1977.
Stchoukine MS	Stchoukine, I., *Les Peintures des Manuscrits Safaris*, Paris 1959.
Stchoukine MT	Stchoukine, I., *Les Peintures des Manuscrits Timurides*, Paris, 1954.
Stchoukine SA	Stchoukine, I., *Les Peintures des Manuscrits de Shah 'Abbas . . .* Paris 1964.
STY	*Sanat Tarihi Yilliği*, periodical of the Institute of Art History, Istanbul University.
Titley	Titley, Norah M., *Miniatures from Persian Manuscripts*. A Catalogue and Subject Index of Paintings . . . in the British Library and the British Museum, London, 1977.
VAM 1951	Robinson, B. W., *Catalogue of a Loan Exhibition of Persian Miniature Paintings from British Collections* (Victoria and Albert Museum) London 1951.
VAM 1952	Robinson, B. W. *Persian Paintings* (Victoria and Albert Museum Picture Book), London, 1952.
VAM 1965	The same, second edition.
VAM 1967	Robinson, B. W., *Persian Miniature Painting from Collections in the British Isles*, London, 1967.
Welch AS	Welch, Anthony, *Artists for the Shah*, Yale University Press, 1976.
Welch KBK	Welch, Stuart Cary, *A King's Book of Kings*, Metropolitan Museum of Art, New York, 1972.
Welch RPM	Welch, Stuart Cary, *Royal Persian Manuscripts*, London, 1976.
W.S.	Written surface.

Introduction

The origins and formation of the Persian collections in the John Rylands Library have been described by Dr Taylor in his article 'The Oriental Manuscript Collections in the John Rylands Library' (*BJRL* liv, pp 1-30), but the basic facts may be repeated here. 'The major part of the Rylands Oriental manuscripts', Dr Taylor writes, 'was acquired in the year after the Library was formally opened, when, in 1901 Mrs Rylands purchased the extensive collection of Eastern and Western manuscripts brought together by the Earls of Crawford and Balcarres'. A general history and account of this remarkable collection will be found in *Bibliotheca Lindesiana*, by Nicolas Barker (London, 1977. Printed for presentation to the Roxburghe Club and published by Bernard Quaritch). A handlist of the Arabic, Persian and Turkish manuscripts by Michael Kerney was published in 1898, and a rather fuller catalogue in manuscript, by the same, with annotations by R. A. Nicholson, is available for consultation in the Library.

The majority of these manuscripts (about two thirds) came from the library of Nathaniel Bland (1803-65), one of the great British orientalists of the nineteenth century. He was of Anglo-Irish descent, and inherited estates in Surrey and Co. Kerry. He went up to Christ Church, Oxford in 1823, took his degree two years later, and from then onwards devoted himself to the study of oriental languages. He was a Fellow of the Royal Asiatic Society, becoming a member of Council and contributing several articles to the *JRAS* between 1843 and 1856.

Several of Bland's manuscripts came from the great French orientalist, Baron Antoine Isaac Sylvestre de Sacy (1758–1838), who became a member of the Académie des Inscriptions in 1785, lay low during the Revolution, but in 1808 was appointed Professor of Persian at the Collège de France. He was later made a Peer of France and Keeper of the oriental manuscripts in the Royal Library, and was a co-founder and first President of the Société Asiatique.

The Library contains one or two manuscripts which can claim other distinguished previous owners. Three of Bland's manuscripts came from the very fine collection made by Sir Gore Ouseley Bt., during his diplomatic mission to the court of Fath'Ali Shah in 1810-12; the great majority of Ouseley's manuscripts eventually found their way to the Bodleian Library via Mr John Bardoe Elliott of the East India Company's Service. Two of the Rylands manuscripts belonged to Turner Macan, the first European editor of the *Shahnama* of Firdawsi (Calcutta, 1829). Another (later acquired by Bland) was the property of William Oliver, a distinguished East India Company servant of strong literary interests, who rose to a place on the Council Board of the Madras Government before his retirement in 1836; he was a Fellow of the Royal Asiatic Society, and died in 1847.

Of other former owners we know practically nothing beyond what they tell us themselves. Two of de Sacy's manuscripts were acquired by a certain Chevalier J. Ferrão de Castello-branco (or Castelbranco), who makes a single appearance in 1847 as a member of the Royal Asiatic Society; they then passed to the Reverend Dr A. Clarke, apparently a friend of Oliver's (see p 237). One of Bland's manuscripts (Ryl Pers 29) was formerly owned by another notable East India Company collector, Edward Galley (c 1750-1804), an account of whom will be found in *JRAS* 1970, p 209, in an article by the present writer on another manuscript of his, the Royal Asiatic Society Qazwini of c 1475. There are a few others: Charles de Ludolf Brousie (1779) and Herbert Lloyd (1781) in the eighteenth century; and in the nineteenth Samuel Robinson of Wilmslow, Mr C. Fox of Bristol (a friend of Dr Clarke), Dr Edward Craven Hawtrey (1832) and a certain Mr Wedderburn. In general it may be said that the majority of the manuscripts have been in Europe for at least 150 years.

Considering that they were collected before Persian miniature paintings were appreciated – or even much noticed – this group of manuscripts provides an excellent representation of the various styles of the Timurid and Safawid periods. Several of them are outstanding in their condition and quality – the Shiraz Nizami of 1445 (p 70), the Turkman 'Assar of c 1490 (p 89), the Herat Nawa'i of 1485 (p 116), the Tabriz *Khusraw and Shirin* of c 1530 (p 148), the Mashhad Jami of 1550 (p 242), the Shiraz Nizami of c 1575 (p 203) and 'Urfi of 1628 (p 226), and the Isfahan Qazwini of 1632 (p 295) are all excellent representatives of their respective styles, and would take a high place in any collection. There are several others which could easily be added to the list.

The collection presents one or two special problems, which will be dealt with as they arise. The most important of these is the question of identifying manuscripts and miniatures originating in pre-Mughal India. The important article by Fraad and Ettinghausen provides a firm base for what had formerly been a vague but growing suspicion. The problem is now to resist the temptation to relegate every recalcitrant Timurid miniature to Sultanate India: firm and definite reasons must be adduced before such an attribution can be accepted.

One may note, in conclusion, that the Library possesses six copies of the *Shahnama* of Firdawsi and three of Qazwini's *'Aja' ib al-Makhluqat*, and that if the miniatures illustrating these be subtracted from the total of 1586, only 148 remain. (The numbering only reaches 1584, but there are three 'a' numbers, 69a, 805a and **1468a**.) There are only three signed works in the collection (Nos **821**, **1581** and **1582**). Transliteration follows *BWG* (Royal Asiatic Society system) but omitting accents and dots except in a few places where their inclusion seemed desirable.

Colour Plates

PLATE I

424 Yusuf sold as a slave. Turkman, *c* 1475

PLATE II

412 Khusraw and Shirin enthroned. Shiraz, 1445

PLATE III

419 Bahram Gur in the Green Pavilion. Shiraz, 1445

PLATE IV

479 Layla and Majnun faint at meeting. Herat, 1485

PLATE V

480 Majnun visited by the camel rider. Herat, 1485

PLATE VI

426 The King visiting the Hermit. Turkman, *c* 1490

PLATE VII

529 Shida slain by Kay Khusraw. Tabriz, *c* 1520-30

PLATE VIII

551 Farhad carries Shirin and her horse. Tabriz, *c* 1530

PLATE IX

552 Khusraw at Shirin's castle. Tabriz, *c* 1530

PLATE X

646 Bahram Gur in the Red Pavilion. Shiraz, *c* 1575

PLATE XI

681 'Aziz at Zulaykha's camp. Mashhad, 1550

PLATE XII

771 Isfandiyar and the Simurgh. Isfahan, c 1590-1600

PLATE XIII

804 Gushtasp slays the rhinoceros. Khurasan, *c* 1580

PLATE XIV

1191 The Great Ocean. Isfahan, 1632

PLATE XV

1581 Shah 'Abbas and the Mughal ambassador. Isfahan, *c* 1650

PLATE XVI

1582 The penitent Magdalene, by 'Ali Quli. Isfahan, *c* 1675

Catalogue

The Timurid Period

The Shiraz Style

This very distinctive school of painting has often been described (e.g. *Robinson B* pp 9-15; *VAM 1967* pp 90, 91) and is now easily recognizable. Shiraz had been the centre of the Muzaffarid style in the late fourteenth century, and at the beginning of the Timurid period Iskandar Sultan was governor; there is reason to believe that more than one of the celebrated manuscripts produced under his patronage (British Library Add.27261, the Gulbenkian *Anthology*, and perhaps British Library Or.2780 and its companion Chester Beatty MS 114) were executed at Shiraz. It is misleading, however, to speak of these as examples of a Shiraz style; it was the court style of the early Timurids, deriving from the Jalayrid school of Baghdad and leading to the Baysunghuri style of Herat. On the fall of Iskandar Sultan in 1414, his painters took service elsewhere – mostly, no doubt, at Herat under Baysunghur Mirza – and Ibrahim Sultan, Baysunghur's brother, became governor of Fars. He was a bibliophile and a noted calligrapher. It appears that, at any rate at first, he found few painters of standing left in Shiraz to work for him. The naïve style of the miniatures in the Berlin *Anthology* of 1420, the earliest illustrated manuscript known to have been commissioned by him (as a present to his brother), is a combination of a latter-day Muzaffarid manner sometimes refined by reminiscences of the work done in the city for Iskandar Sultan. But a few miniatures in that manuscript (e.g. *BWG* pl xxvii B) foreshadow what the Shiraz style was to become in Ibrahim Sultan's later years, when we find it fully developed in his own copy of the *Shahnama* (Bodleian Library Ouseley Add. 176; *Robinson B.* pl 1, IV, etc.). It is a strong, sometimes stark, style, with large figures which are usually confined to those essential to illustrate the incident in question. It is, at this stage, a direct antithesis of the academic refinement of the painting being produced contemporaneously for Baysunghur at Herat. In the 1440s, the period of the John Rylands Qazwini and Nizami manuscripts described below, it was becoming gentler and less violent in its movement and impact, but the bold drawing and broad effects remain. There is evidence of a sly sense of humour. The same style is also found at Yazd (e.g. Topkapi Sarayi R.866), but it seems unnecessary, with Dr Stchoukine, to postulate a separate Yazd style.

It appears almost certain that many Shiraz manuscripts were exported to India and Turkey, and the style was more or less closely imitated in the fifteenth-century paintings of those countries. So far as India is concerned, this question is dealt with on p 95. The Shiraz Timurid style did not long survive the taking of the city by the Turkmans in 1453, appearing in several manuscripts with miniatures of various styles (thought to have been produced for the Black Sheep Turkman princes) down to about 1460, and then vanishing.

Qazwini: 'Aja' ib al-Makhluqat (1-404)
Ryl Pers 37 (ex Bland)
Eighteenth-century oriental (Turkish?) binding of black leather with sunken medallions and pendants coloured with floral designs.

24.8 × 16.5 cm. 295 *ff* (defective beginning and end). Clear *naskhi*, 21 lines to the page. W.S. 18.4 × 10.8 cm. No illuminations or colophon. *c* 1440.

There are 405 miniatures altogether, the majority of

small size, illustrating birds, trees, etc. The painter (or painters) concerned worked very competently in the Shiraz style of the time, many of the miniatures showing great originality, vivid imagination and a sense of humour. He had a particularly strong feeling for animals and birds: his goat (No 316), fox (No 323) and hyena (No 335), though little more than rough sketches, are obviously the result of sympathetic observation, and among the birds, the great crested grebe (No 390) is a small masterpiece. He obviously much enjoyed indulging his fancy with the more mythical beasts and birds, and has produced some very striking dragons and other monsters.

Exhibited: Victoria and Albert Museum, 1967 (*VAM 1967*, 122).

A close parallel to this manuscript is provided by Add.23564 in the British Library, another copy of the same work dated 845/1441 and containing 453 miniatures (*Titley* pp 87-91, MS No 238). This manuscript is complete, and a comparison shows that the missing pages at the beginning and end of the John Rylands copy would probably have contained about twenty-one miniatures, bringing the number to 425. A further eleven or so miniatures would have adorned the replaced folios 49-56, which would make the total about 436. *See Appendix.*

1   *f* 5a A creeping white lizard-like creature called *warak*. 3.8 × 6.3 cm.

2   *f* 5a Only the top 5 mm remains of a miniature that depicted some snake-like creature.

3   *f* 5b Two long-eared men. 6.3 × 6.3 cm.

4   *f* 5b Tiny strip remaining of another miniature – not enough to identify the subject.

5   *f* 6a Winged man addressing two others. 7.6 × 7.6 cm.

6   *f* 6a Top portion only of a miniature representing a two-headed man and another.

7   *f* 6b Elephant-headed man. 6.3 × 5 cm.

8   *f* 6b Winged horse-headed man. 7 × 5 cm.

9   *f* 6b Siamese twins 6.3 × 5.7 cm.

10   *f* 7a Two caterpillars (?).
Defective through rotting green paint. 5.7 × 4.4 cm.

11   *f* 7a Tortoise.
Mostly covered with a paper patch. 4.4 × 4.8 cm.

12   *f* 7a Ibex (?).
Head and forepart covered by marginal restoration. 5.5 cm.

13   *f* 7b A giant with leafy head-dress and green skirt. Rubbed, and a little of it lost by remargination. 16.5 × 6.3 cm.

14   *f* 7b A monkey. A little rubbed. 7 × 6.3 cm.

15   *f* 12b The 'half-man' (*nim-tan*). 7.6 × 3.2 cm.

16   *f* 12b Two-headed man, the heads apparently in disagreement. 9.5 × 5.7 cm.

17   *f* 13a Two-headed man seated. 6.3 × 5 cm.

18   *f* 17a Figure representing the Moon, a golden crescent encircling his head.
Background, plain blue with two gold clouds. 7.6 × 7.6 cm.

19   *f* 20a Bearded man seated writing, representing Mercury. 8.9 × 7 cm. *See illustration.*

20   *f* 20b Girl playing the lute, representing Venus. 8.2 × 8.2 cm.

21   *f* 21a The Lion and Sun (human faced).
Slightly rubbed, and tail and part of hind leg lost through remargination, but a splendid representation. 9.5 × 8.9 cm.
This miniature appears to have been cut out and later replaced.
See illustration.

22   *f* 23a Kneeling warrior (Mars) with drawn sword and severed human head, this latter almost obliterated. 9.5 × 7.6 cm.

23   *f* 23b Jupiter.
A seated, bearded man holding his head and watching an astrolabe suspended between three rods.
Slightly damaged. 8.9 × 8.2 cm.

24   *f* 24a Saturn.
A black-skinned greybeard with six arms, seated like an Indian idol, and holding various objects including a sword, a rosary and a spade.
Slightly damaged. 8.9 × 8.9 cm.

21 The Lion and Sun. Shiraz. *c* 1440

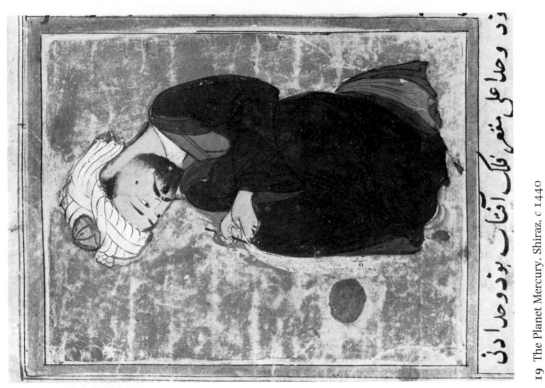

19 The Planet Mercury. Shiraz. *c* 1440

26 The Great Bear. Shiraz, *c* 1440

27 The Dragon constellation. Shiraz, *c* 1440

ميزان خواند وآن دو راكه بربالاى آنست ظليبن كويند كوكبة الدلفين
كوكبة ده است تابع بسرطاير بود وكوكبى نيز كه بردنبال اوست اوراذنب
دلفين خواند ودلفين حيوانيست در
لحرغريق را بربهاند وعرب جهار
كوكب راكه بروسط اوست نعود
خواند وعوام آنرا طبيب كوينند
وازاكه بردنبال است عمود طبيب
كوكبة قطعة الفرس
كواكب اوجهارا است شيع الدلفين

دوازان تضايق اندميان آن مقدار شبرى
بود وميان دوكوكب دكر قدر يك كز وآن
دوكوكب ثك دو فراخ نزد سر
كوكبة فرس الاعظم كواكب
آن بيست است بصورة اسبى واورا دو
دست ون وسر تا آخر پشت واوراكفل
وپايها نيست وآن كوكب كه برسره اوست سلسلة
است كه ياذكرده شود اننا اللهتعالى ودكركوكب كه برپشنن او واخراجناح الفرس
خواند وآن كواكب كه بردوش راست است آنرامنكب الفرس كوينند وازاكه
نزديك كرده دست انراعنق الفرس كوينند وآن كوكب كه براب اوست بس ازان

40, 41 Constellations of the Dolphin and the Half Horse. Shiraz, *c* 1440

62 The East Wind. Shiraz, *c* 1440

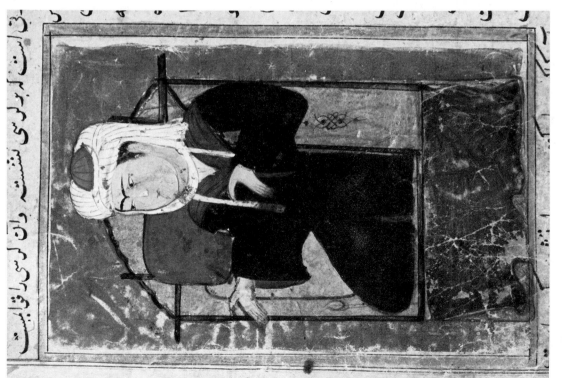

34 The constellation of Cassiopeia. Shiraz, *c* 1440

25 ƒ 26a The constellation of the Bear (Ursa Minor). 6.3 × 7.6 cm.

26 ƒ 26b The Great Bear. 6.3 × 8.2 cm. *See illustration.*

27 ƒ 27a The constellation Draco (*Tinnīn*). 5.7 × 7 cm. *See illustration.*

28 ƒ 27b The constellation Cepheus, shown as a bare-headed man in green, walking with outstretched hand. 9.5 × 6.3 cm.

29 ƒ 28a The constellation Boötes. A bearded man standing with a staff. 8.2 × 5.7 cm.

30 ƒ 28a The Cup (*al-Jathī*). A blue-and-white bowl. Rubbed. 5 × 4.4 cm.

31 ƒ 28b The constellation Lyra. A young man in a brown turban, walking. 8.9 × 5.7 cm.

32 ƒ 28b An astronomical figure of a crested bird. 5 × 5 cm.

33 ƒ 28b The constellation Cygnus. A spread-eagled bird. 5.7 × 5.7 cm.

34 ƒ 29a The constellation Cassiopeia (*Dhāt al-Kursī*), shown as a young man seated on a chair or throne. 12.1 × 8.2 cm. *See illustration.*

35 ƒ 29b The constellation of Perseus. A young man with a severed demon's head. Rubbed. 8.9 × 4.4 cm.

36 ƒ 29b The constellation Ophiuchus. A young man holding a serpent. Rubbed. 7 × 4.4 cm.

37 ƒ 30a The constellation Ophiuchus (again). A bare-headed young man holding a serpent with a head at either end. 7.6 × 5 cm.

38 ƒ 30a The arrow. Roughly drawn on thin gold background: possibly a later addition. 4.4 × 3.2 cm.

39 ƒ 30a The Eagle. 5 × 5.7 cm.

40 ƒ 30b The Dolphin.

A curious fork-tailed, lion-headed, winged fish. 5.7 × 5.7 cm. *See illustration.*

41 ƒ 30b The Horse's Head (*Qit'a al-Faras*). 5.7 × 4.4 cm. *See illustration.*

42 ƒ 31a Pegasus (*Faras al' Azam*). Forepart only, with wings. 8.2 × 7.6 cm.

43 ƒ 31a Andromeda. A kneeling youth with outstretched arms. 7.6 × 7 cm.

44 ƒ 31b The Ram (no horns). 5.7 × 5 cm.

45 ƒ 32a The Bull. 7.6 × 6.3 cm.

46 ƒ 32b The Twins, their lower parts joined and holding a sort of golden staff between them. 7 × 5.7 cm.

47 ƒ 32b The Crab, fat and round with small legs. Rubbed. 5 × 5 cm.

48 ƒ 33a The Lion. 7 × 10.8 cm.

49 ƒ 33a The Virgin. A dark-skinned youth with corn. Rubbed. 7.6 × 5 cm.

50 ƒ 33b The Scales. A crowned youth kneeling and holding a balance above his head. 6.3 × 7 cm.

51 ƒ 33b The Scorpion. Rubbed. 4.4 × 5 cm.

52 ƒ 34a The Archer. A bearded centaur-like figure in a helmet aiming an arrow at the dragon-head that terminates his tail. 8.9 × 7 cm.

53 ƒ 34b The Goat (ibex type). 5.7 × 6.3 cm.

54 ƒ 34b The Water-carrier. Pulling on a rope going into a well-head. Rubbed. 9.5 × 7.6 cm.

55 ƒ 35a The Fishes. A bare-headed youth holding a large fish by the tail, while the latter bites his foot. Rubbed. 7 × 5 cm.

56 ƒ 35a Cetus. The forepart of a winged lion-like monster. Rubbed. 5.7 × 5 cm.

الیازی رحمة الله علیه ابن جزیره رامکلیست نام او مهاج وجنا

خماج اوهسروبرد ویست من زراست بن سشصد درهم   ازان

درخشتها سازند و دراب اندازند بیت المال اوجراست قال ابن

الفقیه برس جدیره قوی هستند

صورة ایشان همچون صورة

ادمی است واخلاق ایشان

جون اخلاق وحوش وکلام

ایشان فهم نتوان کرد واز

درخت بدبخت جهنده

وانجا نوعی هست   از

سناپس وان کرکانرا برا

جون بخفاش ازبن کوش

تا اصل دنب ودرین جزیس نوعی هست ازبر

کوهی بزرک بعضه کودن رنک آن بزان سرخ بود بنقطها سپید ود بال

65 On an island in the China Sea. Shiraz, *c* 1440

57 ƒ 37a The Centaur.
The human part that of a young man in a skull-cap.
7 × 7 cm.

(ff 49-58 inclusive are replacements. The originals no doubt included miniatures of angels: cf. *Titley*, p 87, Nos 39-43. On ƒ 55a is a square divided into 49 smaller squares)

58 ƒ 65a The Moon with a halo. 5 × 5 cm.

59 ƒ 65b The Rainbow, supported by an angel in the middle. Angel's face rubbed. 4.4 × 7 cm.

60 ƒ 67a The North wind.
A human-headed golden cloud. Green background.
6.3 × 5 cm.

61 ƒ 67b The South wind.
As above, slight flaking. 7 × 5 cm.

62 ƒ 68a The East wind.
As above. 7 × 5.7 cm. *See illustration.*

63 ƒ 68a The West wind.
As above, flaking on face. 7.6 × 5 cm.

64 ƒ 68b Thundercloud, represented as the winds.
7 × 5 cm.

65 ƒ 75b Islands in the Sea of Sin (China Sea).
An inhabitant of Java by a tree, and a small winged feline quadruped. 11.4 × 10.8 cm. *See illustration.*

66 ƒ 76a Dragon swallowing an ox, watched by monkeys on a mass of rock. 11.4 × 10.8 cm. *See illustration.*

67 ƒ 76b Native watching four parrots in a tree.
Rubbed. 7.6 × 8.2 cm. *See illustration.*

68 ƒ 77a Naked inhabitants of Sumatra with hairy shoulders climbing a fruit tree. 14.6 × 5.7 cm. *See illustration.*

69 ƒ 77b Fork-tailed fish with tusks. 5.7 × 5 cm.

69a ƒ 77b Crab. 4.4 × 4.4 cm.

70 ƒ 78a Three naked natives by a rock.
This miniature has been cut out and later replaced.
8.9 × 7.6 cm.

71 ƒ 80a Mauve fish with beaked head. 5 × 6.3 cm.

72 ƒ 81a The Burnt Island in the Sea of Zanj.
Dwarf prince and two courtiers conversing with a large man, the latter rubbed and discoloured and the face retouched. 8.2 × 8.9 cm.

73 ƒ 82a The Old Man of the Sea riding his victim.
12.7 × 5.7 cm. *See illustration.*

74 ƒ 82b Fish with long curved horn on its forehead and spikes along its spine. 6.3 × 5.7 cm.

75 ƒ 83b The Western Sea.
The figure on the watch-tower pointing over the sea: two elegant fish swim below the tower.
20.9 × 10.8 cm. *See illustration.*

76 ƒ 84a Two naked natives, one bearded.
7.6 × 7 cm.

77 ƒ 84a Two natives with faces in their chests.
Rubbed. 7.6 × 5.7 cm.

78 ƒ 84b Unicorn with a bushy tail. 5.7 × 6.3 cm.

79 ƒ 85a Fork-tailed fish with human head covered with spots. 4.4 × 5.7 cm.

80 ƒ 85a Two mauve fork-tailed fish. 3.2 × 5.7 cm.

81 ƒ 85b 'Cow-fish'.
A fork-tailed fish with horn, describing a circle.
5.7 × 5 cm. *See illustration.*

82 ƒ 90a The Red Sea.
A spotted sea-snake. 7 × 5 cm.

83 ƒ 90b A hairy frog-shaped creature with white-bearded human head, in the water. 5.7 × 6.3 cm.

84 ƒ 92b The Caspian Sea.
Young man emerging from the head of a large fork-tailed fish. 12.1 × 10.8 cm. *See illustration.*

85 ƒ 93b Large, mauve, horned and bearded demon standing in the water near the shore. 17.8 × 10.8 cm.
See illustration.

86 ƒ 94a A fork-tailed fish with rabbit's head.
5 × 5.7 cm.

67 Islander watching parrots. Shiraz, *c* 1440

66 The dragon of the island of Ranj. Shiraz, *c* 1440

73 The Old Man of the Sea riding a victim. Shiraz, c 1440

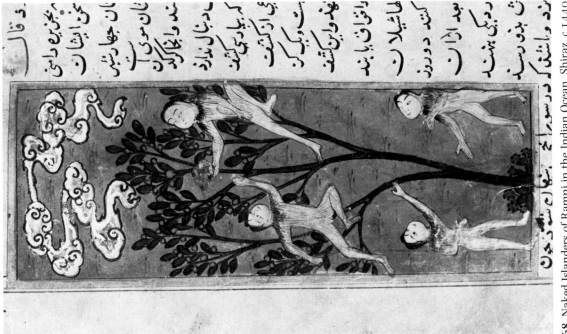

68 Naked Islanders of Ramni in the Indian Ocean. Shiraz, c 1440

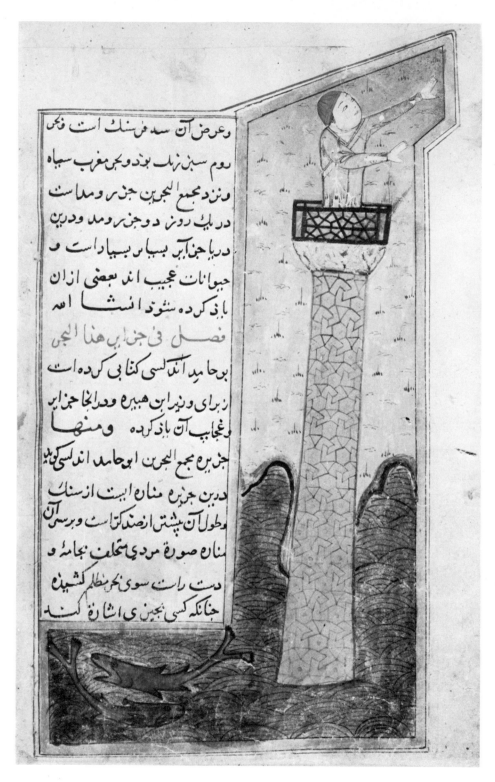

75 The tower in the Western Sea. Shiraz, *c* 1440

حكایت در جنبد کا... در بخشی باطنانلسی آردءو در دلان تابکک در جنه کا با خدا است ان بهرورین حسین و صفا البشین... ان... ی الجکی سدوجخن در رنگی غذ

84 Phenomenon in the Caspian Sea. Shiraz, c 1440

81 'Cow-fish' of the Western Sea. Shiraz, c 1440

85 A sea-demon, Shiraz, c 1440

88 The amber-producing marine cow. Shiraz, *c* 1440

89 Dragon substituting for crocodile. Shiraz, *c* 1440

87 ƒ94b Two naked girls with tails standing in the sea. 6.3 × 5.7 cm.

88 ƒ95a Sea cow.
A splendid blue beast formed like a humped ox with flaming eyes and wings, green horns, and a bushy tail. Background a bit rubbed. 7.6 × 7.6 cm. *See illustration.*

89 ƒ95b *Timsāh* (the crocodile).
A large horned dragon swimming in the sea. 6.3 × 10.8 cm. *See illustration.*

90 ƒ96b The dragon *tinnīn.*
A fantastic blue beast with head like a horned phoenix and tentacles terminating in dragons' heads. 11.4 × 11.4 cm. *See illustration.*

91 ƒ97a An eel-like creature (*jalkā*). 5 × 3.8 cm.

92 ƒ98b The octopus (*sarṭān al-bahr*), pink, with leonine head and fore-paws, the hinder part dividing into five tails. 6.3 × 8.2 cm. *See illustration.*

93 ƒ99a A newt or crocodile-spawn (*saqanqūr*), shown as a mauve lizard-like creature. 4.4 × 6.3 cm.

94 ƒ100b A frog. 4.4 × 4.4 cm.

95 ƒ101b The sea-horse.
Only the head appears above the water, though the original drawing was of the whole animal. 5.7 × 7.6 cm.

96 ƒ101b A small fox-like creature (*qistā*). 4.4 × 6.3 cm.

97 ƒ102a A fork-tailed fish with a kind of plume rising from its head. 5 × 5.7 cm.

98 ƒ102a A horned fish called *qūqī* (beaver). 3.8 × 5 cm.

99 ƒ102b A wild dog. 5 × 7 cm.

100 ƒƒ105b, 106a Map of the World.
Circular, the corners blue with gold clouds, surrounded by the Ocean. India is lower left (ƒ106a), divided from Sistan and Fars on the right by the Jihun (Oxus); to the right again are the Aral and Caspian Seas, and above, the Persian Gulf containing the two circular islands of Wak and Kharak. Beyond them is Zanzibar and the Land of Darkness (*Zulmat*), a blackened arc, top left. At the bottom right (ƒ105b) is

Andalus and the Mediterranean with three circular islands, from which the Nile ascends in a straight line, with the Sahara on the extreme right. The names of the islands are illegible, but are presumably Sicily, Crete and Cyprus. Rubbed. 22.8 × 24.1 cm.

101 ƒ109a The Mountain of Ranis, with a stream issuing from a domed building among rocks.
A small miniature cut from the lower left-hand corner. 7.6 × 7.6 cm.

102 ƒ109b Farhad's sculpture on Mount Bisutun.
A crowned figure (Khusraw) between two others (Farhad and Shirin). A small portion cut away at the bottom with the miniature on the recto, and a strip of white paper repairing the horizon. 9.5 × 10.8 cm.

103 ƒ116a The Mountain of Turquoise (*Firūzaj*).
Dog tethered to a plant growing in small human forms. 7 × 7.6 cm.

104 ƒ117b The Fountain of Two Lions on Mount Maqās.
Some flaking. 7.6 × 8.2 cm.

105 ƒ118a The petrified shepherd, his flock, milk-maid and dog, on Mount Yala Yasham, near Qazwin. 8.9 × 10.8 cm. *See illustration.*

106 ƒ131a Rustam rescuing Bizhan from the pit of Buqir.
Badly rubbed and discoloured along the outside edge which extends into the margin and contains what is left of the figures of Bizhan and Manizha: Rustam's face also somewhat rubbed. 16.5 × 10.8 cm. *See illustration.*

107 ƒ162a The ebony tree 6.3 × 6.3 cm.

108 ƒ162a The myrtle. 5.7 × 5 cm.

109 ƒ162b The orange tree (*turunj*). 5 × 6.3 cm. Cf. No **165**.

110 ƒ163a The plum tree. 7.6 × 5 cm.

111 ƒ163a The 'free tree' (*āzād dirakht*) of Georgia. 7 × 5.7 cm.

112 ƒ163b The Egyptian thorn (*amughailan*). 7 × 5 cm. Cf. No **135**.

113 ƒ163b The mysobalan tree. 7 × 5 cm.

92 The genial octopus. Shiraz, *c* 1440

90 The great dragon *tinnin*. Shiraz, *c* 1440

105 The petrified shepherd and his flock. Shiraz, *c* 1440

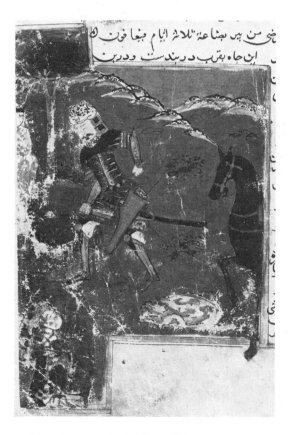

106 Rustam rescuing Bizhan. Shiraz, *c* 1440

[52]

135, 136, 137 A page of trees. Shiraz, *c* 1440

114 *f* 164a The turpentine tree. 7.6 × 5.7 cm.

115 *f* 164a The balsam tree. 6.3 × 4.4 cm.

116 *f* 164b The oak (or chestnut) tree. 8.2 × 5 cm.

117 *f* 165a The apple tree with rabbits and rocks. 7.6 × 7.5 cm.

118 *f* 165a The mulberry tree. 7 × 5 cm.

119 *f* 165b A kind of fir tree (*tanūb*), (but no resemblance to a conifer). 8.2 × 6.3 cm.

120 *f* 166a The fig tree. 8.2 × 6.3 cm.

121 *f* 166b The wild fig. 7.6 × 7.6 cm.

122 *f* 167a The nut tree with rock and fawns. 9.5 × 7 cm.

123 *f* 167b Galangale. 8.9 × 6.3 cm.

124 *f* 167b Palma Christi. 5 × 5 cm.

125 *f* 168a The willow. 8.2 × 6.3 cm.

126 *f* 168a The peach tree. 7 × 5.7 cm.

127 *f* 168b The spikenard tree. 8.9 × 5 cm.

128 *f* 168b The elm. 9.5 × 5 cm.
The miniature of the plane tree (*dulb*) on *f* 169a has been cut out and the folio patched with plain paper.

129 *f* 169b The laurel.
Only the upper portion remains, due to the extraction of the miniature on the recto. 3.8 × 5.7 cm.

130 *f* 170a The pomegranate. 8.9 × 6.3 cm.

131 *f* 171a The olive tree, apparently of two kinds. 10.2 × 6.3 cm.

132 *f* 171b The cypress: two are shown. 11.4 × 4.4 cm.

133 *f* 172a The quince tree. 8.2 × 5.7 cm.

134 *f* 172a The sumach tree. 8.9 × 5.7 cm.

135 *f* 172b The Egyptian thorn (*samurat* – cf. No 112). 10.2 × 6.3 cm. *See illustration.*

136 *f* 172b The cherry tree. 6.3 × 5 cm.
See illustration.

137 *f* 172b The chestnut. 8.9 × 6.3 cm.
See illustration.

138 *f* 173a The sandalwood tree. 7.6 × 7 cm.

139 *f* 173a The fir-tree. 10.8 × 5.7 cm.

140 *f* 173b Unidentified: red leaves. Slightly smudged. 7.6 × 6.3 cm.

141 *f* 173b The tamarisk. 5.7 × 5.7 cm.

142 *f* 174a The juniper or cypress. 8.2 × 4.4 cm.

143 *f* 174a Unidentified: the Tree of Life (?). (Cf. *Titley*, p 88, No 121). Fruit tree with a man, partly visible, looking at it. 7.6 × 8.9 cm.

144 *f* 174b The gall tree. 7.6 × 5.7 cm.

145 *f* 174b The jujube tree. 10.2 × 6.3 cm.

146 *f* 175a The aloes tree. 7 × 5.7 cm.

147 *f* 175a The *ghabrā'* tree. 10.2 × 5.7 cm.

148 *f* 175b The *gharb* tree, common in Hijaz. 13.3 × 5.7 cm.

149 *f* 175b The *fāwaniyā* tree. 8.2 × 5 cm.

150 *f* 176a The pistachio tree. 7.6 × 5.7 cm.

151 *f* 176a The pepper tree. 7.6 × 5.7 cm.

152 *f* 176b The filbert tree. 9.5 × 5.7 cm.

153 *f* 177a The box-thorn tree. 7.6 × 5.7 cm.

154 *f* 177a The clove tree. 8.9 × 5 cm.

155 *f* 177b Reeds. 7 × 7.6 cm. *See illustration.*

156 *f* 178a The camphor tree. 8.9 × 7 cm.

157 *f* 178b The vine. 8.9 × 9.5 cm.

158 *f* 180a Unidentified, named *kamshiri* or *kamthiri*. 7.6 × 6.3 cm.

155 Reeds growing by a rock.
Shiraz, *c* 1440

159 *f* 180a Unidentified, named *lāghiya*. 5.7 × 5 cm.

160 *f* 180b The gum tree. 5.7 × 5 cm.

161 *f* 180b The almond tree. 9.5 × 5 cm.

162 *f* 181a The lemon tree. 8.2 × 6.3 cm.

163 *f* 182a The apricot tree. 7.6 × 6.3 cm.

164 *f* 182b The banana tree. 7.6 × 8.2 cm.

165 *f* 182b The orange tree (*nāranj*). 7 × 6.3 cm. Cf. No **109**.

166 *f* 183a The cocoanut palm. 12.1 × 5.7 cm.

167 *f* 183a The lote tree. 7.6 × 5 cm.

168 *f* 184a The palm tree. 11.4 × 5 cm.

169 *f* 184b The rose tree. 6.3 × 7.6 cm.

170 *f* 185a Jasmine. 7.6 × 7.6 cm.

171 *f* 185b 'Mouse's ear' (*uzn al-fār*). 4.4 × 5.7 cm.

172 *f* 186a Camomile. 3.8 × 3.8 cm.

173 *f* 186a Bog-rush. 4.4 × 3.8 cm.

174 *f* 186a Rice. 3.8 × 4.4 cm.

175 *f* 186a Spinach. 3.2 × 5.7 cm.

176 *f* 186b Wild onion. 4.4 × 4.4 cm.

177 *f* 186b Assafoetida. 4.4 × 4.4 cm.

178 *f* 186b Hyssop. 4.4 × 4.4 cm.

179 *f* 187a Unidentified (*afsitin*). 4.4 × 4.4 cm.

180 *f* 187a Camomile (*aqjuwān* – sic, for *aqhawān*). 4.4 × 4.4 cm. Cf. No **182**.

181 *f* 187a Dodder. 4.4 × 4.4 cm.

182 *f* 187b Camomile (*bābunaj*). 3.8 × 4.4 cm. Cf. No **180**.

183 ƒ187b Unidentified. (*bādrūn*). 4.4 × 4.4 cm.

184 ƒ187b Unidentified (*bādranjūma*). 4.4 × 6.3 cm.

185 ƒ188a Egg-plant (*bādinjān*). 5 × 5 cm.

186 ƒ188a Egg-plant (*bādinjān*). 4.4 × 5 cm.
Cf. No **284**.

187 ƒ188b Beans. 5 × 5 cm.

188 ƒ188b Maiden-hair. 4.4 × 4.4 cm.

189 ƒ189a Mugwort. 4.4 × 5 cm.

190 ƒ189a Onions. 3.8 × 5 cm.

191 ƒ189b Melons. 4.4 × 5 cm.

192 ƒ190a Garlic (*balbūs*). 3.8 × 5.7 cm. Cf. No **198**.

193 ƒ190b Violet. 4.4 × 4.4 cm.

194 ƒ190b Unidentified (*būdālnas*). 3.2 × 5.7 cm.

195 ƒ190b Ox-eye. 3.8 × 5 cm.

196 ƒ191a Dwarf palm. 4.4 × 4.4 cm.

197 ƒ191a Egyptian bean. 3.8 × 5 cm.

198 ƒ191b Garlic (*thūm*). 4.4 × 5.7 cm. Cf. No **192**.

199 ƒ192a Millet. 3.8 × 5 cm.

200 ƒ192a Watercress. 3.2 × 5 cm.

201 ƒ192b Carrots. 3.8 × 5 cm.

202 ƒ192b Unidentified (*jāj*). 4.4 × 5 cm.

203 ƒ193a Purslain. 2.5 × 5 cm.

204 ƒ193a Unidentified (*khurshaf*). 3.8 × 5 cm.

205 ƒ193a Wild rue (*ḥarmal*). 3.2 × 3.2 cm.
Cf. No **207**.

206 ƒ193b Bastard saffron. 3.2 × 5 cm.

207 ƒ193b Wild rue (*ḥarmal*). 3.2 × 4.4 cm.
Cf. No **205**.

208 ƒ193b Saffron (*ḥuṣṣ*). 2.5 × 4.4 cm. Cf. No **230**.

209 ƒ194a Unidentified (*jandqūqī*). 3.2 × 4.4 cm.

210 ƒ194a Wild gourd. 5 × 5 cm.

211 ƒ194b Wheat (*hinṭat*).
But wheat is obviously illustrated by the next miniature: there must have been some slight confusion – cf.
the two *harmals* above. 4.5 × 4 cm.

212 ƒ195a Wheat (*hinṭat*). 4.4 × 4.4 cm.

213 ƒ195a Unidentified (*khānaq al-sanim*).
3.8 × 3.8 cm.

214 ƒ195a House-leek. 3.8 × 4.4 cm.

215 ƒ196b Mallows. 3.8 × 3.8 cm.

216 ƒ195b Hellebore. 3.8 × 5 cm.

217 ƒ196a Mustard. 5 × 3.8 cm.

218 ƒ196b Lettuce. 3.2 × 4.4 cm.

219 ƒ196b Poppy. 3.8 × 3.8 cm.

220 ƒ197a Unidentified (*khaṣī al-taʻ lab*).
3.2 × 3.8 cm.

221 ƒ197a Unidentified (*khaṣī al-kalb*).
3.2 × 4.4 cm.

222 ƒ197a Marshmallows. 3.8 × 5 cm.

223 ƒ197b Red bramble. 3.8 × 3.8 cm.

224 ƒ197b Cucumbers.

225 ƒ198a Mallows. 2.5 × 3.8 cm.

226 ƒ198a Unidentified (*dilfī*). 3.2 × 5 cm.

227 ƒ198b Fennel. 3.8 × 3.8 cm.

228 ƒ199a Sorrel. 3.2 × 4.4 cm.

229 ƒ199a Sweet basil. 3.2 × 5 cm.

230 ƒ199b Saffron (*zaʻfarān*). 5 × 5 cm. Cf. No **208**.

231 ƒ200a Indian spikenard. 3.2 × 3.8 cm.

232 ƒ 200b Rue. 2.5 × 6.3 cm.

233 ƒ 200b Beetroot. 3.8 × 3.8 cm.

234 ƒ 200b Sesame. 3.8 × 5 cm.

235 ƒ 201a Hyacinth. 2.5 × 5 cm.

236 ƒ 201a Iris. 3.8 × 5 cm.

237 ƒ 201b Wild thyme. 3.8 × 5 cm.

238 ƒ 201b Fumitory. 2.5 × 3.2 cm.

239 ƒ 201b Dill. 3.8 × 4.4 cm.

240 ƒ 202a Spurge. 3.8 × 4.4 cm.

241 ƒ 202a Sowbread. 3.8 × 5 cm.

242 ƒ 202a Barley. 5.7 × 3.8 cm.

243 ƒ 202b Anemone. 4.4 × 3.8 cm.

244 ƒ 202b Turnip. 3.2 × 4.4 cm.

245 ƒ 203a Bugloss (*shinjār*). 4.4 × 4.4 cm.
Cf. No **271**.

246 ƒ 203a Hemlock. 4.4 × 4.4 cm.

247 ƒ 203b Coriander (*shūnīz*). 3.2 × 4.4 cm.
Cf. No **277**.

248 ƒ 203b Unidentified (*shaykh*). 4.4 × 5 cm.

249 ƒ 203b Darnel. 3.8 × 5 cm.

250 ƒ 204a Savory. 4.4 × 4.4 cm.

251 ƒ 204a Tarragon. 3.2 × 4.4 cm.

252 ƒ 204a Basil (appears to be ʿ*ashīrān* or ʿ*anthīrān*: perhaps ʿ*īzrān*, medlar?). 3.2 × 5 cm.

253 ƒ 204b Lentils. 3.2 × 4.4 cm.

254 ƒ 204b Indigo. 3.8 × 4.4 cm.

255 ƒ 204b Nightshade. 3.2 × 4.4 cm.

256 ƒ 205a Radish. 4.4 × 5 cm.

257 ƒ 205b Purslain *farqaj?* 3.8 × 5 cm. Cf. No **291**.

258 ƒ 206a Cinquefoil. 3.8 × 5 cm.

259 ƒ 206a Mint. 3.2 × 5 cm.

260 ƒ 206b Wolf's-bane. 3.2 × 4.4 cm.

261 ƒ 206b Dog's-bane. 4.4 × 5 cm.

262 ƒ 206b Tragacanth. 3.8 × 5 cm.

263 ƒ 206b Clover. 3.2 × 5 cm.

264 ƒ 207a Cucumber. 4.4 × 5 cm.

265 ƒ 207b Safflower. 4.4 × 4.4 cm.

266 ƒ 207b Cotton. 3.8 × 4.4 cm.

267 ƒ 207b Wild cucumber. 3.8 × 5 cm.

268 ƒ 208a Hemp. 4.4 × 4.4 cm.

269 ƒ 208b Cauliflower (*qanpaṭ*). 3.8 × 5 cm.

270 ƒ 208b Southernwood. 3.8 × 5 cm.

271 ƒ 209a Bugloss (*gāw-zabān*, ex-tongue). 4.4 × 4.4 cm. Cf. No **245**.

272 ƒ 209a Flax. 4.4 × 5 cm.

273 ƒ 209a Unidentified (*qanpaṭ* – again!). (MS 3 here has *karāth*, leek). 3.2 × 4.4 cm.

274 ƒ 209b Pulse (*karsata* for *karsana*). 4.4 × 4.4 cm.

275 ƒ 209b Parsley. 3.8 × 4.4 cm.

276 ƒ 210a Carroway. 3.8 × 5 cm.

277 ƒ 210a Coriander (*kishnīz*). 3.8 × 4.4 cm.
Cf. No **247**.

278 ƒ 210b Unidentified (*kulū-i asr*). 3.8 × 5 cm.

279 ƒ 210b Cummin. 3.8 × 4.4 cm.

280 ƒ 211a Truffle. 3.8 × 4.4 cm.

281 ƒ 211a Bindweed. 3.8 × 4.4 cm.

282 *f* 211b Plantain. 3.2 × 4.4 cm.

283 *f* 211b Capers. 4.4 × 4.4 cm.

284 *f* 212a Egg-plant (*luffāh*). 3.8 × 4.4 cm.
Cf. No **186**.

285 *f* 212a Pulse. 4.4 × 4.4 cm.

286 *f* 212a Dragon-wort. 3.8 × 4.4 cm.

287 *f* 212b Water-lily. 4.4 × 5 cm.

288 *f* 212b Spurge olive. 3.8 × 4.4 cm.

289 *f* 213a Cherry. 3.8 × 4.4 cm.

290 *f* 213b Long mullein. 3.8 × 4.4 cm.

291 *f* 213b Purslain (*marzangūsh*). 3.8 × 4.4 cm.
Cf. No **257**.

292 *f* 214a Spikenard. 3.8 × 4.4 cm.

293 *f* 214a Aniseed. 4.4 × 5 cm.

294 *f* 214b Narcissus. 3.8 × 5 cm.

295 *f* 214b Dog-rose. 3.8 × 4.4 cm.

296 *f* 215a Mint. 3.8 × 5 cm.

297 *f* 215a Wild cypress. 3.8 × 5 cm.

298 *f* 215a Unidentified (*wasūn*). 3.2 × 5 cm.

299 *f* 215b Asparagus. 3.8 × 4.4 cm.

300 *f* 215b Endive. 3.2 × 5 cm.

301 *f* 216a Gourd. 5.7 × 5.7 cm.

302 *f* 237a A pair of camel-headed *jinn*. 8.9 × 5 cm.

303 *f* 237b Two men, one seated half-naked, by a curious plant. 6.3 × 6.3 cm.

304 *f* 238a Bare-headed youth riding an ostrich (head lost through remargination), watched by another.
Slight flaking. 10.2 × 7.6 cm.

305 *f* 239a Solomon (?) in a golden cloud, pointing to a red flower. Two young spectators cover their eyes and nose respectively. 7.6 × 7.6 cm.

309 The wild ass. Shiraz, *c* 1440

306   ƒ 242a   The horse.
A bit smudged. 7.6 × 8.9 cm.

307   ƒ 243a   The mule. 7 × 7 cm.

308   ƒ   ƒ 244a   The ass. 6.3 × 7 cm.

309   ƒ 245a   The wild ass. 7 × 8.9 cm. *See illustration.*

310   ƒ 246a   The camel. 7.6 × 7.6 cm. *See illustration.*

311   ƒ 247b   The ox, humped and wearing a green coat. 6.3 × 8.2 cm.

312   ƒ 248a   The stag. 7 × 8.2 cm.

313   ƒ 248b   The buffalo. 7 × 8.9 cm. *See illustration.*

314   ƒ 294a   The giraffe (very small head with single horn). 8.2 × 7.6 cm.

315   ƒ 249b   The sheep.
Slight flaking. 4.4 × 5.7 cm.

316   ƒ 250b   The goat. 5 × 5 cm. *See illustration.*

317   ƒ 251b   The antelope (*ẓabī*) by a rock. 5 × 5.7 cm.

318   ƒ 253a   A small dog-like creature (*ibn awī*). 4.4 × 5 cm.

319   ƒ 253b   A jackal (?) (*ibn ghars*). 3.2 × 5.3 cm.

320   ƒ 254a   Two hares running 3.2 × 4.4 cm. *See illustration.*

321   ƒ 255a   The lion. 5 × 9.5 cm. *See illustration.*

322   ƒ 256b   A pair of tigers, with green streamers and bushy tails, derived from Chinese art. 6.3 × 8.9 cm. *See illustration.*

323   ƒ 257a   The fox. 3.2 × 5 cm. *See illustration.*

324   ƒ 257b   A deer-like creature, with a single, slender, curved horn.
It illustrates the rhinoceros (*harish*). 7.6 × 4.4 cm.

325   ƒ 258b   The wild boar. 3.8 × 7 cm.

326   ƒ 259b   The bear. 5 × 7 cm.

327   ƒ 260a   The hay-weasel (*dalaq*). 3.2 × 6.3 cm.

328   ƒ 261a   The wolf (more like a dog). 4.4 × 5.7 cm.

329   ƒ 261b   The elephant giving birth. 5 × 9.5 cm.

330   ƒ 262a   The ermine (*sanjāb*). 2.5 × 5.7 cm.

331   ƒ 262b   The cat. 3.2 × 3.8 cm.

332   ƒ 262b   The wild cat. 3.8 × 4.4 cm.

333   ƒ 263a   *Sarānash.* (*Titley* gives the reading *shir-i-uns*: cf. also No **1402**.)
A bear-shaped beast with a single fungoid horn, flaming red eyes, and a green mane and snout. 5.7 × 7.6 cm. *See illustration.*

334   ƒ 263b   *Shādawār.*
A happy-looking, blue, bear-shaped beast with a single, curved horn on top of his head, by means of which he makes sweet music. 6.3 × 6.3 cm. *See illustration.*

335   ƒ 264a   The hyena. 4.4 × 6.3 cm.

336   ƒ 264b   The lynx (*'anāq*: this word also means a female kid; the artist was not quite certain what he was depicting). 4.4 × 5.7 cm.

337   ƒ 265a   The cheetah. 4.4 × 5.7 cm.

338   ƒ 265b   The elephant ridden by a young Indian mahout. 9.5 × 11.4 cm. *See illustration.*

339   ƒ 266b   The monkey. 2.5 × 4.4 cm.

340   ƒ 267b   The rhinoceros (*karkadann*), represented as the forepart of a large humped ox with a fungoid horn on his nose, by some rocks and a tree. 8.9 × 7.6 cm.

341   ƒ 268b   The dog. 3.8 × 5.7 cm.

342   ƒ 269b   The leopard. 5.7 × 7.6 cm.

343   ƒ 270a   The *nāmūr.*
A stag-like creature with horns like large-toothed saws. 5.7 × 6.3 cm.

344   ƒ 270b   The crane (? *abū-Harūn*). 5 × 5 cm.

310 The camel. Shiraz, *c* 1440

313 The buffalo. Shiraz, *c* 1440

كاو پا بيرند و دركوش جكاتند

كند لجيه التيس بصاحب ث

316 The goat. Shiraz, *c* 1440

320 Hares running. Shiraz, *c* 1440

321 The lion. Shiraz, *c* 1440

322 Pair of tigers. Shiraz, *c* 1440

323 The fox. Shiraz, *c* 1440

333 The beast called *sarānash*, that lives near Kabul. Shiraz, *c* 1440

عان وكويند كه كفتار بله سال نر بود

334 The *shādawār* that makes sweet music. Shiraz, *c* 1440

335 The hyena. Shiraz, *c* 1440

338 The elephant and his mahout. Shiraz, *c* 1440

377 The mighty *'anqā* seizing a 'rhinoceros'. Shiraz, *c* 1440

345 *f 271a* Abū *Barāqish.*
A sort of variegated hen. 3.8 × 4.4 cm.

346 *f 271a* The duck. 5 × 5.7 cm.

347 *f 271b* The falcon. 3.8 × 5 cm.

348 *f 272a* The sparrow-hawk. 3.2 × 4.4 cm.

349 *f 272a* The parrot (rubbed). 3.2 × 3.8 cm.

350 *f 272b* The nightingale, and a small rose-bush.
3.2 × 3.8 cm.

351 *f 273a* The owl. 3.8 × 4.4 cm.

352 *f 273a* The pheasant.
Part of his tail lost. 5 × 5.7 cm.

353 *f 273b* A pair of small crested birds (*shūṭ*?).
3.2 × 4.4 cm.

354 *f 273b* A nondescript brownish bird (*khāṣta al-āf 'ī*). $1\frac{1}{2} \times 1\frac{3}{4}$ in.

355 *f 274a* A pair of bustards. 3.2 × 5 cm.

356 *f 274b* Two sparrow-hawks or kites.
3.8 × 4.4 cm.

357 *f 275b* A pigeon. 3.8 × 4.4 cm.

358 *f 276a* A swallow. 3.8 × 3.8 cm.

359 *f 277a* Two bats in flight. 3.2 × 3.8 cm.

360 *f 277a* The francolin. 5 × 5 cm.

361 *f 278a* The cock. 5 × 5 cm.

362 *f 278b* The hen. 3.8 × 5 cm.

363 *f 279a* A vulture with green wings.
3.8 × 3.2 cm.

364 *f 279a* The quail. 3.8 × 4.4 cm.

365 *f 279b* The hunting falcon (*sunqur*).
3.8 × 5 cm.

366 *f 279b* The royal falcon (*shāhīn*). 3.8 × 4.4 cm.

367 *f 279b* A bird somewhat resembling a curlew (*siftīn*). 3.2 × 3.8 cm.

368 *f 280a* The green magic or woodpecker.
3.2 × 3.8 cm.

369 *f 280a* A whistling bird (*ṣāfir*) which sings all night. 3.8 × 3.8 cm.

370 *f 280a* A hawk (*ṣaqr*). 4.4 × 4.4 cm.

371 *f 280b* The goose (?) (*ṭayr al-jarr*).
3.8 × 3.8 cm.

372 *f 281a* The peacock. 10.2 × 7.6 cm.

373 *f 281a* Two partridges. 3.2 × 5 cm. Cf. No **382**.

374 *f 281b* Two sparrows. 3.2 × 5 cm.

375 *f 282a* The eagle. 5 × 6.3 cm.

376 *f 282b* Two magpies. 3.8 × 5 cm.

377 *f 283a* 'Anqā (depicted like a phoenix) seizing a 'rhinoceros' (deer with fungoid horn) behind a rock. 8.2 × 10.8 cm. *See illustration.*

378 *f 284a* The crow. 3.8 × 5 cm.

379 *f 284b* A pair of beautiful blue and green birds (*gharbīq*: crane?). 5 × 5 cm.

380 *f 284b* A diver (*ghawās*) catching a fish.
3.8 × 3.8 cm.

381 *f 285a* A pair of ring-doves. 3.2 × 4.4 cm.

382 *f 285a* A pair of partridges. 3.2 × 4.4 cm.
Cf. No **373**.

383 *f 285b* The lark. 3.8 × 4.4 cm.

384 *f 286a* The sand-grouse. 3.2 × 3.8 cm.

385 *f 286a* A pair of turtle-doves. 3.8 × 4.4 cm.

386 *f 286a* Qūqnus.
A kind of phoenix or pheasant (more like a crane).
12.7 × 8.2 cm.

387 *f 286b* Kurkī.
A sort of crane, dark grey in colour. 5.7 × 5.7 cm.

389, 390 The stork and the grebe. Shiraz, *c* 1440

دوجشتم بود بزرك ونايها دراز وبارض نو به وهبل بود هرجه

پندم ن وبرید ذ کورآن خبیث تراز اناث بود وجون حیوانی زنک

398 The great dragon *tinnīn*. Shiraz, *c* 1440

401 The *ṣannāja*, the largest beast on earth. Shiraz, *c* 1440

388 *f* 286b *Kadwān.*
A pink-coloured partridge. 3.2 × 4.4 cm.

389 *f* 287a The stork. 7 × 6.3 cm. *See illustration.*

390 *f* 287a The great crested grebe (*mālik al-hazin*). 7.6 × 6.3 cm. *See illustration.*

391 *f* 287b A pair of macaws. 3.8 × 5 cm.

392 *f* 288a The vulture. 5.7 × 6.3 cm.

393 *f* 288a The ostrich, head and feet unfortunately lost in remargination. 7.6 × 7 cm.

394 *f* 288b The mountain swallow. 3.2 × 5 cm.

395 *f* 288b *Yarā'a*, the firefly, represented by two figures of the same bird, one in ordinary light and the other phosphorescent (painted gold) on a background of black. 3.2 × 4.4 cm.

396 *f* 289a A pigeon. 3.2 × 4.4 cm.

397 *f* 290a A viper. 5 × 3.8 cm.

398 *f* 291b The great dragon *tinnīn* (cf. No **27**), pink with flaming appendages. 5.7 × 12.7 cm. *See illustration.*

399 *f* 293a A large venomous lizard (*sāmmi abraṣ*). 5 × 3.8 cm.

400 *f* 293b The tortoise. 4.4 × 5 cm.

401 *f* 294a The *ṣannāja.*
Large, bluish, hairy, lion-footed, boar-headed, with flaming eyes and wings of green and gold. 7.6 × 10.8 cm. *See illustration.*

402 *f* 294a An edible lizard (*ẓabb*). 3.8 × 3.8 cm.

403 *f* 295a A cat-like blue creature (*ẓarbān*). 4.4 × 5.7 cm. *See illustration.*

404 *f* 297b The salamander, represented as a smallish fox-like beast walking through a fire.

403 A cat-like beast called *ẓarbān*. Shiraz. *c* 1440

Nizami: Khamsa (405-423)

Ryl Pers 36 (ex Bland)

Original binding (rebacked, the spine lettered KHEM-SEH I NIZAMI) of dark reddish-brown leather, with exquisitely tooled arabesque medallion and pendants, partly gilt, and narrow gilt frame. Doublures with medallion of fine bold cut-out work of brown leather on a background of blue, green and gold. It is exceptional to find a Timurid book-cover in such good condition outside the Topkapi Library, Istanbul. The whole manuscript is very well preserved. On the upper margin of *f* 3a is the seal of a former owner, Fath 'Ali b. Hidayat-allah, dated 1218/1803.

25.4 × 17.8 cm. 316 ff (the first and the last two blank). Good *nasta' liq* in 4 columns of 25 lines to the page W.S. 16.5 × 10.8 cm. Ff 3b, 4a exquisitely illuminated as a double title-page; headings of equally fine quality on *ff* 29b (*Khusraw u Shirin*), 98b (*Layla wa Majnun*), 147b (*Haft Paykar*), 203b (*Iskandar Nama*, called *Sharaf Nama Iskandari* in the colophon), and 275b (*Sharaf Nama*), the lettering in elegant Kufic. In addition, on *ff* 29a, 202b, 203a, 275a and 314a blank spaces at the end of the poems are covered with geometrical diaper designs in gold and occasional touches of colour. This practice originated under Iskandar Sultan (see the British Library Miscellany of 1411, Add.27261. *ff* 89b, 90a, &c). On *ff* 98a, 147a and 275a smaller spaces are filled with fine floral scrollwork in gold touched with colours. The colophons do not name the copyist, but give dates as follows:

f 29b Monday, 5 Sha'ban 848/17 December 1444
f 98b Tuesday, 12 Ramazan 848/23 December 1444
f 147b Thursday, 12 Shawwal 848/22 January 1445
f 202b Sunday, 14 Dhu'l-qua'da 848/22 February 1445
f 275a Safar 849/May 1445.

(Kerney notes in his MS catalogue, 'I cannot believe it to be so old', which Nicholson endorses with 'Nor I'.) This unusually circumstantial succession of dates may give us some idea of how long an average, competent scribe would take over the transcription of a copy of the *Khamsa*. It is worth noting that the *Khusraw u Shirin*, which is only just shorter than the *Sharaf Nama Iskandari* (the longest poem of the *Khamsa*) only took him six days. He must have had interruptions or taken holidays during the latter part of his task. The manuscript contains 19 miniatures of very good quality in the Shiraz style of the time. Apart from occasional discolouration and smudging, they are in excellent condition.

Exhibited: Victoria and Albert Museum 1967 (*VAM 1967*, 124).

Other works apparently by the same painter are to be found in the Nizami of 854/1450 in the Metropolitan Museum of Art, New York (*Jackson and Yohannan* No 6), MS H.870 (same text) in the Topkapi Library, Istanbul, dated 848/1445, and the Leningrad *Shahnama* of 1445 (Or.Inst.MS C 1654).

405 *f* 2b A princely hunt.
Gold sky, lush green hillside with stream across foreground. The prince in the foreground, his bow drawn, gallops in pursuit of a pair of wild ass, while three terrified hares, one wounded by an arrow, rush away in the other direction. Three other mounted huntsmen occupy the field, one spearing a leopard. Two others are on the horizon attacking a couple of deer.
Some discolouration, and rubbing in the lower right-hand corner.
16.5 × 10.8 cm. *See illustration.*

406 *f* 3a Outdoor court scene.
Wine being offered to the prince, who sits on a carpet, courtiers and musicians before him. The composition is dominated by a group of four magnificent trees, with clouds floating across their topmost branches (a characteristic feature of the style). There is a splendid paeony in the lower left-hand corner. Luxuriant yellowish ground with stream below.
Some discolouration.
16.5 × 10.8 cm. *See illustration.*

407 *f* 6a The Heavenly Ascent of the Prophet.
Ten angels grouped in a circle amid golden clouds, surrounding Muhammad and Buraq.
The faces of both these latter have been scrubbed out, and there is a little discolouration.
12.3 × 10.8 cm. *See illustration.*

408 *f* 18a The hunter, and his dog attacking the fox (6th *maqala* of the *Makhzan al-Asrar*).
The dog is badly smudged.
7 × 10.8 cm. *See illustration.*

409 *f* 36b Prince Khusraw before his father Hurmuzd.
A variation of No **406**, with green ground, large and lush vegetation, and splendid trees, one of which is being nibbled by a horse appearing over the horizon. Courtiers and musicians before the king as usual.
Very slight discolouration.
VAM 1952, pl 12.
12.7 × 10.8 cm. *See illustration.*

405 A princely hunt. Shiraz, 1445

406 Prince holding court out-of-doors. Shiraz, 1445

407 The Heavenly Ascent of the Prophet. Shiraz, 1445

410 *f* 48b Khusraw and his followers at polo with Shirin and her maids.
Plain gold ground. Khusraw and Shirin are the only ones playing, the remainder standing about behind. Shirin and her maids wear gold crowns, Khusraw's side rounded *kullas*. Some curious frontal and rear views of riders.
10.4 × 10.8 cm. *See illustration.*

411 *f* 62a Shirin visits Farhad and his milk-conduit. A towering palace on the right, balanced by the mass of rock on the left. In the margin (though rather discoloured) appears a young shepherd with his staff apparently trying to rescue some of his flock from a precarious position on the mountain.
18.4 × 12.7 cm. *See illustration.*

412 *f* 88b Khusraw and Shirin, seated together on a large throne supported by life-like golden lions, listening to the learned discourse of Buzurg-amid.
Trees above, stream below; maids to the left, courtiers to the right.
Stchoukine MT, pl XLII; *VAM 1965*, pl 4.
16.5 × 10.8 cm. *See colour pl. I.*

413 *f* 107 Layla and Majnun at school.
The fifteen children are grouped very effectively round the master along the lower part of the composition, which gives the painter the opportunity of representing a very fine architectural interior, with central archway, and two oblong windows at the sides, through the grilles of which two figures can be seen.
VAM 1965, pl 5.
11.2 × 10.8 cm. *See illustration.*

414 *f* 132a Majnun in the wilderness seated on a rock, in conversation with his mother (?).
In the foreground is Salim 'Amiri with his camel. Among the animals shown, a crouching fox is badly smudged.
11.2 × 11.4 cm. *See illustration.*

408 The hunter, his dog, and the fox. Shiraz, 1445

409 Prince Khusraw before his father. Shiraz, 1445

410 Khusraw and Shirin at polo. Shiraz, 1445

411 Shirin visiting Farhad. Shiraz, 1445

413 Layla and Majnun at school. Shiraz, 1445

414 Majnun in the wilderness. Shiraz, 1445

415 Layla and Majnun faint at meeting. Shiraz, 1445

416 Bahram Gur and the dragon. Shiraz, 1445

417 'Practice makes perfect'. Shiraz, 1445

418 Entertainment in fairyland. Shiraz, 1445

415 ƒ 140b Layla and Majnun fainting.
They lie side-by-side among palm trees, accompanied by the usual animals. Tents and two spectators on the horizon.
12.7 × 10.8 cm. *See illustration.*

416 ƒ 157a Bahram Gur attacking the dragon, watched by the wild ass.
The depiction of the dragon, rocks and a spreading tree is most effective.
BJRL xxxiv (1951), p 71; *Stchoukine MT*, pl XLI; *Robinson PD*, pl 73.
10.4 × 14.6 cm. *See illustration.*

417 ƒ 164b 'Practice makes perfect'.
Fitna, crowned and veiled, mounting the ladder with a very disgruntled-looking, brown, humped cow on her shoulders. Spectators behind the grille of a window below.
Bahram Gur and his companions on the roof of the towering building are badly discoloured. Slight flaking on the ladder.
19 × 10.8 cm. *See illustration.*

418 ƒ 173a Illustration to the story told in the Black Pavilion.
The hero of the story among the fairies. He sits under a tree holding a wine cup, and another is offered him by a youth in the foreground. Only two fairies are shown. Plain gold ground, with leaf-bordered stream. Round a rock on the horizon a snake coils, hypnotizing four young birds; the parent birds appear to be discussing the situation, left.
Stchoukine MT, pl XLI.
12.7 × 10.8 cm. *See illustration.*

419 ƒ 183b Bahram Gur and the Princess in the Blue Pavilion.
The costumes and dome are in fact green, but there is blue in the surrounding architecture. The throne rests on golden feet shaped as *simurgh* heads, which the artist has whimsically represented biting the candles set in their candlesticks in front. The dome is surmounted by a golden eagle.
17.8 × 10.8 cm. *See colour pl II.*

420 ƒ 196b Bahram Gur and the shepherd who hanged his dog.
In the foreground, the seated king addresses the grey-bearded shepherd who stands by his tent, from which issue several goats. Above, Bahram's black horse, the dog suspended by his hind-legs, and a small heap of dead sheep.
Stchoukine MT, pl XLII.
17.2 × 12.1 cm. *See illustration.*

421 ƒ 218b Victory of Iskandar over the Zangi.
Gold ground; blue sky with large grey clouds and small gold ones. Iskandar clubs a foeman in the foreground, while one of his men shoots another on the horizon. Banner in margin.
13 × 14 cm. *See illustration.*

422 ƒ 267b Victory of Iskandar over the Russians.
General engagement, with the Russians in flight. Pale sand-coloured ground, deep blue sky, central tree.
A smudge across part of the Russian army.
15.8 × 12.1. *See illustration.*

423 ƒ 305b Iskandar and the people of Gog and Magog.
He is interviewing them by a building behind a line of rocks. In the foreground is the sea, with three curious monsters. They are observed by a party of Iskandar's mounted followers, also behind rocks.
Damage to two faces.
12.1 × 10.8 cm. *See illustration.*

The Turkman Style

Turkman supremacy in Persia coincides roughly with the second half of the fifteenth century. Painting under the Turkmans is represented in the John Rylands Library only by a detached miniature in one of the albums, and a single exquisite manuscript of 'Assar's *Mihr u Mushtari*; both these are in what has come to be known as the 'Commercial' Turkman style.

The first appearance of this style in a recognizable form, so far encountered, is in a manuscript of *Mihr u Mushtari*, whose colophon is dated 822/1419 by Ja'far al-Tabrizi (see *Sotheby* 23.XI.1976, lot 387; *Spink* No 5); this is now in a Persian private collection. Tabriz seems the most likely place of origin for this manuscript, and the style may therefore have originated under the early Black Sheep Turkman rulers of Azarbayjan. By the middle years of the fifteenth century it is occasionally found alongside Shiraz-Timurid and Herat-inspired miniatures in several mixed-style manuscripts, such as the Berlin Nizami (*Pertsch* 719) and the Hakim *Shahnama* (*Stchoukine MT* pl XXXIV, XXXV). It seems to have been given its final form by the painter Farhad, who signed a number of miniatures in a *Khawaran Nama*, adding the date 881/1477. For the remainder of the century and well into the Safawid period (see Nos **568–574** below), examples abound, several of the manuscripts containing colophons dated 'at Shiraz'; so numerous, indeed, are they that one cannot avoid the conclusion that Shiraz was continuing to produce manuscripts on a commercial scale and had now hit on an ideal style for the purpose.

Of the John Rylands miniatures in this style, No **424** exemplifies its earlier form, while the *Mihr u Mushtari* illustrations are perfect examples of its maturity. It is a simple style, broad and effective, with rather childlike little figures, and landscape either lush green or pale with regular grass tufts. By about 1510 it had developed into the Shiraz-Safawid style (see below, p 155.

For the style in general, see *Ars Or* 1 (1954), pp 105-112; *Robinson B*, pp 26-29; *VAM 1967*, pp 94, 95. Turkman court painting (not represented in the John Rylands Library) is dealt with by the present writer in the forthcoming UNESCO Album of Timurid Painting.

Album (424)
Ryl Indian Drawings 16.

424 *f* 24a Miniature from a manuscript perhaps of poems by Katibi.
Yusuf sold as a slave. He stands, haloed, on a curious throne-like structure; the green-clad auctioneer makes his play, and there are six prospective purchasers, two holding up bags of money. Plain pale green hillside with a few flowering plants and a single tree.
'Commercial' Turkman style c 1475.
12.7 × 7.6 cm. *See colour pl III.*

'Assar: Mihr u Mushtari (425–430)
Ryl Pers 24 (ex Bland, de Sacy)
Contemporary binding of high quality and in good condition. Flap missing, and spine replaced apparently in France in the eighteenth century, with one inscribed in gilt AMOURS DE MEHER EN LANGUE PERSIENNE, and also bearing the crest of a castle. A seal of a capital L surmounted by some sort of coronet appears in one or two places in the manuscript. The covers are of dark leather with sunken gilt medallions, pendants and corner-pieces embossed with floral arabesques. Doublures similar, with one or two leaves etc. picked out in blue. An exquisite little MS in excellent condition throughout.

22.8 × 12.1 cm. 220 *ff.* Fine *nasta'liq* in two columns of 12 lines to the page. W.S. 14 × 6.3 cm. The colophon (*f* 220a) does not give the name of the copyist nor the date of the manuscript, but contains the author's name and the date of composition of the poem, i.e. 788/1386. The manuscript itself is about a century later (or a few years more). The pencilled foliation omits the first folio. F*f* 1b, 2a are superbly illuminated in a fine Turkman style as a double title-page. The condition is impeccable and the execution faultless.

425 *ff* 0b and 1a Double-page frontispiece within an illuminated border, of a hunt, watched by a prince riding under an umbrella on the horizon.
Six hunters are busily employed among the game, one being attacked by a lion and another by a bear. Gold sky with white clouds. There is some discolouration and a few small patches of damage where the thick green paint of the ground has stuck to the opposite page. Each side 14 × 5.7 cm (without border). *See illus.*

426 ƒ15a Visit to the hermit.
Six figures altogether. Rocks projection into the margin. 10.2 × 7.6 cm. *See colour pl IV.*

427 ƒ54b Badr and Mushtari, blindfolded and bound, before the king, are about to be executed.
The figure of the executioner has been badly scrubbed.
9.5 × 6.3 cm. *See illustration.*

428 ƒ94b Battle with the beast-men.
Three mounted archers (including Mushtari, crowned) charging from the left and six beast-men, two wounded by arrows and the others hurling stones, represented as wolf-like creatures.
Excellent condition.
10.4 × 5.7 cm. *See illustration.*

429 ƒ134a Mihr playing the lute before King Kaywan.
Outdoor court scene.
9.5 × 6 cm. *See illustration.*

430 ƒ167b The battle between King Kaywan and Qara Khan.
9.5 × 6.3 cm. *See illustration.*

Timurid painting in Western India

This is a problem of fairly recent growth, but one which has quickly swelled to considerable proportions. Until about twenty years ago, the possibility of fine illustrated manuscripts being produced at any of the Muslim courts of India in the pre-Mughal period seems not to have been envisaged. Miniatures that could not be fitted into any of the established categories were simply labelled 'provincial', meaning, of course, Persian provincial. But suspicions began to stir. Manuscripts such as Mohl's *Shahnama* in the British Library (Or.1403: *VAM 1967*, No 111) appeared in many respects quite un-Persian – the dancing-girls in the frontispiece, for example, with their hair loose and hanging down anyhow (*FE*, fig 138), as they perform their contortions, are surely no kin to the well-dressed, trim and apparently decorous ladies who perform in a less abandoned manner in authentic Persian court scenes. One of the purposes of *VAM 1967* was to draw attention to a body of material of which such suspicions might be entertained, and a few examples were brought together in Part 2, section 11 (pp 85-90).

Two years later appeared the article by Fraad and Ettinghausen entitled 'Sultanate Painting in Persian Style, primarily from the first half of the Fifteenth Century: a Preliminary Study', here referred to as *FE*. This appeared in the Golden Jubilee volume of *Chhavi* (Benares, 1969, pp 48-66), a publication not readily available in the West, and in view of the article's great importance it may be well to give here a summary of its content.

In their opening section, *The Issue*, the authors state the problem, namely the grouping of certain recalcitrant 'provincial' paintings and the possibility of their assignment to India, noting that such a possibility had already been suggested on more than one occasion by S. C. Welch and the present writer. There follows an invaluable annotated list of the relevant material divided into three groups.

Group A – Dated Manuscripts. Eight manuscripts are listed, dating from 1417 to 1440. In addition to comparatively well-known volumes such as Mohl's *Shahnama* of 1438, (*VAM 1967*, No 111), the Uppsala Nizami of 1439 (*BWG*. No 58), and the Chester Beatty Anthology of 1435–36 (*VAM 1967*, No 110), this group contains two manuscripts in the National Museum, New Delhi (notably a *Shahnama* of 1428) and two in the Vever collection, that almost legendary body of material for whose renewed manifestation many of us continue fervently to hope and pray.

Group B – Undated Dispersed Manuscripts contains only three items: an early fifteenth-century *Miscellany* sold at Sotheby's 11.XII.1968, lot 148 (this is not dispersed, but is now in the British Library, MS Or.13163), the *Shahnama* of about the second quarter of the fifteenth century of whose dispersed miniatures twelve are in the Metropolitan Museum of Art, New York (see *VAM 1967*, No 107), and a late fifteenth-century *Shahnama*, twenty-eight of whose miniatures are in the Museum of Fine Arts, Boston (one is also illustrated in *Spink*, No 9).

Group C – Detached Leaves from Manuscripts. This group, which it is difficult to distinguish from Group B, is divided into eight items, five of which are *Shahnamas*; (one of them includes *VAM 1967*, No 113; see also *Spink* No 31). Like those in the previous group, they are widely scattered, the majority being in the United States.

From this material the authors deduce their next section, *General Characteristics*. These may be summarized as follows.

1 The miniatures seem to belong to the Shiraz orbit, or at least to have something in common with it, though details have been 'adopted in a dry and reduced form'.
2 Nevertheless they form a distinct group, somewhat differing from the normal styles of Timurid painting, characterized by archaisms – shallow format of miniatures with 'stepped' upper edge, Mongol clothing and facial types, cross-hatching to indicate ground plane, the use of outmoded iconography and, occasionally, a text in six columns.

This leads naturally to the next section, *Specific stylistic and iconographic Features of Indian Origin*, which are given as follows.

1 Groups of figures in serried rows and identical poses.
2 Incompetent spacing of figures.
3 Flat compositions.
4 Use of colour for dramatic impact, rather than for corresponding values and contrasts.
5 Many details of furniture, accessories, landscape, and architecture have no Persian counterparts.
6 Certain decorative details (especially decorated bands unrelated to the miniature) suggest Jain manuscripts from Western India.

The next section is *General Expression of Indian Attitudes* which begins, 'Certain miniatures have an Indian "look". The characters have long faces, and their gestures and stances render expressive Indian attitudes.' It proceeds to adduce further examples: the size of figures sometimes varies with their importance, there is an obvious unfamiliarity with any representation of the Ka'ba, and the treatment of clouds and clothes is as found in later Rajput miniatures; one or two other features are specified.

The article continues with a masterly analysis of *Calligraphic Features*. This was the work of Dr Ettinghausen, who demonstrates that the Indian addiction to what he calls 'rhythmic parallelism' is often found in the chapter headings of this group of manuscripts: this he defines as 'the deliberate parallel delineation of letters of the same general outline, and even of neighbouring letters which are different and yet were made to conform to the overruling pattern'. He clearly shows its popularity in India as a calligraphic device by illustrating twelve monumental inscriptions from various parts of India dating from 692/1293 to 967/1560.

Features indicating Translation from Persian Models, the next section, brings a number of examples from the material under consideration to show that 'while many of the miniatures . . . have neither specific Indian features, nor express general Indian attitudes, they reveal themselves, nevertheless, as copies from Persian models, for some use well-known Persian prototypes in a novel fashion, while others misunderstand some of the Iranian objects, which they depict'. In their *Conclusion*, the authors, while deploring the absence of incontrovertible evidence and documentary proof, consider that the circumstantial evidence and reasoning they have adduced in the article, as well as the 'stylistic, iconographic and calligraphic features in these miniatures make a Sultanate [Indian] origin seem most likely'.

It seemed necessary, before discussing the particular problems presented by the John Rylands Library manuscripts included under this head, to ensure that the reader was aware of what Fraad and Ettinghausen had written, and no apology is therefore offered for the above *précis*. The present writer agrees fully with their conclusion, while venturing to doubt the Indian origin of one of the manuscripts they list (Group B, No 11) which he is inclined, tentatively, to place at Samarqand.

Two of the John Rylands manuscripts are here placed in this 'Indian Timurid' category. The first is a *Shahnama* with Nizami's *Khamsa* in the margins, whose miniatures are the work of two clearly distinguishable painters. The one here called Painter A displays a number of the features noted as Indian by *FE* – a generally archaic and primitive character, unfamiliarity with Persian iconography, a predilection for plain oblong brickwork in the architecture (derived from the Muzaffarid style – cf. *Stchoukine MT* pl X), and

a particular mode of painting the folds of turbans frequently found in the miniatures listed by *FE*. Painter B, on the other hand, would pass for a normal Shirazi, though some of his colouring is a little exotic. But there is a closely parallel situation in the Chester Beatty *Anthology* of 1435 (CB MS 124; listed by *FE*) where one painter is exuberantly Indian, whilst another works in quite orthodox Shiraz style. It is not, perhaps, necessary to postulate the migration of Shirazi painters to India (though that is by no means impossible); it may simply be that B was more attuned to the Persian style than A, or was a better painter and copyist. In either case an Indian rather than a Shirazi provenance for the manuscript seems the most probable.

The other manuscript is a clearer case altogether. It is a *Shahnama* of wide format, the text in six columns, its proportions inevitably recalling Inju manuscripts of the fourteenth century though its original miniatures and text are surely of the fifteenth century. The miniatures are also of the wide shallow shape, the upper edge often 'stepped', that was usual at that time. But only four of them are contemporary with the manuscript, and a comparison with several miniatures illustrated by *FE* leaves little or no doubt that they come from the same stable. Apart from anything else, Rustam's tiger-skin cuirass is coloured *black* in the two where he appears in arms (unthinkable in a Persian representation) and it will be recalled that the unorthodox use of colour is among the characteristic features of Indian work listed by *FE*. For the remainder of the miniatures, which may also have been executed in India, see below, Nos **694-768**.

Neither of these manuscripts has a colophon (the last folios of both are replacements), and it is disappointing that none of the dated manuscripts in *FE* have any information about where they were completed. The same is true of *FE*'s MS C.17, the body of whose text, still containing five miniatures, came up at Sotheby's among the Kevorkian Collection on 7.iv.1975 (lot 186), and of a *Kalila wa Dimna*, also sold at Sotheby's and later with Messrs. Spink & Son. This last is an important addition to the 'Indian' corpus, notable for its anomalies (from a Persian standpoint) of architecture, costume and accessories.

The next stage should be an attempt to allocate the various styles of the miniatures cited by *FE* to the different Muslim princedoms of fifteenth-century India – Delhi, Sind, Malwa, Gujerat, and so forth. But failing the discovery of an informative colophon, it is difficult to see how this problem is to be approached. Painstaking research among the princely and other libraries of India and Pakistan is the only course that suggests itself at this stage.

Firdawsi: Shanama & Nizami: Khamsa

(431-474)

Ryl Pers 9 (ex Bland and Ouseley)

Early nineteenth-century half-calf gilt binding, the spine lettered: SHAH NAMEH KHEMSEH I NIZAMI. Inscribed on fly-leaf 'From Sir Gore Ouseley's Collection'.

23.5 × 15.8 cm. 702 ff. Fine *nasta'liq*, 4 columns of 21 lines in the central text (*Shahnama*) and 42 written diagonally in the margins (*Khamsa*). W.S. 20.2 × 13.3 cm. Illuminated headings on ff 1b ('old' preface to the *Shahnama*: much damaged by damp), 7b (text of *Shahnama*: damaged at outer edge), and 359b (reign of Luhrasp); small ones in the marginal text on ff 1b (*Makhzan al Asrar*, damaged by damp), 56b (*Khusraw u Shirin*), 219b (*Layla wa Majnun*), 332b (*Haft Paykar*), 457a (*Sharaf Nama*), and 620b (*Khirad Nama*). All these are in the un-outlined style of illumination associated with Shiraz from the Muzaffarid period to the second half of the fifteenth century. The colophons contain no information (the last folio is a modern replacement). The text includes the *Barzu Nama*. The manuscript may be assigned to the middle years of the fifteenth century.

There are 42 miniature paintings, 2 unfinished preliminary sketches, and 11 spaces left blank, showing that the manuscript was planned for 55 illustrations. The miniatures have suffered very considerable damage and deterioration, a great deal of it due to deliberate scrubbing and smudging, and to clumsy redrawing in black ink. They appear to be the work of two painters of uneven ability. Painter A is rather primitive and naïve, often with attenuated figures recalling the Jalayrid style. In all probability he at least was an Indian. His colours, especially orange and mauve, have an Indian flavour, as do some of his idiosyncrasies of drawing, like the oblong brickwork and the manner of rendering folds of a turban, which can be paralleled in manuscripts shown to be western Indian by *FE*. Painter B's style, however, is unquestionably Persian. A competent practitioner of the Shiraz-Timurid style who may perhaps have helped to illustrate the Teignmouth *Shahnama* some years later, he may have been a visiting Persian artist, or, just as likely, an Indian painter more attuned to the Persian style than A.

431 *f* 18a The Blacksmith Kawa and his two sons before Zahhak.
Faded by damp. Painter A.
7.6 × 10.8 cm.
See illustration.

432 *f* 28b The murder of Iraj by his brother Tur.
Slight flaking towards outer edge, and Iraj's features retouched. Painter B.
The central group as here portrayed became a 'stock' group in the Commercial Turkman style (cf. *Ars Or* I (1954) p 106, fig 15 from the Hakim *Shahnama*).
7.6 × 10.8 cm. *See illustration.*

433 *f* 38b Zal brought down the mountain from the *Simurgh's* nest by his father Sam, whose elephant awaits him in the lower right-hand corner.
Group round the elephant badly smudged. Painter A.
No Persian illustration of this particular moment in the story is known, nor is Sam elsewhere provided with an elephant.
11.4 × 10.8 cm. *See illustration.*

434 *f* 44a Meeting of Zal and Rudaba in the palace of the latter's father, Mihrab.
They stand hand-in-hand by an orange-red carpet under an open window.
Both faces damaged, and that of Rudaba touched in with black ink. Painter A.
A strong contrast to the normal Persian representations of the happy couple.
8.9 × 10.8 cm.

435 *f* 52a Sam meets Sindukht, mother of Rudaba, in a landscape, whilst an axe-bearing groom holds his horse.
Rather rubbed. Painter A.
8.2 × 10.8 cm. *See illustration.*

436 *f* 78a Rustam about to slay the witch: his arms are piled on a stool behind.
Badly rubbed and smudged in the middle, and the two faces touched in. Painter B. 8.2 × 10.8 cm.

437 *f* 80b Rustam slays the White Demon in his cave.
This is the classical Shiraz composition for this favourite subject: Awlad tied to a tree, and Rakhsh, left, and the two principals in the cave, right.
Slight flaking, and the demon's head smudged.
Painter B. 8.9 × 10.8 cm. *See illustration.*

438 *f* 90b Kay Ka'us in his flying-machine, represented like a golden boat in which the king sits, impiously aiming an arrow up to heaven.
His face has been scrubbed. The background is plain blue, slightly flaked, on which a tear has been repaired with narrow strips of white paper. Painter A.
7.6 × 10.8 cm.

431 The blacksmith and his sons before Zahhak. W. India, mid 15th century

432 The murder of Iraj. W. India, mid 15th century

[98]

433 Zal restored to his father. W. India, mid 15th century

435 Sam meets the mother of Rudaba. W. India, mid 15th century

440 The death of Suhrab. W. India, mid 15th century

441 The fire-ordeal of Siyawush. W. India, mid 15th century

445 Suicide of Jarira on her son's body. W. India, mid 15th century

446 Ashkabus and his horse shot by Rustam. W. India, mid 15th century

447 The Khaqan lassoed by Rustam. W. India, mid 15th century

448 Rustam carried by the demon Akwan. W. India, mid 15th century

450 Bizhan rescued by Rustam. W. India, mid 15th century

451 Barzu saved by his mother. W. India, mid 15th century

454 Battle between Kay Khusraw and Afrasiyab. W. India, mid 15th century

453 Combat of Gudarz and Piran. W. India, mid 15th century

456 Execution of Afrasiyab and Garsiwaz. W. India, mid 15th century

455 Rustam attacking Gang Dizh. W. India, mid 15th century

470 Chess introduced at the court of Nushirwan. W. India, mid 15th century

467 Bahram Gur wrestling in India. W. India, mid 15th century

471 *f* 641a Combat of Bahram Chubina and Kut the Roman.
Some damage to faces. Painter B.
10.8 × 10.8 cm. *See illustration.*

472 *f* 652b Murder of Bahram Chubina.
The murderer, and Bahram's face obliterated, and the remainder of the miniature (which includes two spectators) slightly damaged by a damp patch. Painter A.
8.9 × 10.8 cm.

473 *f* 662b Khusraw at Shirin's castle.
This has been so thoroughly and viciously scrubbed out that little more than the outlines of the building remains. A horse has been crudely drawn in with black ink. Probably Painter A.
12.1 × 10.8 cm.

(*ff* 665b and 685a. Blank spaces left for miniatures of Barbad playing music to Khusraw, and of the encounter of Rustam with Sa'd b. Waqqas, respectively.)

474 *f* 691a The body of Yazdagird flung into the millstream after his murder by the miller.
Somewhat rubbed and damaged, and one face touched in with ink. Painter A.
8.2 × 10.8 cm. *See illustration.*

(*f* 694a. Blank space left for a miniature of the combat of Bizhan and Mahwi.)

Firdawsi: Shahnama (475-478)

Ryl Pers 933 (ex Nichetti of Venice)
Oriental brown leather binding with stamped border, sunk medallions, pendants, and corner-pieces, with remains of inlaid grey paper. Rebacked and repaired. A pencilled note on the back fly-leaf reads as follows: 'Bought from G. A. Nichetti di Venezia – conduttore of a caravan which goes [year] by year from Als . . . ine to Teheran – bought by him at Teheran. Last year he was the fourth conductor of a general caravan that went to Mecca from Cairo – and the 3 first died and he carried the caravan to the gates of Mecca. For 4 generations he and his fathers have all been conductors of caravans'. Kerney's MS catalogue observes: 'Although bought in Tehràn, this is undoubtedly an Indian MS and is of no great importance'. It would be interesting to know his reasons for the first of these conclusions, which seems to be correct (see below); as to the second, we must beg leave to question it.

40 × 29.2 cm. 266*ff* remargined throughout. Fifteenth-century *nasta' liq* in 6 columns of 31 lines to the page. W.S. 26.7 × 19.7 cm. On *f* 1b is an elaborate illuminated *shamsā* of 16 points, with 2 principal and 6 minor pendants, in a fairly rough late sixteenth-century style. F 2a is the remaining half of an illuminated double title-page, also apparently late sixteenth-century, but of superior execution; rubbed in the lower left-hand corner. There is an illuminated heading on *f* 2b in a style similar to that of the *shamsa*. *Ff* 6b, 7a are illuminated as a double title-page at the beginning of the poem itself: the style is broad and not highly finished, and appears to be of the fifteenth century, i.e., contemporary with the text. *f* 266a is illuminated in the same late sixteenth-century style as *ff* 1b, 2b. It seems to have been the left-hand half of a double page, and consists of a circle between two rectangular panels, containing an inscription in praise of Firdawsi. In a brief colophon in the last two columns of text on *f* 265b the scribe describes himself as 'the feeblest of the slaves' (*aẓ'af al-'ibād*), but does not give his name; he dates his work 1195/1781. However *ff* 255-260 and 262-265 are clearly replacements, and this date may be presumed to apply to them only. They are on European paper, and *f* 262 has a watermark of a shield of scrolled outline, charged with a double bend and surmounted by a fleur de lys. The restored margins are also of European paper.

Section headings, written in gold (crimson on the replaced folios) against a diagonally-shaded background of pale blue or pink. The original text is given the same background throughout.

Three Persian seals occur at intervals throughout the manuscript, being often stamped on the miniatures. The largest (1) bears the title Shujā' al-Mulk and a reference to the Shahinshāh, and the smallest (3) the name 'Isā with the date 1178/1764-65. The middle-sized one (2) has the name Bābā Khān.

There are 79 miniatures in all, of which 4 (Nos **475-478**) are probably Western Indian and contemporary with the text of the manuscript, and 3 (Nos **749, 751,** and **752**) are imitations of the Inju style, probably executed in the late sixteenth century, which is the period of all the remaining miniatures. These latter are in a rather rough and hurried style based on that of Qazwin, and will be found noted under Nos **694-768**. Particulars of the four original miniatures are as follows:

475 *f* 25b Suhrab about to kill Rustam.
Both faces damaged.
(This folio has been displaced, and should follow *f* 41).
7.6 × 19.7 cm. *See illustration.*

471 Combat of Bahram Chubina and Kut. W. India, mid 15th century

474 Death of Yazdagird. W. India, mid 15th century

475 Suhrab about to kill Rustam. W. India, mid 15th century

476 Tahmina comes to Rustam's chamber. W. India, mid 15th century

477 The fire-ordeal of Siyawush. W. India, mid 15th century

478 Rustam carried by the demon Akwan. W. India, mid 15th century

476 *f* 37a Tahmina comes to Rustam's chamber.
Rustam's face badly damaged and retouched.
7.6 × 19.7 cm. *See illustration.*

477 *f* 43b The fire-ordeal of Siyawush.
The faces of Sudaba and of the palace door-keeper
badly damaged, and the former retouched. Single 'step'
at left-hand end of upper edge.
10.2 × 19.7 cm. *See illustration.*

478 *f* 87b Rustam carried by the Demon Akwan.
In all three original miniatures where it occurs,
Rustam's tiger-skin cuirass or surcoat is coloured black
with white stripes. Single shallow 'step' in upper edge.
A bit creased, but condition reasonable, and colours
good.
JIS I (1951) p 83.
8.9 × 19.7 cm. *See illustration.*

As will have been gathered from the introductory
remarks and the detailed list of miniatures (see also
below, p 244) this is an extraordinary manuscript that
has passed through many vicissitudes. It seems most
likely that its origin was somewhere in Western India
towards the middle of the fifteenth century. The form
and proportions of the volume are alien to Persia at this
date, and so is the style of the original illumination on
ff 6b, 7a. No Persian *Shahnama* written in *six* columns
is known between the mid fourteenth and late
sixteenth centuries. This archaism is extended to the
shape and proportions of the miniatures – shallow in
depth with frequent 'stepping' of the upper edge –
recalling those in *Shahnamas* produced under Inju
patronage.

The four original surviving miniatures have been
formerly dubbed 'provincial Persian', but of late years,
and especially since the publication of *FE*, one needs to
examine this catch-all classification more narrowly. In
fact they have several points of resemblance to some of
the miniatures published convincingly in that article
as Western Indian: the helmets with rounded crowns

and two little red streamers; the curious shape of the
feet; the fondness for symmetry; the straight lines of
oblong bricks in the wall of a building (as opposed to
the intricate brick patterns found in fifteenth-century
Persian miniatures); and some un-Persian (at this
period) colours, like purple and orange.

So much for its origin. We may suppose that the four
miniatures already mentioned were the only ones
completed at this time; there is no sign of the later
miniatures having been painted over earlier work. By
the late sixteenth century it was decided to fill in the
spaces with miniatures. This was obviously something
of a rush job, but the artist (or artists – it is difficult to be
sure with hurried or second- and third-rate work) had
some originality and imagination, as witness his
version of Iskandar in the Land of Darkness (No **741**);
but his most remarkable contribution was the three
Inju style miniatures (Nos **749**, **751**, **752**). Considering their date (and there is no reason to put them any
later than the bulk of the miniatures) they are very
creditable performances. The artist was clearly familiar
with work of the fourteenth century, and the wide
pages, 6 columns, and shallow miniature-spaces of the
present volume, brought it irresistibly to his mind. So
far as is known at present, these are unique among the
many Persian archaizing miniatures that imitate
Timurid and Safawid work (certainly imitation Mongol
work has been seen, but it is mostly poor, late stuff).
Illuminations were also added at this time.

The last stage came in the late eighteenth century,
when the owner was no doubt one of those whose seals
have been noted. The manuscript was probably in a
bad state at the back and front, especially the former,
necessitating the replacement of ten folios and a
certain rearrangement of the illuminations. Half the
double title-page was gone, and perhaps an answering
page to the curious *f* 266. Also, the whole volume had
to be remargined and probably a new binding supplied.

So it was that it finally caught the eye of the
nineteenth-century Venetian caravan conductor as he
looked over the stock of a *dallal* or strolled through the
Tehran bazaar.

The Herat Style

Full accounts of Bihzad and his school at Herat, under the enlightened and munificent patronage of Sultan Husayn Mirza will be found in all the standard textbooks (see especially *BWG* chapter IV; *Stchoukine MT*, pp 21 *ff.*, 68 *ff*, etc) and in an article 'Bihzad and his School: the Materials' (*Marg* XXX.2, March 1977, pp 51-76) the present writer endeavoured to gather together all the basic materials in convenient form. As has been frequently stressed, Bihzad was a reformer, not a revolutionary; he always respected and observed the basic canons of Persian painting. His main contribution was to relax its sometimes over-stiff formality, and to give it as much humanity and naturalism as was consistent with its essential character. Amongst his followers at Herat there must have been one or two senior to him in age, trained in an earlier style, who nevertheless tried to keep up with the new trends he set. As suggested in the *BJRL* article referred to in the following entry, the painter of the two miniatures in this superb Nawa'i volume may well have been such a one.

When the Bodleian volumes of this same set were shown at Burlington House in 1931, nobody realized the existence of this John Rylands manuscript: 'the volume containing the *Layla and Majnun* is missing', said *BWG* (p 96). It must somehow have escaped the eye of Mr J. B. Elliott when he purchased over 400 of the Ouseley manuscripts for eventual donation to the Bodleian in 1859.

Nawa'i: Layla wa Majnun (479-480)

Ryl: Turk. MS 3. (ex Bland and Ouseley)

Modern European binding of green half-calf with marbled paper sides. Sir Gore Ouseley's bookplate appears at both ends, and on the fly-leaf is a note on the text and manuscript in his writing, dated 'Hall Barn Park, 1838'.

27.9 × 19.7 cm. 48 *ff*. Very fine *nasta'liq* in 4 columns of 21 lines to the page. W.S. 15.5 × 9.5 cm. Extremely fine illuminated heading on *f* 1b. No colophon, but the manuscript is in a set with the other four volumes of Nawa'i's *Khamsa*, or Quintet, in the Bodleian Library (see the present writer's article in *BJRL* xxxvii) one of which is dated 890/1485. The set was executed for Prince Badi' al-Zaman, son of Sultan Husayn Mirza of Herat. The whole is in excellent condition.

There are two miniatures in the best Herat style of the late fifteenth century. As suggested in the article to which reference has already been made, the anonymous painter is probably to be identified with the painter of Bodleian MS Elliot 317 *f* 14a (*Robinson B*, No 611).

Exhibited: Victoria and Albert Museum 1967 (*VAM 1967*, No 27)

479 *f* 16b Camp scene, with Layla and Majnun fainting.

Three black tents against a pale mauve hillside dotted with exquisitely painted flowers and plants bounded by a horizon of delicately tinted rocks from which spring a tamarisk and a convoluted tree with bare branches. Sky of intense blue dotted with stars. The fainting couple are on the left, Layla tended by an old woman; to the right, a bearded man carrying a candle approaches a young woman in one of the tents, and below, a young man, also carrying a candle, converses with a greybeard who leans out of his tent.

A classic composition for this scene (as for several other favourite subjects) seems to have been established by the painter of Iskandar Sultan's *Miscellany* of 1411 (British Library Add.27261), which was followed in a detached miniature of *c* 1425-30, probably made for Baysunghur (*Keir* III.75), in Shah Rukh's Nizami of 1431 in the Hermitage, Leningrad, in the Nizami of Turkhan Khatun, 1446 (Topkapi Library, Istanbul, H.781), and in the Nizami of Amir'Ali Farsi Barlas, 1494 (British Library, Or.6810). But the present miniature does not follow the canon. This may be due either to the individual and independent character of the artist, or to the fact that the text here illustrated is

that of Nawa'i, not Nizami. *BJRL* xxxvii (1958) p 264;
VAM 1965, pl 18.
15.5 × 9.5 cm. *See colour pl V.*

480 *f* 34a Majnun visited by the camel-rider.
Majnun sits under a large *chinar* tree, left, his visitor
before him, and the latter's camel resting on the other
side of a stream, right. Antelopes and mountain sheep
appear lower left, and among the tumbled rocks of the
horizon is a leopard stalking an ibex. Delicate peacock-
blue ground dotted with exquisite flowers, a lush green
border to the stream, and scattered stones. A fine
poplar in the centre, and tamarisks and bare-branched
trees and shrubs among the rocks. Gold sky.
This miniature takes a high place among those
executed by Bihzad and his school for the court of
Herat.
BJRL xxxvii (1958) p 265; *Robinson PD*, pl 25; *VAM
1965*, pl 17.
14.3 × 9.5 cm. *See colour pl VI.*

The Safawid period

The Tabriz Style

The style associated with Tabriz, the capital during the reign of Isma'il I and the early years of Tahmasp his son and successor, had a double root in the meticulous and academic style practised by Bihzad and his pupils at Herat, and the freer and more fantastic court style of Ya'qub Beg and the later Turkman princes. Among Isma'il's court painters Shaykhzada was at first the protagonist of the former, and Sultan Muhammad of the latter. The two styles fused in the crucible of the great Houghton (formerly Rothschild) *Shahnama*; in the early part of the volume the style of Sultan Muhammad prevailed, but in the later miniatures we find the smoother style of Mirak predominating, and his was the style that set the trend for the remainder of Tahmasp's reign. Even Sultan Muhammad himself conformed to it in the great British Library Nizami of 1539/43 (Or.2265).

Two of the John Rylands manuscripts provide excellent examples of this sumptuous court style. In the *Shahnama* of 924/1518 the miniatures nearly contemporary with the text seem to be the work of three different artists of whom the best, here called C, was a painter of very high attainments. The miniatures in the *Khusraw u Shirin* of perhaps about ten years later, are also fine specimens of mature Tabriz work; it is sad that the best miniature in the volume (No **550**) is also the least well preserved. Both manuscripts contain work by some of the best of Tahmasp's court painters.

The Tabriz style is well covered in all the standard text-books, but they should be read in conjunction with Mr Cary Welch's lively and penetrating treatment of the Houghton *Shahnama* miniatures (*Welch KBK* and *Welch RPM*, and a full-scale study of the manuscript shortly to be published by the Harvard University Press).

Firdawsi: Shahnama (481-549)

Ryl Pers 910

Eighteenth-century Indian binding of claret-coloured leather with white medallions, pendants, corner pieces and border panels inlaid and embossed. Doublures with medallions and pendants painted in silver. Modern slip-case of scarlet morocco.

31.1 × 22.8 cm. 564 *ff*. Good *nasta'liq* in four columns of 25 lines to the page. W.S. 22.8 × 15.2 cm. Colophon (*f* 562a) gives no copyist's name, but the date, somewhat rubbed and interfered with, was probably 6 Jumāda I 924/1518. The fly-leaf at the beginning bears an inscription in English (early nineteenth century) stating that 'this must have been the very copy presented to the Sultan (Mahmud of Ghazna)'! The foliation numbering includes 5 fly-leaves at the beginning and 2 blank folios at the end. To the base of each folio where a miniature occurs a paper tag is attached (some are missing) inscribed with the subject in Persian and English (not always correctly).

Good illuminated heading for the Preface on *f* 6b, slightly damaged, and the text and margins of this opening embellished with gold. This heading seems to be at least half a century later than the text, and must be a replacement of a lost original. On *ff* 16b, 17a fully illuminated double title-page of excellent quality in a fairly broad style recalling Commercial Turkman work of a generation earlier.

The miniatures in this manuscript, of which there are 101 (not counting an Indian addition under the colophon), are clearly divided into two main groups.

1 The first 52 and 17 others are probably the work of

three painters, and seem to be a little later than the date of the text – perhaps *c* 1520-30. One artist was a man of great ability and technical refinement; the others, inferior in vision and technique, still carried a flavour of the Commercial Turkman style, or of the early Shiraz-Safawid style that grew from it.

2 The last 26, and 16 others, seem to be the work of three different painters, and probably date between 1580 and 1590. They will be found noted below, Nos **769-800**. The best of these later artists, who only seems to have contributed three paintings, was an equal in ability to the best painter of the earlier group; his work foreshadows the Isfahan style. The other two seem to have imitated his style (perhaps they were pupils?) but with less ability and frequent signs of hurry.

The individual painters may be particularized as follows.

Earlier Group

A An artist of mediocre attainments, probably brought up in the Commercial Turkman style (see especially No **487**). His compositions often dispense with horizon and sky: his drawing is rather weak; and he is fond of cloud-scroll designs. 14 miniatures are here attributed to him, with 7 more doubtful.

B A capable exponent of the rising court style of Tabriz though sometimes harking back to less academic Turkman habits, such as faces in the rocks, and conventional trees with red fruit. 26 miniatures are attributed to him, with 3 doubtful.

C A painter of great distinction and fine technique, who must later have served Shah Tahmasp. He maintains a high standard in the 19 miniatures (and one or two doubtful ones) here attributed to him, but his work is sometimes difficult to distinguish from that of B when the latter is on form. They are both fond of a certain type of tree with beautifully painted and shaded foliage (Nos **494**, **503**, **506**, **508**, **516**, **529**, **531**, **533**, and **536**). This painter seems to have been a young man, influenced by Mirak and Sultan Muhammad; it might be possible to identify him as Mir Sayyid 'Ali or even Mirak himself in his earliest years. I am much indebted to Mr Cary Welch for this suggestion.

Later Group

D The better of E's pupils. Competent and, one would imagine, capable of working at high speed. He follows

483 Murder of Iraj. Tabriz, *c* 1520-30

E's mannerisms that lead to the normal Isfahan style of the early seventeenth century. His hand may perhaps be seen in the India Office *Shahnama* of 1604 (*Robinson IO*, Nos 1005-1067).

D¹ A more naïve and awkward painter than D, but in a very similar style. He was evidently responsible for two drawings in the India Office Library (*Robinson IO*, Nos 146, 151).

E The master of the emerging new style. Both drawing and colour-scheme are bold and effective.

There has been a certain amount of Indian 'restoration' of faces etc. Particulars of the earlier group of miniatures are as follows.

481 *f* 23a The sons of Kawa the blacksmith before Zahhak. The faces of the two courtiers seated in the foreground have been repainted in India, but less crudely than usual. A trifle rubbed. Painter A.
10.8 × 15.2 cm.

482 *f* 28b Faridun strikes Zahhak with his mace in the palace.
One of Jamshid's sisters behind.
The face of Faridun and the lower part of the lady's repainted in India. Painter A.
8.9 × 15.2 cm.

483 *f* 34a Murder of Iraj by his brothers Tur and Salm.
Only the three principal figures are shown, in a tent. Curiously enough, Tur is shown cleanshaven and Iraj bearded: Salm has a moustache. Painter A.
12.1 × 15.2 cm. *See illustration.*

484 *f* 46a Zal feasting with Rudaba.
Six figures altogether, the faces of Rudaba and one of her maids repainted in India. (The candlesticks are of blue-and-white porcelain). Painter A.
12.7 × 15.2 cm.

485 *f* 56b The young Rustam, crowned, armed, and mounted on an elephant, meets his grandfather Sam, before whom Zal and another warrior make obeisance. Painter A.
19 × 15.2 cm. *See illustration.*

486 *f* 57b Young Rustam kills the mad elephant with his mace.
Gold ground: no horizon. The elephant's head retouched in India, making it more realistic, with a rather melancholy expression. Painter A.
8.9 × 15.2 cm. *See illustration.*

487 *f* 64a Afrasiyab beheading Nawdar.
This miniature is strongly reminiscent of the Commercial Turkman style of the previous century, especially in the luxuriant green ground: there is no horizon or sky. Painter A.
7 × 15.2 cm. *See illustration.*

488 *f* 67a Rustam catches his horse Rakhsh.
He wears a three-fold plume in his leopard's-head helmet, and is still cleanshaven. Rakhsh's dam, a grey, makes for him with ears laid back. Herdsman on the horizon. Painter B. 12.7 × 15.2 cm.

489 *f* 68b Young Rustam, having spitted Qulun on his spear, plants it in the ground.
The hero's figure is splendidly portrayed: Qulun, a tree, and banners in the upper margin, also Rustam's threefold helmet-plume. Painter C.
14.6 × 19 cm. *See illustration.*

490 *f* 69a Rustam lifts Afrasiyab from the saddle.
An inferior painter to the last: the figures are smaller and Rustam has grown a moustache and beard. Slight retouching on one or two faces. Painter A.
13.3 × 16.5 cm.

491 *f* 71b Zal before Kay Ka'us.
A modest little miniature, probably by the same painter as the last. Painter A.
8.9 × 15.2 cm.

492 *f* 73a Rustam sleeping while Rakhsh kills the lion.
Vestiges of the Turkman Commercial style in vegetation bordering the stream and a tree with red fruits. Painter B.
13.3 × 15.2 cm. *See illustration.*

493 *f* 74a Rustam, Rakhsh, and the dragon.
The composition largely framed in orange-coloured rock. Painter B.
12.1 × 15.2 cm. *See illustration.*

494 *f* 76b Rustam and the White Demon.
The cave is surrounded by rocks of a rather phallic appearance, with many hidden faces: Awlad tied to a large tree. A certain flavour of Shiraz. Painter B.
13.3 × 15.2 cm. *See illustration.*

495 *f* 94b Combat of Rustam and Suhrab.
The horizon convention recalls Shiraz-Timurid work. Painter A.
17.8 × 15.2 cm. *See illustration.*

485 Rustam meets his grandfather. Tabriz, *c* 1520-30

486 Rustam kills the mad elephant. Tabriz, *c* 1520-30

487 King Nawdar beheaded by Afrasiyab. Tabriz, *c* 1520-30

489 Qulun slain by the young Rustam. Tabriz, *c* 1520-30

492 Rustam, Rakhsh, and the lion. Tabriz, *c* 1520-30

493 Rustam, Rakhsh, and the dragon. Tabriz, *c* 1520-30

494 Rustam and the White Demon. Tabriz, *c* 1520-30

495 Combat of Rustam and Suhrab. Tabriz, *c* 1520-30

496 *f* 97a Rustam mourning the dead Suhrab.
The latter's head and bare arm repainted in India.
Painter A.
19 × 17.8 cm.

497 *f* 105b The fire-ordeal of Siyawush.
The head of Sudaba, on the balcony with Kay Ka'us, has been repainted in India, giving her a brown moustache and beard! Another lady in a tower in the top margin also repainted. Painter A.
13.3 × 15.2 cm (plus tower and cupola in upper margin).

498 *f* 112b Siyawush displaying his skill at polo.
All figures wear baton-turbans, which appear throughout the manuscript.
Slightly rubbed. Painter B.
9.5 × 15.2 cm.

499 *f* 115a Marriage feast of Siyawush and Firangis.
Lush green ground with no horizon: two dancing-girls performing under a large umbrella (flaked): Siyawush enthroned, right.
His face, those of the two dancing-girls and of one of the seated courtiers on the right, have been repainted in India. Painter B.
13.3 × 15.2 cm.

500 *f* 118a Siyawush lifting an opponent from the saddle.
The face of the principal figure repainted in India. Painter B.
13.3 × 15.2 cm.

501 *f* 123a The murder of Siyawush.
The pale green ground has partly flaked away. Painter B.
13.3 × 15.2 cm.

502 *f* 127a Rustam lifting Pilsam from the saddle on his spear.
Rustam's panoply is not differentiated. Painter A.
12.7 × 15.2 cm.

503 *f* 129b Rustam struck on the head by Human's mace in single combat.
Painter B.
14.6 × 15.2 cm. *See illustration.*

504 *f* 135b Captive Piran led in by a running footman.
King and two others on horizon.

Piran's face repainted in India. Painter B.
15.2 × 15.2 cm.

505 *f* 139a Kay Khusraw attacking the demon castle of Bahman.
Demons on the walls and in the gate.
Slight flaking on pale green. Painter B.
15.2 × 15.2 cm. *See illustration.*

506 *f* 146b Farud from his castle wall shoots Riwniz.
Faces in the rocks: grey castle outlined with gold. Painter B.
16.5 × 15.2 cm. *See illustration.*

507 *f* 152a Night attack of the Turanians on the Persian camp.
Black ground. Painter A.
10.3 × 15.2 cm. *See illustration.*

508 *f* 156b Bahram slain by Tazhaw.
Wounded Gustaham lies back in the right-hand corner. Painter B.
11.4 × 15.2 cm.

509 *f* 164a Rustam before Kay Khusraw on arriving to help the Persians against Kamus.
Rustam's face repainted. Painter B.
12.7 × 15.2 cm.

510 *f* 170b Rustam shoots Ashkabus and his horse.
Painter B. 12.7 × 15.2 cm.

511 *f* 172a Rustam lassoing Kamus.
No horizon: face of Kamus repainted: no other figures. Painter B.
8.2 × 15.2 cm.

512 *f* 178a Shangul speared by Rustam.
The face of one of the warriors on the left has been repainted. Painter B.
11.4 × 15.2 cm.

513 *f* 180a Rustam dragging the Khaqan from his elephant.
Rustam's face repainted. Painter B.
17.8 × 15.2 cm.

514 *f* 183a Rustam slays Kafur the man-eater outside his fortress.
Kafur and his followers are shown dark-skinned, with human faces in front and dogs' faces behind. Painter B.
13.3 × 15.2 cm. *See illustration.*

503 Rustam in combat with Human. Tabriz, *c* 1520-30

505 Kay Khusraw attacking the castle of Bahman. Tabriz, *c* 1520-30

506 Farud shoots Riwniz. Tabriz, *c* 1520-30

515 *ƒ* 199b Rescue of Bizhan.
All details correct: 7 warriors, Manizha, stone cover, fire – even the head of the apocryphal demon Barkhyas.
Bizhan's head repainted in India. Painter B.
16.5 × 15.2 cm. *See illustration.*

516 *ƒ* 215b Bizhan remounting after taking the head of Human.
The severed head (on the saddle-bow) repainted in India. Painter B.
13.3 × 15.2 cm (plus banners in the top margin).

517 *ƒ* 221a First of the Rukh duels.
Fariburz and Kulbad. Fariburz cuts Kulbad through the body while he holds his bow. No horizon.
A bit rubbed and Kulbad's face repainted. Painter A.
7.6 × 15.2 cm.

518 *ƒ* 221b Giw captures Gurwi.
Painter B. 8.9 × 15.2 cm.

519 *ƒ* 222a Guraza throws Siyamak.
Painter B. 8.9 × 15.2 cm.

520 *ƒ* 222a Furuhil shoots Zangula.
Flaked. Painter B. 7 × 15.2 cm.

521 *ƒ* 222b Barman unhorsed by Ruhham.
Discoloured at the top. Painter B. 10.8 × 15.2 cm.

522 *ƒ* 223a Ruīn vanquished by Bizhan.
Painter B. 6.3 × 15.2 cm.

523 *ƒ* 223a Hajir cuts down Sipahram.
Painter A. 7 × 15.2 cm.

524 *ƒ* 223b Zanga unhorses Akhwast.
Rubbed. Painter A. 7.6 × 15.2 cm.

525 *ƒ* 224a Gurgin rides away with the head of Andariman.
The head retouched. Painter B. 7.6 × 15.2 cm.

507 Night attack on the Persian camp. Tabriz, *c* 1520-30

514 Kafur the man-eater slain by Rustam. Tabriz, *c* 1520-30

515 Bizhan rescued by Rustam. Tabriz, *c* 1520-30

526 ƒ224a Barta leading back the horse of Kuhram with his body across the saddle.
Head of Kuhram retouched. Painter B.
7.6 × 15.2 cm.

527 ƒ224b Piran fleeing up the mountain from Gudarz.
Painter B. 12.1 × 15.2 cm.

528 ƒ228a Gustaham kills Lahhak and Farshid-ward.
The faces of the two combatants repainted in India. Painter B.
11.4 × 15.2 cm.

529 ƒ237b Shida slain by Kay Khusraw.
Perhaps the best miniature in the book. Painter C.
19 × 20.2 cm. *See colour pl VIII.*

530 ƒ244b Capture of Gang Dizh by Rustam.
Rustam shown on the walls receiving severed heads (one of them repainted) while his men capture terrified females on the tower above. Painter C.
22.8 × 18.4 cm. *See illustration.*

531 ƒ254a Execution of Afrasiyab and Garsiwaz by Kay Khusraw.
Painter C. 15.8 × 19 cm. *See illustration.*

532 ƒ257b Zal, Rustam, and the other paladins in audience with Kay Khusraw.
Splendid green background. Painter C.
21.6 × 19.7 cm. *See illustration.*

533 ƒ287b Isfandiyar and the lions.
Painter C. 15.8 × 15.2 cm. *See illustration.*

534 ƒ291a Isfandiyar takes Gurgsar, who rides a camel, with two other camels in what appears to be a morass.
Painter C. 20.2 × 20.2 cm. *See illustration.*

535 ƒ294a Isfandiyar slays Arjasp in the Brazen Hold.
A dead man in the doorway. Painter B.
11.4 × 15.2 cm.

536 ƒ300a Rustam kicks back the rock rolled by Bahman.
Painter C. 15.8 × 15.2 cm. *See illustration.*

537 ƒ303a Meeting of Rustam and Isfandiyar.
Rustam is exceptionally well painted. Painter C. *JIS* I

(1951) p 85. 20.2 × 20.2 cm. *See illustration.*

538 ƒ309b Combat of Rustam and Isfandiyar, with maces, their swords lie broken on the ground.
Painter C. 17.2 × 19.7 cm. *See illustration.*

539 ƒ314b Rustam shoots Isfandiyar in the eyes.
Again, Rustam is very well painted and the artist has given his eyes a staring look, as if in horror at what he has done. A little discoloured. Painter C.
19 × 19 cm.

540 ƒ317a Gushtasp receives the body of his son Isfandiyar, surrounded by weeping women.
All faces (with the possible exception of that of the corpse) repainted in India. Gold ground. Probably Painter C.
10.8 × 15.2 cm.

541 ƒ322a The death of Rustam.
A very dramatic effect with the spears in the pit converging.
Shaghad a bit rubbed. Painter C.
21.6 × 20.2 cm. *See illustration.*

542 ƒ347a Queen Qaydafa enthroned.
One or two of the faces have been slightly retouched. The throne is unfinished. Painter B or C.
15.8 × 18.4 cm.

543 ƒ387a Bahram Gur seated on the throne after killing the lions.
Very symmetrical composition: two dead lions, two large trees, Bahram in the middle. Painter C.
12.7 × 15.2 cm. *See illustration.*

544 ƒ395a Bahram Gur entertained by ladies in a garden.
All the ladies' faces, and the king's have been repainted in India. Painter C.
15.2 × 19 cm.

545 ƒ396a Bahram Gur hunting lions.
A vigorous representation: the wounded lions recall some of those in the Assyrian reliefs, being excellently shown. Painter C.
17.8 × 18.4 cm.

546 ƒ402b Bahram Gur beheads the dragon to free a man it has swallowed.
(Story of Bahram Gur and the *dihqan*). The dragon, in shaded gold, is excellent. Painter C.
15.2 × 20.2 cm.

530 Rustam captures Gang Dizh. Tabriz, *c* 1520-30

531 Execution of Afrasiyab and Garsiwaz. Tabriz, *c* 1520-30

532 Paladins in audience with Kay Khusraw. Tabriz, *c* 1520-30

533 Isfandiyar and the lions. Tabriz, *c* 1520-30

534 Gurgsar captured by Isfandiyar. Tabriz, *c* 1520–30

536 Rustam kicks back the rock. Tabriz, *c* 1520-30

537 Meeting of Rustam and Isfandiyar. Tabriz, *c* 1520-30

538 Combat of Rustam and Isfandiyar. Tabriz, *c* 1520-30

541 The death of Rustam. Tabriz, *c* 1520-30

543 Bahram Gur enthroned after killing the lions. Tabriz, *c* 1520-30

547 Victory of Bahram Gur over the Khaqan. Tabriz, *c* 1520-30

548 Bahram Gur slays the 'wolf'. Tabriz, *c* 1520

547 *f* 405a Victory of Bahram Gur over the Khaqan of Chin.

The enemy are all shown in conical Tartar caps. One has a cheetah on the crupper behind him, another holds a falcon as he is speared from behind and a pink-legged white hound runs beside (Bahram Gur had surprised them on a hunting expedition). Painter C.

17.2 × 20.2 cm. *See illustration.*

548 *f* 411b Bahram Gur kills the 'wolf'.

The wolf is a fantastic pink monster, founded on the Chinese 'Dog of Fo', but with horns and golden streamers. Painter C.

22.2 × 20.2 cm. *See illustration.*

549 *f* 412b Bahram Gur in India beheading a black dragon with gold streamers. Painter C.

12.7 × 15.2 cm.

Nizami: Khusraw u Shirin (550-554)

Ryl. Pers 6 (ex Bland and Ouseley)

Early sixteenth-century binding of splendid quality; the outer faces consist of a sunk gilt panel of floral and cloud scrolls, surrounded by a frame of small panels and corner-pieces of similar design. The doublures have each a large medallion with pendants and corner-pieces, all of the finest cut-out work of brown on blue, on a sunk gilt ground with clouds and floral scrolls, the flowers picked out with colour. On the medallions themselves the cut-out work has disappeared and has been replaced by a spray of roses painted on paper stuck on to the medallion (Indian, eighteenth century?). 4 *ff* of fly-leaves at the beginning are occupied by an account, in the handwriting of Sir Gore Ouseley, of the poem and its author. This is signed and dated 'Hall Barn Park, January, 1837'. His bookplate appears on the end fly-leaf. At the end of the text is the impression of a seal in the form of a lion, inscribed 'Abd Muhammad Ibrahim, with the date 197 (presumably 1097/1686).

30.5 × 20.2 cm 66 *ff*, remargined throughout with gold-dusted pink paper, the edges trimmed down so that the covers overlap about 3 mm in the European manner. Very fine small *nasta'liq* in 4 columns of 25 lines to the page. W.S. 17.8 × 11.2 cm. Illuminated heading on *f* 1b of the highest quality and (like the whole manuscript) in very good condition, and the whole text decorated at this opening. Sub-headings and triangles (where lines are written diagonally) fully illuminated throughout, and two small decorative panels above the colophon. All the illuminations are in the best early sixteenth-century style. Colophon on *f* 66a, dated 24 Rabi' 11, 824/28 April 1421, by the

well-known calligrapher Azhar al-Sultani. The various questions raised by this colophon were discussed by the present writer in *Ars Or.* 11, p 387. The middle digit of the date certainly appears to have been altered and the left-hand one possibly, yet as it stands it is in agreement with Azhar's known *floruit*. On the other hand the final triangular portion of the colophon, which reads '*khadam bi-kitāb al-hā al-'abd al-muftaqir ila rahmat Allāh al-ghanī Azhar al-Sultānī. M.*' may not belong to the rest, from which it is divided by the gold marginal ruling, possibly masking a join in the paper. The script appears a trifle smaller, too, though its inclusion in the gold-dusting of the margin may produce an illusion. These fine points must be decided by qualified epigraphists, but for the purposes of this catalogue, it is sufficient to emphasize that the illuminations and miniatures are all consistent with a date about 1530. Mr Cary Welch's tentative attributions of the latter are included in the entries below.

There are five miniatures, all superb examples of court artists' work at the beginning of Tahmasp's reign.

Exhibited: Victoria and Albert Museum 1967 (*VAM 1967* No 26).

550 *f* 10b Shirin sees the portrait of Khusraw, displayed in a tree.

Beautiful green foreground, with a stream and numerous plants and flowers; between it and the rising hillside of delicate mauve is a group of four trees, on one of which the picture hangs; gold sky. In this beautiful setting Shirin and no fewer than 19 of her maids are represented, standing, sitting, picking flowers, offering wine and fruit and playing music.

Very slight rubbing near inner edge. This might, perhaps, be the work of 'Abd al-Samad.

19.3 × 10.8 cm. *See illustration.*

551 *f* 37b Farhad carries Shirin and her horse.

A beautiful pale-toned landscape of pink and green under a gold sky with delicately convoluted grey clouds; in the foreground a mass of rock that still retains a trace of Bihzad. Farhad and Shirin are preceded by one of her maids riding, and a running footman, and followed by two pairs of mounted maids. *VAM 1965*, pl 23. This may be a youthful work of Mir Sayyid 'Ali.

17.8 × 11.2 cm. *See colour pl VIII.*

552 *f* 43b Khusraw at Shirin's castle.

This gorgeous building rises on the left, with Shirin at the window, four of her maids on the roof, and a doorman below. In the tiled courtyard Khusraw sits on

550 Shirin sees the portrait of Khusraw. Tabriz, *c* 1530

a small throne in the shadow of a richly decorated tent, surrounded by courtiers; others appear outside the courtyard railings, and others again, with two saddled horses, on the horizon. Garden of green merging into gold, with a fine flowering tree. Blue sky with impressionistic streaky white clouds.
Ars Or. 11 (1957), p 384, fig 2. This strongly suggests the work of Mir Sayyid 'Ali.
17.3 × 11.2 cm.
See colour pl IX.

553 *f* 55a Khusraw and Shirin after their wedding-feast.
They relax in the upper floor of a splendid palace, attended by a maid, Khusraw in loose undress wearing a fur-edged cap. Other maids appear at the door, window and balcony. In the courtyard are two guards, one of them asleep, and a courtier carrying a ewer and basin. Beyond the courtyard railings, against a gold hillside, is a gardener with his spade on his shoulder. Possibly the work of 'Abd al-Samad.
17.8 × 11.2 cm. *See illustration.*

554 *f* 60a Suicide of Shirin on Khusraw's coffin. The coffin is exquisitely painted as *khatambandī* work, and the tragedy takes place in the beautifully tiled and painted interior of a fine palace. Outside, everything proceeds as usual; maids gossip on the roof, courtiers gossip in the courtyard and on the horizon, a groom holds a saddled horse and mule in readiness. Blue sky slightly darkening in streaks at the top edge. Possibly the work of 'Abd al-Samad.
Ars Or., 11 (1957), p 384, fig 3.
17.8 × 11.2 cm. *See illustration.*

'Attar: Jawab Nama & 'Arifi: Guy u Chawgān (555-561)

(also *Ahli Khursani: Diwan* – see p 196)
Ryl Pers 45 (ex Bland, Horkssia (?) and Brousie)
Seventeenth-century oriental (probably Turkish) brown leather binding with flap; sunk medallions and pendants. Rebacked and repaired. On the back doublure is written the name Francisci Horkssia (?) and on the front fly-leaf, Charles de Ludolf Brousie 1779. The front doublure is covered with Persian verses written in ink on the leather.
18.4 × 12.7 cm. 156 *ff,* some of pinkish hue. Good *nasta'liq,* 2 columns of 12 lines to the page. W.S., gold-dusted, 10.2 × 5 cm, 10.2 × 5 cm & 11.4 × 5.3 cm – sequence as given in heading above. Delicate illuminated headings on *ff* 62b *Guy u Chawgan-i 'Arifi* and 92b

Diwan-i Mawlana Ahli Khurasani. Minor headings, on plain gold panels, on *ff* 88b *Fī al-munājāt* (On Prayer), and 52b *Abiyāt* (Distichs). Text decorated on *ff* 92b, 93a. On *f* 1b is a lightly tinted design of a rose bush with two nightingales, butterflies, and rabbits below, inscribed (signed?) in the lower left-hand corner, *Darwish.* Colophons on *ff* 86a, dated 939/1532-3, but unsigned, and 152a, completely uninformative: inscriptions round the end of the text on *f* 155a have been erased and painted over with gold. Arabic prayers and Persian verses on *ff* 155b, 156a.

The seven miniatures illustrating the first two works in this volume are minor examples of the Tabriz style of the 1530s, of small scale and modest execution. Several of them are a bit rubbed. The last work seems to have been copied and illustrated at Shiraz about twenty years later. Notices of the miniatures illustrating it will be found under Nos **632-635.**

Attempts have been made to erase some of the batons from the turbans in these miniatures and the later ones in the same manuscript listed under Nos **632-635.** This was presumably the work of the Turkish owner who had the manuscript rebound.

555 *f* 22b Young prince on the roof of a building shooting birds with a gun, watched by an astonished dervish in the courtyard below.
Slight rubbing and smudging.
8.9 × 5 cm. *See illustration.*

556 *f* 38b Young mounted prince by a stream addressing a dervish seated on a green hill.
The prince's attendants appear over the horizon.
10.2 × 5 cm. *See illustration.*

557 *f* 45a Mounted prince addressed by a dervish in a landscape.
Stream, pink hillside, and tree; four spectators on the horizon.
3.6 × 5 cm. *See illustration.*

558 *f* 55b Battle between Persians and Uzbeks (?).
A Persian champion beheads one of the enemy in single combat.
Some damage to faces.
13.3 × 5.3 cm.

559 *f* 67a A game of polo.
Three players are engaged, and three others watch from the horizon.
Slightly rubbed.
8.2 × 5 cm.

553 Wedding feast of Khusraw and Shirin. Tabriz, *c* 1530

554 Suicide of Shirin on Khusraw's coffin. Tabriz, *c* 1530

556 The prince and the dervish. Tabriz, 1533

555 Young prince shooting. Tabriz, 1533

560 ƒ73b Two youths playing polo watched by four
others, and a bare-headed dervish, on the horizon.
Rubbed.
7.6 × 5 cm.

561 ƒ82b Mounted prince addressed by a dervish in
a landscape.
Very similar in all respects to No **557** above.
Figure of dervish rubbed and scratched.
8.2 × 5 cm.

557 The dervish and the prince. Tabriz, 1533

The Shiraz Style

As already mentioned (p 89) the Shiraz-Safawid style evolved smoothly and naturally from the Commercial Turkman style that had been extensively practised in that city during the last quarter of the fifteenth century. The process took about fifteen years, and by at least 1520 all obvious traces of the Timurid period had been shed. Nevertheless freak survivals of Timurid-style miniatures do sometimes occur, as in Ryl Pers 55 of 1531-33 (p 158) and, the latest so far recorded, Chester Beatty MS 214, a *Shahnama* dated 955/1548, but illustrated throughout in the Commercial Turkman style. Shiraz painters took their cue from the court artists of Tabriz and (later) Qazwin, but continued their role of producing illuminated manuscripts on a commercial basis. Ryl Pers 20 below gives us the name of one of the establishments where this work was carried on – the Foundation (*asitāna* – literally 'holy tomb') of Hazrat Mawlana Husam-al-Din Ibrahim.

This *asitāna* must have been one of a number of similar establishments at Shiraz where illustrated manuscripts were produced commercially; it is the only one whose name has come down to us, occurring in five manuscripts so far recorded apart from the present one, as follows:

c 1510/15. Sa'di. Oxford, Bodleian Library, Fraser 73. *Robinson B*, No 695.
922/1516. Nizami. (formerly) New York, Kevorkian Collection. *Sotheby* 7.XII.1970 Lot 191.
926/1519. Ahmad i Rumi. Istanbul, Museum of Turkish and Islamic Art, No 1921. *Çiğ*. No 1.
926/1519. Hafiz. Istanbul, Nurosmaniye 3816. Unpublished.
928/1522. *Shahnama*. Istanbul, Topkapi Sarayi, H.1485. Güner Inal, 'A manuscript of the Shahnameh . . .' in *STY* v (1973) pp 497-545.

Naturally enough, with manuscripts produced in these circumstances, the quality varies widely, depending, one imagines, on the status and means of the client in question. They run a gamut from small volumes with two or three routine illustrations hurriedly dashed off by some hack painter, through a rising scale of quality and magnificence, to ponderous royal (or near-royal) volumes such as the *Shahnama* of Warren Hastings in the India Office Library (*Robinson IO* pp 124-136). Sixteenth-century Shiraz manuscripts in the John Rylands Library are in general of high quality, showing the style at its best. Perhaps the choicest is the Nizami of *c* 1575 (Ryl Pers 856), though several of its miniatures have been abstracted.

The pioneer work of Miss Grace Dunham Guest *Shiraz Painting of the Sixteenth Century* (Washington 1949) as its title implies, did not pursue the subject beyond 1600. But the John Rylands Library possesses a pair of Shiraz manuscripts (Ryl Pers 35 and 908, Nos **668-672**) from the end of Shah 'Abbas's reign which show that volumes of great magnificence continued to be produced there, and that their miniatures retain a certain individuality. On the whole, however, it must be admitted that the illuminations are of higher quality than the miniatures; the latter, of course, are modelled on the contemporary metropolitan style of Isfahan.

Jami: Yusuf u Zulaykha (562-566)
Ryl Pers 20 (ex Bland, and de Sacy)

Contemporary binding with flap, rebacked and repaired, of reddish leather with beautiful sunk relief gilt panels back and front of dragon, phoenix, hares and other birds and beasts in a landscape; at the base is a stream with fish and ducks swimming. Border of sunk gilt panels of floral scrolls. Doublures of reddish leather, gilt, with medallions, pendants, and corner-pieces of black cut-out work on blue ground (slight damage).

22.2 × 13.3 cm. 176 *ff*. Good *nasta'liq* in 2 columns of 12 lines to the page: W.S. 13.3 × 5.7 cm. Small illuminated heading of unusual design and colour-scheme on *f* 1b; section headings in blue and gold on plain background. The colophon (*f* 176a) states that the copy was made at the holy tomb (*asitāna*) of Hazrat Mawlana Husam al-Din Ibrahim, at Shiraz, in the year 924/1518, but no scribe's name is given.

There are 5 small miniatures in a characteristic Shiraz style of the time, fine and meticulous, but sometimes a little weak in drawing. Their condition, on the whole, is good.

These are charming little miniatures, of comparatively early date as illustrations to Jami's most popular poem.

563 Yusuf restrains Zulaykha from suicide. Shiraz, 1518

564 Yusuf entering Zulaykha's apartment. Shiraz, 1518

562 ƒ 48b Arrival of 'Aziz of Misr at Zulaykhā's tent. A running footman (face smudged) holds his horse, while a young man does homage before him. Large tent, pale mauve hillside, plain gold sky.
10.4 × 6.3 cm.

[A ƒ seems to have been removed between 70 and 71, and a few spots of colour which have come off on ƒ 71a indicate that it bore a miniature. Presumably it represented Yusuf in the slave market.]

563 ƒ 107b Yusuf restrains Zulaykha from suicide in the chamber decorated with amorous frescoes.
Yusuf, with a flame halo, wears a baton turban gay with colours and gold.
10.4 × 6.3 cm. *See Illustration.*

564 ƒ 118a Yusuf enters Zulaykha's apartment where she sits with her maids.
The latter, overcome by Yusuf's beauty, cut their fingers with their fruit-knives. Zulaykha wears the golden aigrette, of which this must be an early instance. Yusuf has a coloured turban throughout the manuscript.
10.4 × 3.2 cm. *See illustration.*

565 ƒ 148a Yusuf riding, attended, encounters Zulaykha as an old woman.
He is preceded by a running footman. A mounted attendant holds a large parasol over his head, which has been deliberately erased.
10.4 × 7 cm.

566 ƒ 162b Zulaykha mourning at Yusuf's tomb.
Yusuf's turban and folded clothes rest on stools on either side of the rear window, making this a highly symmetrical composition.
Zulaykha's face has been scrubbed out and the features roughly retouched in black.
9.5 × 6.3 cm.

Anthology (567-574)
Ryl Pers 55 (ex Bland)
European binding of dark red leather, probably early nineteenth-century. On ƒ 9a is an obliterated seal impression, large, circular, and probably royal, and three more on ƒ 233b.
  20.2 × 12.1 cm. 233 ƒƒ. The European foliation which is followed here is in pencil, and includes all the fly-leaves etc. at the beginning. The manuscript begins with ƒ 9. Fine *nasta'liq*, though deteriorating a little towards the end of the volume, in two columns of 16 lines, and a marginal column, written diagonally, of

14 lines to the page. W.S. 15.8 × 9.5 cm. A number of the folios are of dark-coloured paper, blue, greenish or black, with text written in white. The manuscript has suffered through damp, and especially towards the beginning. Fine illuminated headings on ƒƒ 10b (much damaged: the whole opening decorated), 11b (badly damaged), 18b (damaged at outer edge), 46b (slight damage at either end), 84b (rubbed; gold on green paper), 110b (upper part damaged), 118b (ditto), 130b (ditto, inferior quality), 141b (ditto, ditto), 156b (damaged), and many smaller headings of inferior quality.
  The colophon, on ƒ 233a, is dated 938/1531-2 by the copyist Muhammad *al-kātib* al-Lari, and the date 939/1532-3 appears in the marginal column of ƒ 11a. This manuscript, whose original beauty can still be appreciated even through the terrible damage and defacement it has suffered, is one of the latest in a succession of anthologies, often featuring coloured paper and decorated pages, which seem to have been a Shiraz speciality from early Timurid times. They normally assumed the oblong format known as *safina* ('boat shape'), and the fact that this one is in normal book shape may be due to the fact that it is not a random or capricious anthology, but is the *Majalis al-Nafa'is* ('Assemblies of Delicacies') of Mir'Ali Shir Nawa'i (though the title given in the heading is *Khulasat al-Ash'ar*, 'Abstract of verses').
  Three, or even four, different hands can be detected in the miniatures. The first, an excellent exponent of the current Shiraz style, seems to have contributed no more than the frontispiece, always the most prestigious painting in a manuscript. He was assisted by a past master of the Turkman Commercial style – perhaps a man in late middle age who had been trained in pre-Safawid times – and two other Shiraz painters who were presumably called upon to adjust their style to the archaistic ideas of the patron. One of them (No **572**) succeeded better than the other.
  The manuscript contains 8 double-page miniatures, all of them, except the first, being late survivals of the Commercial Turkman style, and all more or less severely damaged. There are also 14 decorative pages at intervals throughout the volume; these are listed below, for information, but will not be numbered in the catalogue.
ƒƒ 49b, 50a All-over geometrical design picked out in gold.
ƒ 58a A découpé floral design was formerly here, of which hardly a trace remains. A few rough sketches of leaves.
ƒ 73b Découpé in blue (damaged) of two trees with birds.

f 103a Découpé floral design in two lozenge shapes, blue and black.

f 129b A couplet of elegant *nasta'liq* cut out of thin pink paper.

f 137b Elegant *nasta'liq* calligraphy on decorative background.

ff 153b, 154a *Nasta'liq* calligraphy cut out of thin pale paper.

f 168a Floral design in blue touched with gold.

f 175b Découpé *nasta'liq* calligraphy.

f 183b Symmetrical design of a vase of flowers, découpé and roughly coloured.

f 192a Découpé design of trees and birds (black).

f 215b Découpé design of trees and birds (blue).

567 *ff* 9b, 10a Double-page court scene.
On the right a prince and princess with attendants in an *iwan*; on the left other courtiers and attendants in a walled courtyard, one of them apparently overcome by liquor, and a gardener in the doorway leading from the terrace to the garden.
The miniature has lost almost all its colour – in some places even the outlines have disappeared – it is damaged and patched, and several of the faces have been childishly inked in. But enough remains to show that it was once a charming and finely executed Shiraz miniature of the period. It is enclosed in an illuminated frame or border, composed of two panels and 49 circles inscribed with the book's various contents.
Each half 14.6 × 7.6 cm.

568 *ff* 13b, 14a Two mounted youths hunting, the one a leopard and the other a lion that has leapt on the crupper of his horse.
Both halves are very badly flaked and damaged, but the style is clearly intended for Commercial Turkman. The margins, which have survived pretty well, are decorated with graceful floral scrolls on a brown stippled ground, with fully painted animals at intervals.
Each half 9.5 × 6.3 cm.

569 *ff* 21b, 22a On the right-hand side a young prince seated on a mat in a landscape (pond with duck, foreground), reading from a book, whilst an attendant pours him a cup of wine; on the left, two other young men by a tree, and a bottle on a tray.
On dark blue paper. Flaked and a bit discoloured. Broad border of floral scrolls picked out with gold, on white-stippled ground, with pairs of confronted fish at intervals. Pure Turkman style.
21b: 8.2 × 5.7 cm 22a: 7.9 × 4.8 cm. *See illustration.*

570 *ff* 41b, 42a Eight angels, arranged in four pairs, two on each half, amid conventional clouds on white-stippled background.
On black paper. Despite damage and flaking this is still a strikingly decorative composition in pure Turkman style.
Each half 15.2 × 7.6 cm. *See illustration.*

571 *ff* 65a, 66a On the right, a seated man in a landscape has wine poured for him by an attendant; on the left, three attendants carrying dishes, and a groom squatting beside a saddled horse.
This is evidently the work of a painter used to the current Shiraz style (as exemplified in the frontispiece) but who has been told to archaize and produce a picture in the old Commercial Turkman style. A comparison with *ff* 21b, 22a, which is true Turkman work, will make this point clear. The wide border is of conventional arabesque scroll panels, the corners being occupied by brick-like geometrical designs incorporating the name of 'Ali, all on brown stippled background.
A little damage and flaking mostly to faces and turbans.
Each half 8.2 × 7 cm. *See illustration.*

572 *ff* 94b, 95a On the right, a young prince and a companion seated *al fresco* on mats, are served wine by an attendant; on the left a dancing-girl and two musicians.
Water in the foreground of both halves, with a duck on the right.
On dark blue paper. This again is very badly rubbed and flaked; the coloured paper does not hold the thick colours at all well.
The style is closer to Turkman originals than the preceding, but not so faithful to them as Nos **569** and **570**. Above and below each half is a panel of arabesque scrollwork picked out with gold on a white-stippled background.
Each half 8.9 × 7.6 cm.

573 *ff* 109b, 110a Two very similar representations of a young prince riding out hawking preceded by his running footman, against a green hillside.
The margins are decorated with trees and foliage, freely drawn in pale brown and touched with gold, among which are animals and birds, fully painted.
Badly rubbed and damaged.
Each half 9.2 × 6.3 cm.

569 Young prince and attendants *al fresco.* Shiraz. 1533

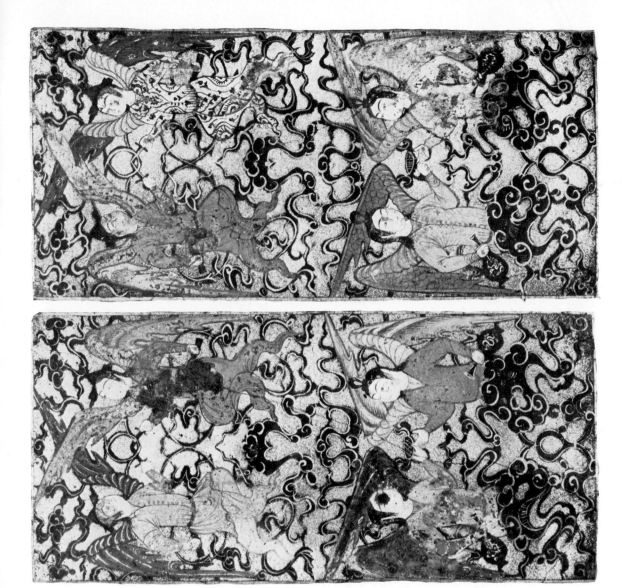

570 Angels and clouds. Shiraz, 1533

571 *Fête champêtre.*
Shiraz, 1533

574 *ff* 117b, 118a Two mounted youths hunting, as in No **568**. The one on the left pursues a gazelle, while the one on the right tackles a bear. The marginal border is virtually the same as that on No **568**.
Badly damaged as usual, especially *f* 117b.
Each half 9.5 × 6.3 cm.

Firdawsi: Shahnama (575-612)

Ryl Pers 932 (ex Hawtrey, Turner Macan, and the Kings of Oude)

Modern European binding of scarlet morocco, gilt-stamped with the name and arms of Dr Edward Craven Hawtrey. On *f* 1a is the signature of Turner Macan, the first European editor of the *Shahnama*, and a note below: 'This beautiful Manuscript of Firdousi's immortal poem was the finest in the library of the King of Oude. It was written in the year 949 of the Hegira (AD 1542) and is therefore 290 years old. It was one of the copies used by Captain Macan in collating this work.'

33 × 20.2 cm. 604 *ff* remargined throughout. 644 is the number given in the MS catalogue, a figure arrived at, presumably, by counting the blank sheets that have been bound in to protect the miniatures. Good *nasta'liq* in 4 columns of 23 lines to the page. W.S. 20.2 × 10.8 cm. The colophon (*f* 602a) is unsigned, but gives the date Muharram 949/April 1542. *Ff* 1b, 2a are exquisitely illuminated in Shiraz style as a double title-page and there are fine illuminated headings on *f* 15b at the beginning of the poem, and on *f* 298b for the reign of Luhrasp. Section headings written in blue against delicate scrollwork, in the normal Turkman/Shiraz style.

There are 38 miniatures of characteristic Shiraz type, apparently the work of two artists, A and B.

A, who executed the first 16 paintings, was painstaking, but lacked a professional touch in his drawing, and many of his faces are childish. His compositions, too, are sometimes stiff and awkward. But he could rise to an occasion and display a lively imagination (e.g. No **587**).

B, to whom the remaining 22 miniatures are attributed, was a well-trained Shiraz professional, with confident drawing and grouping, and a sure line. He occasionally 'looks back' stylistically, as in the horizon rocks and feathery white clouds (e.g. in Nos **591**, **592**, **595** etc.), the former of which is a vestigial relic of the early fifteenth-century Shiraz style, and the latter of the Commercial Turkman.

Both painters made extensive use of the many available stock groups and figures that are such a feature of Shiraz painting of the sixteenth century (see

Robinson IO, pp 85*ff*).

   Exhibited: Victoria and Albert Museum 1967 (*VAM* 1967, No 143).

575 *f* 7b The Court of Sultan Mahmud.
Carefully executed but rather naïve and childish drawing. Painter A.
16.5 × 10.8 cm. *See illustration*.

576 *f* 18b Gayumarth seated on a tiger-skin among rocks, surrounded by his courtiers in animal skins.
Painter A. 17.2 × 10.8 cm. *See illustration*.

577 *f* 27b Faridun feasting with Kundraw, minister of Zahhak.
Painter A. 17.2 × 11.4 cm. *See illustration*.

578 *f* 42a Enthronement of Minuchihr.
Naïve and childlike. Mauve ground with flowers: blue sky covered with fine feathery white clouds. Painter A.
15.8 × 10.8 cm.

[Persian foliation in top left-hand margin ceases with 48, which is followed by two unnumbered folios. Numbering is resumed at top left-hand corner of text with 49. Thus this Persian foliation is two behind (49 = 51).]

579 *f* 64a Rustam and the mad elephant.
The scene takes place in a landscape similar to the preceding, with spectators occupying the middle ground. Rustam wears a crown with his night-attire; the elephant is white, spotted. Painter A.
16.5 × 14 cm. *See illustration*.

580 *f* 70b Battle between the Persians and Turanians in which Nawdar is captured by the latter.
Includes some 'stock' figures, especially the Bihzadian group of a horseman attacked by two men on foot. The figures are smaller than in A's previous miniatures, and the effect thereby improved. Painter A.
17.2 × 10.8 cm. *See illustration*.

581 *f* 78a Rustam lifts Afrasiyab from the saddle.
Stock figures of trumpeter and man falling from horse duplicated from No **580**. Painter A.
16.5 × 10.8 cm.

582 *f* 87b Rustam and the White Demon.
Effective. Two large demons in middle ground; Rakhsh, and Awlad tied to tree, right. The tree is tall, projecting into upper margin. Painter A.
23.5 × 14 cm. *See illustration*.

575 The court of Sultan Mahmud. Shiraz, 1542

576 Gayumarth, the legendary first King, and his court. Shiraz, 1542

577 Faridun feasting with Kundraw. Shiraz, 1542

579 Rustam and the mad elephant. Shiraz, 1542

580 Defeat of Nawdar by the Turanians. Shiraz, 1542

582 Rustam and the White Demon. Shiraz, 1542

583 *f* 96b Kay Ka'us in his flying machine.
In it with him are two youths, one dark-skinned, and courtiers stand by in groups. Magnificent eagles. Gold clouds as well as the white feathery variety in the blue sky. Painter A.
15.8 × 15.2 cm. *See illustration.*

584 *f* 112b Rustam bewailing the dying Suhrab.
The hero tears his chest and weeps drops of blood. Two lines of warrior-spectators in middle ground and on horizon, the latter including a not very successful effort at frontal foreshortening. But the figure of Rustam is good. Rakhsh is shown with bowed head, exactly as in No 582, which is unusual. Painter A.
20.2 × 14.6 cm.

585 *f* 122a The fire-ordeal of Siyawush.
Kay Ka'us on foot, left, Sudaba at the window, and three groups of courtiers in the foreground. The fire seems to have been painted with a gold pigment that rots the page. It is holed and patched with light brown paper in two places. Painter A.
20.9 × 14.6 cm.

586 *f* 164b Kay Khusraw attacking the fortress of Bahman.
The defenders include both humans and demons. Symmetrical composition: in the centre two soldiers attack the gate with axes: on either side a scaling ladder: large central tower in upper margin. One of Painter A's better efforts.
26 × 17.2 cm. *See illustration.*

587 *f* 193b Fariburz consummates his marriage to Firangis, widow of Siyawush and mother of Kay Khusraw.
Vigorous and explicit central group, with male and female spectators at every window and doorway.
The miniature has formerly been stuck over with paper, and the surface is somewhat damaged in consequence. Painter A.
20.9 × 14.6 cm.

588 *f* 211a Rustam drags the Khaqan from his elephant.
The latter differs somewhat from the beast in No 579, but there can be little doubt that the same painter is involved. Painter A.
20.9 × 14.6 cm. *See illustration.*

589 *f* 226a Captive Bizhan brought before Afrasiyab.
Outdoor court scene. A very slim and formal gold cloud

among the white feathery ones. Painter A.
16.5 × 14.6 cm.

590 *f* 247b Nastihan's night-attack on the Persian camp, during which he was killed by Bizhan.
The ground is painted black and stock figures appear, especially the Bihzadian trio and the trumpeter (cf. Nos **580, 581**). Painter A.
26.7 × 15.8 cm. *See illustration.*

[Two successive folios are numbered 253, so from the second of these the true foliation is *three* ahead of the Persian]

591 *f* 273a Kay Khusraw and Shida wrestling.
This is a different artist. His drawing is surer and his faces less childish: plants, vegetation and rocks are also quite different. Feathery white clouds are neater. Painter B.
20.9 × 14 cm. *See illustration.*

592 *f* 292a Execution of Garsiwaz and Afrasiyab by Kay Khusraw.
Afrasiyab has just been beheaded (his head is nowhere to be seen, though a young man in the middle of the painting is looking skywards in what appears to be a significant manner). Garsiwaz awaits his turn, still wrapped in the ox-hide in which he was beaten so that his cries should bring his brother (Afrasiyab) from his hiding-place at the bottom of the lake. The lake itself, with fish, is shown in the foreground. Painter B.
21.6 × 11.4 cm. *See illustration.*

593 *f* 301b Enthronement of Luhrasp.
Scene in the palace courtyard: building right, garden behind. Neat and highly professional work. Painter B.
14 × 10.8 cm. *See illustration.*

594 *f* 308a Gushtasp and the dragon.
An excellent portrayal of this subject. Brownish 'desert' ground. Painter B.
17.2 × 12.7 cm. *See illustration.*

595 *f* 318a Battle between the Persians and Turanians in which Zarir was killed.
Stock figures and groups again. Painter B.
25.4 × 13.3 cm. *See illustration.*

596 *f* 329b Isfandiyar enquires of Gurgsar concerning the Brazen Fortress.
Outdoor scene with tents and awnings: dark olive ground. A man in the foreground (a bit damaged) playing the lute left-handed. Painter B.
15.2 × 13.3 cm.

583 Kay Ka'us in his flying-machine. Shiraz, 1542

586 Kay Khusraw attacks the castle of Bahman. Shiraz, 1542

588 The Khaqan lassoed by Rustam. Shiraz, 1542

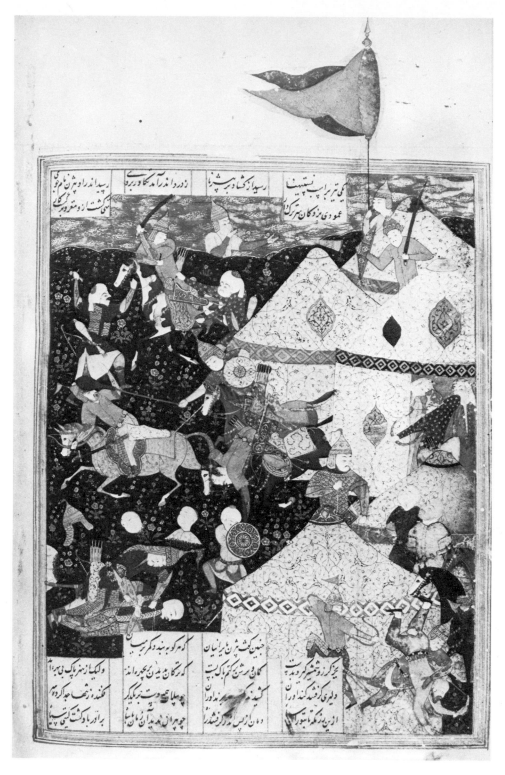

590 Night attack by Nastihan on the Persians. Shiraz, 1542

591 Kay Khusraw and Shida wrestling. Shiraz, 1542

592 Execution of Afrasiyab and Garsiwaz. Shiraz, 1542

593 Enthronement of Luhrasp. Shiraz, 1542

598 Iskandar, disguised, at the court of Dara. Shiraz, 1542

599 Iskandar's iron horsemen in battle against Fur. Shiraz, 1542

600 Iskandar and the dragon. Shiraz, 1542

602 Ardashir recognizes his son Shapur. Shiraz, 1542

603 Bahram Gur winning the crown. Shiraz, 1542

605 Shangul of Hind entertained by Bahram Gur. Shiraz, 1542

606 Nushirwan going to war with Caesar. Shiraz, 1542

608 Bahram Chubina going to see King Hurmuzd. Shiraz, 1542

612 Shirin before Shirwi the parricide. Shiraz, 1542

597 *f* 355a Rustam shoots Isfandiyar in the eyes. Isfandiyar's coat and bow were painted in rotting green pigment which has destroyed the paper; the holes have been patched from the back. Painter B. 24.1 × 11.4 cm.

[*ff* numbered 365 and 366 are missing]

598 *f* 371a Iskandar, disguised as a legate, before Dara.
Outdoor court scene with Iskandar and Dara seated on a large carpet. Painter B.
15.8 × 12.7 cm. *See illustration.*

599 *f* 381b Discomfiture of the Indian army of Fur by Iskandar's fire-breathing iron horsemen.
A striking representation of this rare subject. Painter B.
26 × 12.7 cm. *See illustration.*

600 *f* 389b Iskandar and his men destroying the dragon among the rocks.
Slightly damaged in one place by rotting green pigment. Painter B.
16.5 × 10.8 cm. *See illustration.*

601 *f* 402b Battle between Ardashir and Ardawan.
Stock figures. Experimental clouds in blue sky. Painter B.
23.5 × 14 cm.

602 *f* 408a Ardashir recognizes his son Shapur playing hockey with other boys.
The ground is brown 'desert' and all the boys are dressed in blue. Painter B.
17.2 × 11.4 cm. *See illustration.*

603 *f* 433b Bahram Gur winning the crown from between the two lions.
He uses an ox-headed mace. Painter B.
16.5 × 12.7 cm. *See illustration.*

604 *f* 449b Battle between Bahram Gur and the Khaqan in which the latter was captured.
A very energetic drummer mounted on a camel is duplicated from No **601**. Painter B.
26.7 × 16.5 cm.

605 *f* 460a Shangul King of Hind entertained by Bahram Gur.
The left-handed lutenist and accompanying tambourine player in the left foreground are duplicated from No **596**. Painter B.
17.8 × 14.6 cm. *See illustration.*

606 *f* 477b Nushirwan leading his army to war with Caesar.
Painter B. 15.8 × 14 cm. *See illustration.*

607 *f* 510a Nushirwan and the grey-bearded Indian envoy with his puzzles.
Interior court scene with slight damage from rotting green pigment. Some lively figures. Painter B.
15.2 × 10.8 cm.

608 *f* 525a Bahram Chubina riding to visit King Hurmuzd.
He is preceded by a young warrior on foot carrying a golden ball (?). Some boldly foreshortened horsemen in the background. A rather striking miniature. Painter B.
22.8 × 16.5. *See illustration.*

609 *f* 539b Execution of Ayin Gashasp before Khusraw enthroned.
He is hung head downwards. Courtiers watch. Executioner wears his red fur cap. Painter B.
15.8 × 10.8 cm.

610 *f* 561b Battle between Khusraw and Bahram Chubina in which the former escapes.
Stock figures. Brown 'desert' ground. Painter B.
21.6 × 14 cm.

611 *f* 574a Gurdiya displaying her horsemanship before Khusraw, who is shown enthroned with Shirin. Ladies' white headcloths embroidered with red and blue, and with gold aigrette, the points terminating in rubies and emeralds. Painter B.
17.2 × 11.4 cm.

612 *f* 591b Shirin before the parricide Shirwi.
Outdoor court scene with an elaborate and remarkable throne and a number of courtiers. Painter B.
15.8 × 11.4 cm. *See illustration.*

Firdawsi: Shahnama (613-631)

Ryl Pers 8 (ex Bland)
Oriental black morocco binding with sunk medallions and pendants, much worn, and with European early nineteenth-century light brown gilt calf back inscribed SHAN (*sic*) NAMEH. Doublures of Indian kincob. Back cover detached.

36.2 × 21.6 cm 581 *ff*, the last one being a replacement on which the last few couplets of the epic have been copied: if there was a colophon, it is lost. *Nasta'liq*, in 4 columns of 23 lines to the page. W.S. 19.7 × 10.2 cm (gold-sprinkled for the preface only). *Ff*

1b, 2a magnificently illuminated in Shiraz style as a double title-page; a heading of equally fine quality on ƒ15b at the beginning of the poem, and another on ƒ270b for the reign of Luhrasp. Fine illumination in spaces left at the conclusion of the text on ƒƒ15a and 270a. Section headings written in gold or blue on panels of lightly drawn scrollwork. The whole manuscript in excellent condition, apart from deliberate damage to the miniatures.

Of these there are 19, all originally excellent examples of the Shiraz style of the mid sixteenth century, but most of them have been barbarously defaced, as will appear from the list below. They are remarkable in their choice of subject in the first part of the poem. The only two 'old favourites' here are Rustam and the White Demon, and the Death of Rustam. There is no sign of the Court of Gayumarth, Zal and the Simurgh, Rustam and Suhrab, the Rescue of Bizhan, or half a dozen more than one expects to find in a manuscript of this kind.

It seems likely that these miniatures were shared between two painters. Painter A was notable for his bold and individual treatment of clouds; otherwise his work is competent and characteristic of its time and place. Painter B is also unmistakably Shirazi, but his drawing is rather stiffer than A's, his figures are generally larger, and their faces are characterized by a rather long pointed chin. He enjoyed painting demons, and was probably the illustrator of the 1560 Jami in the India Office Library (*Robinson IO* Nos 297–301).

613 ƒ34a The head of Iraj laid before Faridun.
Court scene on a terrace with garden gate and large tree behind.
The head of Iraj has been smudged, but otherwise the miniature is in good condition. Painter A.
22.8 × 10.4 cm. *See illustration.*

614 ƒ57b Pre-nuptial feast of Zal.
He is seated on a mat in a pale landscape, drinking with friends and entertained by musicians.
The miniature has been wantonly scored and scratched, especially across Zal's face and the instruments of the musicians; this would seem to be the work of an idle and spoiled child, rather than of the usual religious bigot. Painter A.
16.5 × 10.4 cm. *See illustration.*

615 ƒ63b Capture of Nawdar in battle by Afrasiyab.
Gold ground dotted with flowers. Swirling, light clouds or mist in the sky and a clawed cloud of variegated hue. One or two stock figures and groups (camel drummer on horizon and man leaning over horse's neck to grasp

opponent by the girdle).
A fine miniature in good condition. Painter B.
27.3 × 17.2 cm. *See illustration.*

616 ƒ78b Rustam and the White Demon, Awlad tied to a tree and Rakhsh grazing.
The composition is exactly the same as that of No **582** but with four instead of two demons appearing above the cave. A large tree of rather original form projects into the upper margin.
It must have been an impressive miniature, but has been most savagely smudged and defaced; the figure of Rustam, in particular, is almost obliterated. Painter B.
26.7 × 17.2 cm.

617 ƒ81a Encounter of Rustam and the King of Mazandaran.
Unusual sky, with shaded white clouds and a clawed gold cloud of the usual Shiraz type.
The heads of both principal figures, and that of a trumpeter, and his long trumpet, have been scrubbed out. Painter A.
24.1 × 17.8 cm.

618 ƒ127a Combat of Faramurz and Warazad.
Same shaded clouds. Eyebrows of Faramurz retouched. Painter A.
24.1 × 17.8 cm. *See illustration.*

619 ƒ155a Council meeting of Kay Khusraw with Rustam and the other Persian leaders.
A well-executed interior court scene. (The doorkeeper, bottom left, seen frontally, is a striking figure.)
The faces of the king and of a lady at a window have been badly damaged. Painter A.
17.8 × 15.2 cm.

620 ƒ187b Rustam wrestling with Puladwand.
Again, the wild cloudy sky.
The eyes and noses of the two principal figures have been childishly redrawn with black ink, and the colour has flaked off the leopard's head on Rustam's helmet. Painter A.
22.8 × 12.7 cm. *See illustration.*

621 ƒ206a Rustam brings captives to Kay Khusraw after his sack of Afrasiyab's palace.
Outdoor court scene in a pale, finely painted landscape; the captives are painted with great expressiveness and sympathy.
Rustam's features have again been childishly redrawn, and the face of Kay Khusraw badly rubbed. Painter A.
16.5 × 12.7 cm.

613 Faridun receives the head of Iraj. Shiraz, mid 16th century

614 Zal feasting before his marriage. Shiraz, mid 16th century

615 King Nawdar captured by Afrasiyab. Shiraz, mid 16th century

618 Combat of Faramurz and Warazad. Shiraz, mid 16th century

620 Rustam wrestling with Puladwand. Shiraz, mid 16th century

622 ƒ233a Kay Khusraw weeping as he views the dead after the battle of the Twelve Rukhs.
A very slight patch of discolouration, otherwise good condition. Painter A.
16.5 × 10.4 cm.

623 ƒ270a The enthronement of Luhrasp.
A well-painted interior court scene: slight rubbing here and there, but not serious. Painter A.
12.1 × 10.2 cm. *See illustration.*

624 ƒ307b Interview of Isfandiyar with his father Gushtasp.
A beautifully painted court scene on a walled terrace opening onto a garden. Shaded white clouds in the sky again.
The king's face has been scrubbed out and then the features crudely redrawn in ink: Isfandiyar's turban partly smudged. Some flaking of green pigment. Painter A.
17.8 × 16.5 cm.

625 ƒ328b The dying Rustam shoots his treacherous brother Shaghad through the tree.
The last agony of the hero and his faithful horse in the death pit are well shown – Rustam's half-closed eyes, and Rakhsh's desperate struggle.
The figure of Rustam and the face of Shaghad are smudged and rubbed, and the outlines of some of the rocks have been childishly followed in black ink. Painter A.
24.1 × 16.5 cm. *See illustration.*

626 ƒ341b The dying Dara comforted by Iskandar, while the captive murderers are brought on.
A striking miniature with the same vivid colour scheme of gold and blue as No **615**, but the faces of the central group of courtiers have been deliberately smudged out, and one or two of them then roughly touched in with black ink. Painter B.
20.2 × 17.2 cm.

627 ƒ375a Interview of Iskandar and Queen Qaydafa. Court scene round a terrace; building on left.
This miniature seems to be untouched and almost undamaged except for a tiny smudge below the throne. Painter A.
17.8 × 15.8 cm. *See illustration.*

628 ƒ394b Bahram Gur hunting with Azada.
They ride on separate camels. A wonderful turbulent sky, with shaded white clouds and gold ones with claws. The treatment is unusual, but is closely

parallelled in the India Office *Shāhnāma* of 1560. (*Robinson IO*, No 287).
Bahram Gur's face and adjacent area smudged. Painter A.
18.4 × 15.8 cm. *See illustration.*

629 ƒ447a Nushirwan's erring wife and her lover brought before him.
Court scene: walled terrace and garden, building left. Almost every face has been obliterated and the surface of the paper torn in one or two places. Painter A.
17.8 × 15.2 cm.

630 ƒ496b Sawa Shah shot by Bahram Chubina.
Unlike the usual composition, Bahram is here shown above, near the horizon, and Sawa immediately below him.
Some smudging and a little discolouration at the outer edge. Painter A.
26.7 × 17.8 cm. *See illustration.*

631 ƒ543a Gurdiya, sister of Bahram Chubina, displaying her equestrian and military skills before Khusraw and Shirin.
The composition is the same as that of No **611**, but the treatment here is far more lively.
Gurdiya's face deliberately damaged, her sword smudged and clumsily redrawn, and a little smudging elsewhere. Painter A.
18.1 × 15.4 cm.

Ahli Khurasani: Diwan (632-635)
Ryl Pers 45
(For description of the whole manuscript and other miniatures, see p. 150.)
Four miniatures in the Shiraz style of the mid sixteenth century, on a small scale, but of good quality. They have suffered a certain amount of rubbing and other damage.

632 ƒ106b Two youths and three companions in a rocky landscape.
They are looking with astonishment at a panel of sculpture on the rock representing a prince and princess seated together.
The outlines of the rocks in the lower part of the miniature have been crudely emphasized with black ink.
9.5 × 7.6 cm. *See illustration.*

623 Enthronement of Luhrasp. Shiraz, mid 16th century

624 Isfandiyar before Gushtasp. Shiraz, mid 16th century

625 The death of Rustam. Shiraz, mid 16th century

627 Iskandar and Queen Qaydafa. Shiraz, mid 16th century

628 Bahram Gur hunting with Azada. Shiraz, mid 16th century

632 Youths inspecting a rock sculpture. Shiraz, mid 16th century

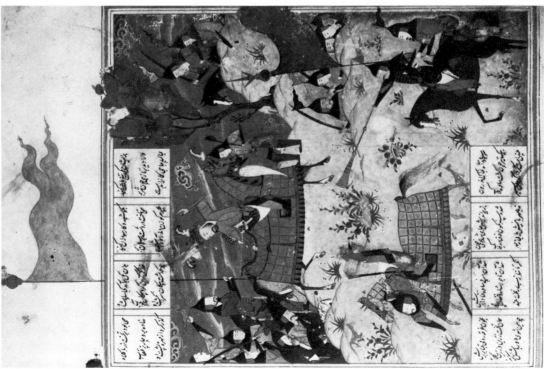

630 Sawa Shah shot by Bahram Chubina. Shiraz, mid 16th century

633 ƒ119a A princely *fête champêtre*.
The prince, seated on a mat, right, is offered a dish by a page, while two young courtiers on either side of a bearded man seen full-face, seem to be encouraging him to empty the wine-cup he holds. Green landscape with graceful trees: gold sky.
10.2 × 8.2 cm.

634 ƒ128b Sermon in a mosque.
The women and children are in the gallery, and the male congregation on the floor.
9.2 × 7.3 cm. *See illustration.*

635 ƒ142b A bearded man (the poet?) by a stream.
He sits in a luxuriant green landscape with blossoming trees and cypresses, listening to the song of the birds. This must have been a very fine miniature in its original state, but it is now a bit rubbed and discoloured.
14 × 9.5 cm. *See illustration.*

Nizami: Khamsa (636-651)
Ryl Pers 856
Nineteenth-century oriental binding of red leather (rebacked) with medallions and pendants inlaid with gilt paper. Pencil note on a front fly-leaf gives the price, £14.14s.
    31.1 × 20.9 cm 222 ƒƒ (I follow the small pencil foliation: there is also one in ink, in Persian, which breaks off at 226, and a rough and clumsy European *pagination* reaching 440). Good *nasta'liq* in 4 columns of 20 lines to the page; gold-dusted W.S. 19 × 10.8 cm. Very richly illuminated double title-page, ƒƒ 1b, 2a, but somewhat damaged and the edges trimmed. Illuminated headings of great richness on ƒƒ 40b (*Layla wa Majnun*), 94b (*Haft Paykar*), 144b (*Iqbal Nama Iskandari*), 192b (*Sharaf Nama Iskandari*). A completely uninformative colophon on ƒ222a, and others at the end of each poem. The text is defective in several places, and some pages with miniatures have been removed.
    The manuscript at present contains 16 miniatures, (there must originally have been about 25) in good condition for the most part, and excellent examples of the Shiraz style of *c* 1575. The painter's touch is sure and delicate. The exquisite shading of the rocks is especially noteworthy, and the drawing of the tents in No **643**, and such small details as the arabesque door behind the schoolmaster in No **640**, attest his skill and competence.

[Folio extracted between the present ƒƒ 3 and 4; it probably carried a miniature of the *Mi'raj*, or heavenly ascent. Several more missing between ƒƒ 7 and 8.]

636 ƒ9b The old woman's petition to Sultan Sanjar.
Slightly rubbed and discoloured, and somebody has drawn crosses and asterisks on the small stones in the upper right-hand part of the miniature. Very finely shaded rocks, and leaves growing *all round* the stones.
19 × 15.8 cm. *See illustration.*

[A considerable lacuna between ƒƒ 15 and 16, from *maqala* 11 of the *Makhzan al Asrar* to the beginning of the story in the *Khusraw u Shirin*; this may have contained a *Mi'raj* miniature].

637 ƒ17a The ministers of Hurmuzd plead with him for his disgraced son Khusraw, lower left, carrying his sword.
Tall building left, with doorkeeper and ladies on the balcony.
Very slight discolouration along outer edge.
19 × 16.5 cm. *See illustration.*

638 ƒ25a Khusraw spies Shirin bathing.
Classic composition. Khusraw, on a splendid dappled horse, is preceded by a running footman.
19 × 18.4 cm. *See illustration.*

[A number of ƒƒ are missing between ƒƒ 32 and 33, probably including a miniature of Khusraw and the lion, and again between ƒƒ 38 and 39, comprising the whole episode of Farhad, which no doubt contained at least one miniature.]

639 ƒ39b Khusraw at Shirin's palace.
He sits on a small throne set in the courtyard, holding a flower, and looking up at the balcony on which Shirin appears. Several attendants behind Khusraw, and the courtyard has a very handsome wall and door. Cf. No **552**.
21.6 × 15.5 cm. *See illustration.*

[ƒƒ 39/40. A further lacuna, possibly with a miniature of the murder of Khusraw.]

[ƒƒ 41/42. Several ƒƒ missing. Another *Mi'raj* passage occurs in the missing portion.]

640 ƒ45b Layla and Majnun at school.
Crowded composition with numerous pupils, book-rests and small white ink-pots. The schoolmaster wears a baton turban. In the upper floor of the tall building, right, two ladies are receiving instruction, whilst a latecoming parent enters the door below, ushering in his small boy to join the class.
19 × 16.5 cm. *See illustration.*

641 *f* 50a Majnun and his father at the Ka'ba.
A number of pilgrims and worshippers are present, and in the upper margin, much discoloured, are two men on a hilltop between two minarets. The man seated with his rosary in a tiny domed building of his own in the bottom left-hand corner could almost be a self-portrait of the artist.
26 × 16.5 cm. *See illustration.*

642 *f* 71a Majnun, among the beasts in the wilderness is visited by Salim riding on a mule.
Other travellers and watchers appear behind rocks. Majnun has *'ya Layla'* tattoed on his chest.
Discoloured along the outer edge.
19 × 17.8 cm. *See illustration.*

643 *f* 85b Layla and Majnun faint at meeting.
The background is a busy camp scene, with travellers behind a group of three tents in which women appear. In the foreground Majnun's four-footed friends attack various innocuous bystanders.
A little discoloured along the outer edge.
19 × 17.2 cm. *See illustration.*

644 *f* 106b Bahram Gur entertained on the roof while Fitna carries the cow upstairs.
She wears no veil, and her sponsor watches her progress anxiously through a doorway at the top of the ladder. Courtiers and attendants in the courtyard below, most of them wearing baton turbans.
A little discoloured along the outer edge.
19 × 17.2 cm. *See illustration.*

645 *f* 116b Bahram Gur and the princess in the Yellow Pavilion.
Numerous female attendants, a dancer, musicians and a gardener energetically digging beyond the terrace gateway. There is very little yellow indeed in the miniature.
Slight discolouration at the lower right-hand edge.
24.1 × 17.2 cm. *See illustration.*

[One *f* missing between *ff* 118 and 119; no doubt it carried a miniature of the Green Pavilion.]

646 *f* 121b Bahram Gur and the Princess in the Red Pavilion.
Usual composition.
23.5 × 17.2 cm. *See colour pl X.*

647 *f* 125b Bahram Gur and the Princess in the Blue Pavilion.

Most of the shades used, including the dome in the upper margin, are green rather than blue.
A crease runs across the lower part of the miniature.
24.1 × 17.2 cm. *See illustration.*

648 *f* 130b Bahram Gur and the Princess in the Sandalwood Pavilion.
Discoloured and damaged along the outer edge: the top of the dome also discoloured.
23.5 × 17.2 cm. *See illustration.*

649 *f* 135a Bahram Gur and the Princess in the White Pavilion.
Discolouration along the outer edge and on the dome in the upper margin.
24.1 × 18.4 cm. *See illustration.*

[A lacuna between *ff* 149 and 150, covering Iskandar's battle with the Zangi, of which there was no doubt a miniature.]

650 *f* 163b Iskandar comforting the dying Dara.
Warriors stand round in a circle, and the captured murderers are brought on, right.
Creased, and a little damaged and discoloured along the outer edge.
20.2 × 17.2 cm. *See illustration.*

[One *f* is missing between *ff* 173 and 174; it probably carried a miniature of Iskandar at the Ka'ba. A further lacuna between *ff* 178 and 179, covering Iskandar's battle with the Russians. Here, too, a miniature is almost certainly missing.]

651 *f* 207a Iskandar, leaning on his stick at the entrance of a state tent, and with wise men in attendance, interviews a shepherd.
Rocky landscape behind with a number of birds. The man holding a sheep immediately in front of Iskandar is one of the stock figures often found in early Safawid-Shiraz painting. See *Robinson IO*, p 89 (x).
Rather more discolouration than usual along the outer edge.
19 × 17.2 cm. *See illustration.*

635 Poet listening to birds in a wood. Shiraz, mid 16th century

634 Sermon in a mosque. Shiraz, mid 16th century

636 Sultan Sanjar and the old woman. Shiraz, *c* 1575

637 Khusraw before his father Hurmuzd. Shiraz, *c* 1575

638 Khusraw spies Shirin bathing. Shiraz, *c* 1575

639 Khusraw at Shirin's palace. Shiraz, *c* 1575

640 Layla and Majnun at school. Shiraz, *c* 1575

641 Majnun at the Ka'ba. Shiraz, *c* 1575

642 Majnun visited by Salih. Shiraz, c 1575

643 Layla and Majnun faint at meeting. Shiraz, *c* 1575

649 Bahram Gur in the White Pavilion. Shiraz, *c* 1575

650 Iskandar and the dying Dara. Shiraz, *c* 1575

651 Iskandar and the shepherd. Shiraz, *c* 1575

Hafiz: Diwan (652-655)

Ryl Pers 945

Lacquer covers painted with a mass of flowers within double frame of gold scrollwork, the doublures with gold floral scrolls on dark green ground (second quarter nineteenth century).

13.7 × 8.6 cm. 214 *ff*, the last one a replacement (blank), remargined throughout. Fine small *nasta'liq* in two columns of 12 lines to the page. W.S. gold-sprinkled, 8.6 × 4.1 cm. This little manuscript is beautifully decorated and illuminated; *ff* 2b, 3a, where the preface begins, is minutely and sumptuously illuminated as a double title-page, and the following opening, *ff* 3b, 4a, is almost entirely covered with gold, both text and margins having a gold background enriched with floral scrolls; the effect is extremely rich. F 8a has a small illuminated heading, and the whole opening, text and margins, is decorated. At the end of the *qasidas* on *f* 17b the residue of the W.S. is covered with a magnificent square panel of illumination, and the *ghazals* begin on *f* 17a with a sumptuous illuminated heading and a fully decorated opening. There is no colophon, the original last folio being lost, but in the lower margin of *f* 213b the date 1027/1618 has been written, presumably when the manuscript was re-margined and rebound in the nineteenth century. What its significance, if any, may be is doubly hard to determine, because the digits appear to have been tampered with already. It seems best to disregard it. The miniatures in any case can be quite confidently assigned to Shiraz *c* 1580, and are excellent small scale examples of the style.

652   *ff* 1b, 2a A hunting party.
Despite the very small scale, fourteen humans and about twenty animals of various kinds are represented, yet there is no sense of clutter; all the usual incidents are portrayed. Especially noteworthy on *f* 2a is a falcon seizing a heron on the wing, and on *f* 1b a bear, seen backview, climbing in a tree on the horizon.
Each half 8.9 × 4.8 cm, within a richly illuminated border. *See illustration.*

653   *f* 57b Dervishes dancing, watched by a ring of spectators.
Green ground, gold sky. Margins and text of opening as *ff* 3b, 4a.
7.6 × 6 cm. *See illustration.*

654   *f* 123b Young prince playing polo, accompanied by an orchestra.
Rather discoloured and damaged, especially at the outside edge. Margins and text as before.
8.9 × 6 cm.

655   *f* 167a Battle scene against a mauve hillside with a youthful champion cleaving the head of an opponent.
Margins and text lavishly decorated and illuminated as before.
8.9 × 7 cm. *See illustration.*

Sa'di: Bustan (656-659)

Robinson Pers 1 (ex Samuel Robinson)
European brown calf binding of the early nineteenth century (covers loose). Bookplate of Samuel Robinson, Blackbrook Cottage, Wilmslow; bequeathed by him to Owen's College in 1884.

26 × 18.4 cm. 86 *ff*, the last one a replacement. Fair *nasta'liq* in two columns of 17 lines, and a marginal column of 12 lines written diagonally, to the page. W.S., gold sprinkled, 19 × 10.2 cm. Damaged and patched illuminated heading on *f* 1b. Decorated sub-headings and corners of marginal columns throughout, also text of *ff* 1b, 2a and all openings with miniatures. No colophon.

There are four miniatures, good examples of the Shiraz style of *c* 1600.

656   *f* 24a Bearded man in gold turban addressing youth in a landscape.
Other young men stand round, and a horned sheep appears in the lower right-hand corner.
14 × 10.2 cm. *See illustration.*

657   *f* 36b Mounted prince with attendants in a landscape addressed by a greybeard.
14 × 10.2 cm. *See illustration.*

658   *f* 57b Courtier shooting the old woman's cat found in the royal kitchen.
Building in the background, and 9 other figures, one full-face.
14 × 10.2 cm. *See illustration.*

659   *f* 82a Yusuf tempted by Zulaykha in the House of Idols.
She places a golden figure on a throne, while he gestures, sitting in the foreground on a rug with pillow. Two ladies at windows, left.
Slight discolouration and damage.
14 × 10.2 cm.

652 Hunting party. Shiraz. *c* 1580

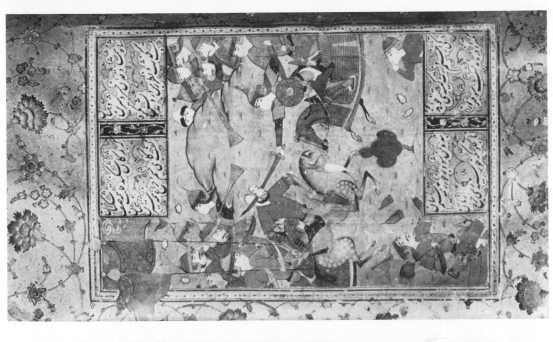

655 Battle scene. Shiraz, c 1580

653 Dancing dervishes. Shiraz, c 1580

657 Mounted prince addressed by a greybeard. Shiraz, *c* 1600.

656 Bearded man addressing a youth. Shiraz, *c* 1600

659 Yusuf and Zulaykha in the house of idols. Shiraz, *c* 1600

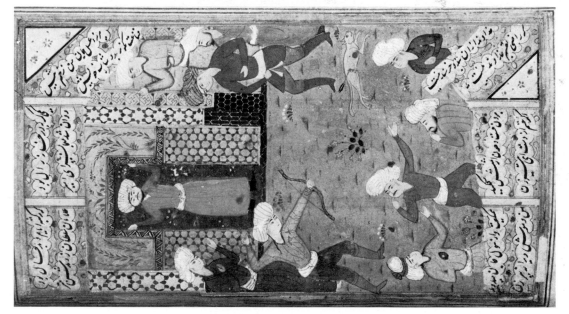

658 The old woman's cat shot by a courtier. Shiraz, *c* 1600

Ahli: Kulliyat (660)
Ryl Pers 868

In slip-case. Splendid contemporary binding in very good condition (repaired and flap replaced), of characteristic Shiraz type. On each outer face a gilt panel with medallion, pendants and corner-pieces, surrounded by a double frame of sunken gilt panels and corner-pieces; the doublures with similar designs, but executed in gilt cut-out work on variously coloured backing; slight damage in places.

34.9 × 22.8 cm. 338 ff. Fine *nasta'liq* in 2 columns of 12 lines and a marginal column (three sides) of 28 lines; W.S. 20.2 × 12.1 cm. Splendid illuminated heading on *f* 2b, and the text decorated for this opening; other good illuminated headings on *ff* 55b, 163b, 269b, 270b, 287b, 288b, 307b and 309b, and a number of minor ones. Uninformative colophon on *f* 338b.

660 *ff* 1b, 2a Double-page frontispiece, within a bold and effective illuminated border.

The miniature has been subjected to an extreme of bigoted vandalism; all the figures (occupying the greater part of the painted area) have been viciously scrubbed, smeared and defaced. So far as one can see, the scene was of men in discussion in the courtyard of a mosque, and among tombs. The quality appears to have been very good, and the style is that of Shiraz in the first years of the seventeenth century.

Each half 19.7 × 11.4 cm.

Sana'i: Hadiqa (al-Haqiqa) (661-667)
Ryl Pers 12 (ex Bland and Turner Macan)

Fairly modern oriental binding of dark red leather, inlaid with gilt medallions and pendants, the spine inscribed HUDDEEKA HUKEEM SUNNAIE; a bit wormed. The original doublures, of fairly rough gilt cut-out work on various coloured backgrounds, have been incorporated, but are somewhat damaged.

23.8 × 13.3 cm. 318 ff. Good *nasta'liq* in 2 columns of 16 lines to the page. W.S. 16.5 × 7 cm. Good illuminated headings on *ff* 2b (Preface, with the signature of Turner Macan beside it) and 10b (beginning of text), the text of these and the facing pages decorated. Sub-headings in red; central column-ruling of each page is not formed of the usual pair of fine gold lines outlined in black, but of a narrow gold stripe flanked by pale green lines.

There are colophons on *ff* 10a and 317a, the former giving the scribe's name. Muhammad al-Qiwami, and the latter the date 'End of Rajab the revered, the year 1016' corresponding to mid November 1607.

The manuscript contains 7 miniatures, three of which are double-page compositions, in the Shiraz style of the time.

661 *ff* 1b, 2a Double-page frontispiece. An outdoor court scene within a rich illuminated border. On the right, the prince enthroned, and surrounded by courtiers; on the left, preparation of an *al fresco* meal, supervised by a stout courtier in vermilion. Background of pastel-shaded rocks; foreground dark green with yellowish-green plants.

F 1b a bit cracked and damaged at the edges.

Each half (without border) 14 × 7.6 cm. *See illustration.*

662 *f* 60b Abraham seated calmly on his mat amid the flames into which he has been cast by a great catapult.

Nimrod and attendants watch from the palace roof, and an executioner stands ready with a heavy chain.

11.4 × 10.8 cm. *See illustration.*

663 *ff* 163b, 164a Scene in a public bath.

On the right is the dressing-room, and on the left a customer is having his head shaved.

The little cupola in the margin of *f* 164a was left by the artist without support in mid-air; a previous owner of the manuscript has drawn the supports roughly in black.

F 163b, 8.9 × 8.9 cm; *f* 164a, 12.1 × 9.5 cm.

664 *f* 196a Scene in a tavern.

Several men drinking, a prostitute enticing a customer, and large wine-jars and jugs standing about.

15.8 × 8.9 cm. *See illustration.*

665 *f* 221b Illustration of the story of the sick maiden and her nurse frightened by a black humped ox with a cooking-pot stuck on its head. The story also occurs in *Anwar i Suhayli*.

15.2 × 8.9 cm. *See illustration.*

666 *f* 247b King Mahmud Zawuli addressed by a woman whilst out hunting.

Several faces damaged.

13.3 × 8.9 cm.

667 *ff* 317b, 318a Double-page tail-piece of a royal hunt.

On the right, the quarry is presented to the young mounted prince; on the left, an encounter with a lion and, above, a man with a gun considers shooting at a group of ibex.

The whole enclosed in a good illuminated border, rubbed and cracked in places.

Each half 14 × 7.6 cm (without border). *See illustration.*

Nizami: Khamsa (668-670)

Ryl Pers 35 (ex Bland)

Original seventeenth-century binding of exquisite quality, restored with gilt morocco back ('NIZAMI'S WORKS. PERSIAN MANUSCRIPT. M.DC.') and edges. The outer surfaces each have a central gilt panel very finely tooled in relief with animals and birds round a large central tree, and clouds above; above and below this are two narrow gilt panels each containing two pheasants and foliage in relief. These are surrounded by a frame composed of six panels of inlaid crimson leather, with verses cut out in fine *nasta'liq*; the writing and its background of foliated scrolls were formerly inlaid with white and green leather respectively, but most of this has disappeared. The panels are separated by gilt rosettes. Finally, there is an outer frame of inlaid gilt relief panels and corner-pieces of foliated scroll-work. The black morocco background to these various panels is painted with leafy designs in gold, but these are much worn away. The central panels of the doublures have been replaced by marbled paper, matching the present end-papers; above and below them are oblong panels of finely cut-out gilt floral scrolls (damaged) on green ground, and the whole is enclosed in a frame of gilt cut-out scrolls set in blue panels, and corner-pieces. This magnificently luxurious binding may be compared with those of the Victoria and Albert Museum *Khusraw u Shirin* of 1632 (No 364-1885) signed by Muhammad Muhsin Tabrizi and one in the Gulbenkian Foundation, Lisbon, signed Muhammad Salih Tabrizi on a manuscript of the *Qiran al-Sa'dain* of Amir Khusraw, of about the same date.

26 × 15.2 cm. 319 *ff*, the majority remargined. Good *nasta'liq* in 4 columns of 22 lines to the page. W.S., gold-powdered, 15.8 × 7.9 cm. Magnificent double-pages of illumination on *ff* 2b, 3a (*Makhzan al-Asrar*), *ff* 29b, 30a (*Khusraw u Shirin*: heading and fully decorated margins and text on gold ground), *ff* 97b, 98a (*Layla wa Majnun*: heading and richly decorated margins on plain ground), *ff* 149b, 150a (*Haft Paykar*: as *ff* 29b, 30a: damaged at inner edges), *ff* 205b, 206a (*Iskandar Nama*: as *ff* 97b, 98a), *ff* 269b, 270a (*Iqbal Nama*: as the preceding, but with Waq-waq scrolls containing human and animal faces). Fully illuminated sub-headings and gold intercolumnar scrolls throughout. On *f* 269a, seal-impression reading *rukh i 'Abbas shad 'z Mihr 'Ali* with the date 1107/1696. Decorated but uninformative colophons at the end of

the first five poems; the last one (*f* 318a) gives the copyist's name as Mir 'Ali, with the date 3 Dhū'l-qa'da 1037/5 July 1628, 'at Shiraz, the abode of plenty' (*dār al-fā'iz*).

The manuscript contains two double-page miniatures within decorated margins, as follows:

668 *f* 1b A young prince seated on a chair, resting after the hunt, approached by a dark-skinned servant, whilst another servant roasts kebabs on a spit.

In the foreground are two groups: three courtiers on the right, and a row of six young men on the left. The latter are in seventeenth-century costume and diminish in scale from front to rear. They would seem to be additions to the original composition.

This miniature does not belong to the manuscript, and was inserted to replace the lost half, perhaps when the manuscript was restored. It may originally have been a fairly modest Tabriz painting of *c* 1530, but has been very extensively repainted.

14.6 × 7.3 cm.

669 *f* 2a Shah 'Abbas and his court.

He is surrounded by courtiers, including two seated ladies, and there is a group of musicians in the foreground. In front of the enthroned monarch is a row of six gold wine-bottles ranged along the edge of an ornamental tank in which are two ducks.

Creased.

This was originally the *right-hand* half of the double-page frontispiece.

14.6 × 7.3 cm. *See illustration.*

670 *ff* 318b, 319a Crowded royal hunt, with Shah 'Abbas on the right, about to release his falcon.

To the right of the middle of *f* 318b is a row of six young men recalling those added to *f* 1b; in the foreground a dramatic incident with a lion. On *f* 319a, hawking is in progress at the top of the composition (distant figures reduced in size), the remainder being occupied by the pursuit of antelopes, and a young man defending himself from a tiger (*very* rarely found in Persian miniatures) which has leaped upon his horse's crupper. Most of the ground of both halves is gold and silver, and the sky has rather impressionistic streaky white clouds.

Each half 14.6 × 7.3 cm. *See illustration.*

This is a manuscript of great magnificence, but it must be admitted that the quality of the miniatures, which imitate the Isfahan style of the time, is not quite up to that of the binding and illuminations. A close parallel is the India Office Sa'di of 1624 (*Robinson IO*

662 Abraham and Nimrod. Shiraz, 1607

665 The sick maiden, the ox, and the cooking-pot. Shiraz. 1607

664 Scene in a tavern. Shiraz, 1607

670 Hunting party of Shah 'Abbas. Shiraz, 1628

671 Outdoor court scene. Shiraz, 1628

675 Prince watching polo. Bukhara, c 1560

674 A game of polo. Bukhara, c 1560

680 Youth attempting to detain a girl. Bukhara, 1579

676 Prince enthroned, with attendants. Bukhara, c 1560

678 Two enthroned youths listening to music. Bukhara, 1579

676 *f* 20a Prince enthroned under a blossoming tree.

A kneeling courtier (perhaps intended for the author?) offers him a book, whilst another courtier stands respectfully by, hands hidden in sleeves. Dark green foreground with plants and flowers; gold behind.
14 × 7 cm. *See illustration.*

Shahi: Diwan   (677-680)

Ryl Pers 43 (ex Bland, Wedderburn, Fox)

European red leather binding, *c* 1800, the spine inscribed DIVAN SHAHY: MS PERS. The manuscript was apparently acquired by a Mr C. Fox in 1800, the text then being in some confusion. Fox consigned it to a friend, Dr A. Clarke, evidently a Persian scholar (cf. the preceding manuscript), who rearranged the *ff* in their proper order, and had the manuscript rebound. A note from him to Fox, mounted on the front fly-leaf, reads, in part, 'Rejoice with me that I have had the very good fortune to restore poor misplaced *Shahee* to his original order, and find, that there is not a page missing. The book is a prize.' It was subsequently 'Bought at Mr Fox's sale' by a Mr Wedderburn.

26.7 × 19.7 cm. The manuscript is numbered by *pages* not folios, the last being 100, remarginated throughout in Bukhara style with stiff paper of various colours, the margins adorned with stencilled floral scroll designs and inlaid medallions of coloured paper, all picked out with gold. Fine *nasta'liq*, 2 columns of 13 lines to the page. W.S., gold dusted, 15.2 × 7.6 cm. Pp 1, 4 and 5 are decorated with large floral scrolls, freely drawn in gold, and on p 5 is a beautiful illuminated *shamsa* enclosing the *bismillah* (formerly, perhaps, the patron's name and titles). Pp 6 and 7 are splendidly illuminated as a double title-page (slight damage and trimming at the edges). Sub-headings are written in white on illuminated panels. Colophon (much decoration added later) signed by Muhammad Salih, and dated 987/1579.

The miniatures are typical Bukhara products of the time, but except in No **678** all the faces and figures, as well as some other details, have been heavily repainted in a style of European inspiration, probably not long before the acquisition of the manuscript by Mr Fox (cf. MS 907 on p 270).

677 pp 2, 3 Double-page court scene within illuminated frame.

A prince enthroned in an *iwan*, attended by courtiers, being offered refreshment (p 2). In the adjoining courtyard, separated by a red fence and wooden door from a garden and golden hillside, are more courtiers, one overcome by drink, and two musicians (p 3). Above and below the miniatures are verses from Hafiz.
P 2. 19 × 11.4 cm; p 3 17.8 × 10.8 cm.

678 pp 38, 39 Double-page outdoor court scene, within illuminated frames.

Two youths seated on a throne, holding hands, with six other young men, one of whom offers them refreshment (p 38). They are being entertained by a lady harpist and two youths playing lute and tambourine, while four other youths are in attendance (p 39). Usual background of golden hillside.

This miniature is in almost pristine condition; there is only very slight retouching on the faces of the musicians on p 39.
Each half, 15.5 × 7.9 cm. *See illustration.*

679 p 63 Lovers seated on a mat by a garden wall, entertained with music and wine.
Golden hillside above.
15.2 × 7.6 cm.

680 p 81 Lovers on a walled terrace opening on a garden.
The girl makes to depart, and the man catches the tail of her robe. Golden hillside above. This was a popular composition, and a number of versions exist. Cf. for example, *Kühnel* pl 67.
15.2 × 7.9 cm. *See illustration.*

The Mashhad and Qazwin Style

Shah Tahmasp moved his capital from Tabriz to Qazwin in 1548; the former had proved uncomfortably near the Turkish frontier, and had been taken by the Ottoman armies on three occasions. It is interesting to note that Milton seems to have been aware of this situation:

> As when the Tartar from his Russian foe,
> By Astracan, over the snowy plains,
> Retires; or Bactrian Sophie, from the horns
> Of Turkish crescent, leaves all waste beyond
> The realm of Aladule,* in his retreat
> To Tauris or Casbeen.
>
> (*Paradise Lost*, x, ll.431-6)

It was about the time of the move of the capital that 'Bactrian Sophi' began to develop that vein of religious bigotry which eventually turned him against painting altogether and, incidentally, caused his markedly uncivil reception of Sir Anthony Jenkinson, our first envoy to the Persian court, in 1561 ('Oh thou vnbeleeuer, we haue no neede to haue friendship with the vnbeleeuers'). Court painting at Qazwin, in fact, was in a languishing condition during the third quarter of the sixteenth century.

But the tradition of royal patronage was well kept up at Mashhad in the north-east, where Tahmasp's nephew Ibrahim Mirza was appointed governor in 964/1556. He managed to gather a gifted group of painters and calligraphers round him, and despite the unpredictable and often trying behaviour of his uncle, he brought to completion the celebrated manuscript of Jami's poems in the Freer Gallery, Washington, after nine years' work (1556-65). Several fine manuscripts of this period may have originated at Mashhad; the miniatures in the John Rylands *Yusuf u Zulaykha* (Nos **681-685**) are close to some of the work done for Ibrahim Mirza in colour and drawing, though the text (1550) antedates his governorship there by a few years. It is the only Rylands manuscript of this group that merits special mention.

Tahmasp died in 1576 and was succeeded by his son Isma'il II, one of whose first acts was to put to death his brilliant cousin Ibrahim Mirza and several other princes of the blood. During his short reign of less than two years he commissioned a very splendid copy of the *Shahnama*, which was broken up by the dealer Demotte some sixty-five years ago. It was unfinished, no miniatures being executed beyond the reign of Iskandar; they are now widely scattered in public and private collections on both sides of the Atlantic (see the present writer's 'Isma'il II's copy of the *Shahnama*' in *Iran* XIV, 1976, pp 1-8).

For a full and clear account of this confused and difficult period, *Welch AS*, should be consulted.

---

* Presumably 'Ala'al-Dawla b. Baysunghur (*d* 1449) is intended; but the poet's chronology and geography may be somewhat confused.

Jami: Yusuf u Zulaykha (681-685)

Ryl Pers 23 (ex Bland, de Sacy)

Contemporary binding with flap, rebacked and repaired. It would appear that in the course of repair the covers and flap were reversed, to make the doublures the present outer surface and vice versa. The original outside surfaces (now doublures) are of leather, painted black and covered with very finely painted gold medallions, pendants, corner pieces and arabesque scrolls, the surface being then varnished over. Small parts of this surface are missing. Such bindings were the forerunners of the painted and varnished papier-mâché book covers, mirror cases and pen boxes of the Zand and Qajar periods. The original doublures (now the outer surfaces) are of crimson leather, painted with floral scrolls in gold, and with medallions, pendants and corner-pieces of cut-out work on backgrounds of blue and green. Round this is a frame of strips and squares of green and yellow silk let into the leather and covered with cut-out work of black and brown (some missing, and the silk a little worn). This is a beautiful and remarkable binding.

24.1 × 16.5 cm. 153 *ff*. Fine *nasta'liq* in 2 columns of 14 lines to the page. W.S., gold-sprinkled, 15.2 × 7.6 cm. *Ff* 1b, 2a most exquisitely illuminated as a double title-page in a blend of the Herat and Tabriz styles characteristic of Khurasan manuscripts of the later sixteenth century. Section headings written in gold on a background of scrollwork, and spaces in the text and round the colophon similarly adorned. Colophon (*f* 153a) signed by Muhammad Amin b. 'Abdallah, and dated 957/1550.

There are 5 miniatures. They are small but brilliant examples of their period, and may have been executed at Mashhad, though a trifle early for the patronage of Prince Ibrahim Mirza. Drawing is firm and confident, and colours bright and striking. The whole manuscript is in excellent condition apart from waterstaining on the inner top corner (which does not affect the miniatures).

681 ƒ 42b 'Aziz at Zulaykha's camp.
She peeps at him through the tent-curtains. A beautiful landscape scene with a stream flowing through stippled greenery, and delicate mauve rocks. 12.7 × 7.6 cm. *See colour pl XI.*

682 ƒ 63b Yusuf sold as a slave.
Gold ground, buildings above. A greybeard presides, seated on a mat and Zulaykha, attended by three maids, watches from a window.
14.6 × 7.6 cm. *See illustration.*

683 ƒ 89a Yusuf tempted by Zulaykha.
Interior scene with a large *chinar* tree behind. She leads him by the hand, wearing a tailed Safawid crown. Two maids at windows.
15.2 × 7.6 cm. *See illustration.*

684 ƒ 103b Yusuf, bearing a dish of fruit, enters the apartment where Zulaykha sits on a splendid golden throne.
Her maids are overcome by his beauty, and one of them has fainted.
15.2 × 7.6 cm. *See illustration.*

685 ƒ 133b Yusuf standing before Zulaykha.
Interior scene with ornamental tank and two attendant maids; trees, flowers and a pool in the outer margin.
16.5 × 10.2 cm. *See illustration.*

Jami: Subhat al-Abrār (686)
Ryl Pers 29 (ex Bland, Galley)
Modern European binding of plain brown leather. On the fly-leaf is the signature and seal of Edward Galley. 19.7 × 12.7 cm. 111 ƒƒ. Good *nasta'liq* in 2 columns of 14 lines to the page. The first folio is missing, but the present ƒ 1a has a decorated text and gold margins painted with floral scrolls in blue and pink. The colophon gives no date, but the copyist is Shah Muhammad *al-kātib*, a well-known late sixteenth-century scribe (e.g. British Library, Or.4122).

686 On the verso of the last folio is the ruin of the right-hand half of a double-page miniature representing a scene in a garden. Besides being almost completely obliterated, it seems to have been stuck over at some stage with a sheet of paper, the remains of which still adhere to it. So far as one can tell, the style was probably that of Qazwin in the third quarter of the sixteenth century.

Anwar i Suhayli (687-690)
Ryl Pers 18 (ex Bland?)
Fine contemporary binding (rebacked and repaired) of black morocco with sunk and inlaid gilt medallions, pendants, corner-pieces, and frame. Doublures of brown leather with similar designs of fine cut-out work on blue and green backgrounds (some damage).

34.2 × 21.6 cm. 353 ƒƒ. Fine *nasta'liq* of fairly large size, 17 lines to the page. W.S. 21.6 × 12.1 cm. Two illuminated arabesque medallions with pendants and corner-pieces, in a bold style, on ƒƒ 2b, 3a; ƒƒ 3b, 4a sumptuously illuminated as a double title-page; illuminated border to the text on ƒƒ 351b, 352a, rather damaged. Margins throughout decorated with large floral scrolls, animals, birds, trees, clouds, etc. in thin gold. Colophon, on ƒ 352a, dated mid-Muharram 910/late July 1504, by the celebrated Herat calligrapher 'Ali (*al-kātib*). The text, however, must have lain undecorated for some 75 years, as all the illuminations, marginal decoration, and miniatures, undoubtedly date from *c* 1580.

The manuscript contains two double-page miniatures and one below the colophon, on a large scale, but of rather less than first-rate quality, in the Qazwin style. They have suffered a good deal of damage from rubbing, flaking, and discolouration.

687 ƒƒ 1b, 2a A princely hunt.
On the right, a young prince rides off after shooting a sitting lion with an arrow; another huntsman draws his bow on the same animal at point-blank range; below, a mounted huntsman attacks wild pig in a reed-brake, whilst above, among the rocks two leopards are threatened by an archer and a man with a gun. Gold sky, blue ground with highly variegated rocks. On the left a central tree dominates the composition, in which are two monkeys, one having his tail pulled by another on the ground; under the tree is a young mounted falconer (right) and a pair of lions (left) threatened from below by an archer apparently kneeling in a river; on the horizon a mounted huntsman, a fox (?), a bear and a leopard. Blue sky with white clouds, gold ground, and variegated rocks. In view of the difference in

dimension and in the colouring of sky and ground, it may perhaps be doubted whether these two paintings were originally designed as a double-page composition, though they are clearly the work of the same hand.

F 1b, 27 × 15.8 cm; *f* 2a, 27.9 × 15.8 cm. *See illustration.*

688 *f* 352a Two young men seated in a pink landscape with flowering trees, one playing the tambourine and the other holding a paper.

Miniature fitted in below the colophon, a practice that seems to have arisen in the late fifteenth century (*Keir* III, 180, 186, 192) and continued well into the seventeenth century (*Colnaghi* 1976 43.ix).

12.7 × 12.1 cm. *See illustration.*

689 *f* 352b Outdoor court scene.

Sloping dark green ground; gold sky with blue clouds. A prince seated on a mat under an awning by a large tree with variegated leaves. As on *f* 2a, which must be by the same hand, a stream issues from the base of the tree. Courtiers surround the prince, one offering fruit, one holding arrows, and a third seated. In the foreground musicians and a dancing-girl, bare-headed and wearing a sort of check skirt, provide entertainment.

24.1 × 14.6 cm.

690 *f* 353a A young prince (centre), galloping off and looking behind him, having just discharged his bow. Above, among the rocks, a bear is about to drop a large stone on a man who takes aim at a leopard with his gun.

This miniature seems to be by a different, and slightly superior, hand to the rest. In any case the subject and the markedly different dimensions make it clear that it has no connection with No **689**, though it does seem to have had a right-hand half originally.

The foreground of the miniature (i.e. the bottom 5 cm), looks as if it had been added by an inferior hand to make the miniature fit the page. It contains a stream, a lion, and a pair of antelopes.

23.8 × 14 cm.

Amir Khusraw: Kuwalrani u Khizrkhan (691-693)

Ryl Pers 49 (ex Bland)

Modern European (French?) binding of a brown leather, gilt, with flap.

24.1 × 12.7 cm. 144 *ff*. (*paginated* in pencil). Fair *nasta'liq* in 2 columns of 15 lines to the page. W.S. 15.3 × 6.7 cm. Rather rough illuminated heading on

f 1b. Colophon at the end signed by Qutb al-Din *al-kātib*, and dated Rajab 989/August 1581.

There are three miniatures in a rough and provincial version of the Qazwin style.

691 p 88 Interior, with the hero and heroine seated on a carpet, attended by maids.

Damaged. 17.2 × 8.9 cm. *See illustration.*

692 p 196 The princess seated listening to music played by her maids.

Damaged and a bit discoloured.

19 × 8.2 cm.

693 p 189 The princess lounging at ease in a landscape reading a love-letter, whilst her maids fan her, offer her refreshment and play her music.

19.7 × 8.9 cm. *See illustration.*

Firdawsi: Shahnama (694-768)

Ryl Pers 933 (see above, Nos **475-478**)

694 *f* 10b Meeting of Iraj and his brothers Tur and Salm.

It takes place in a cross between a building and a tent with central column. Upper edge of miniature double 'stepped'.

8.2 × 19.7 cm. *See illustration.*

695 *f* 13b Tur slain by Minuchihr.

Smudged and some damage to faces.

7.6 × 19.7 cm.

696 *f* 15a Zal and the *Simurgh*.

Upper edge double-stepped up to the left. Beige sky. Rubbed. 11.4 × 19.7 cm. *See illustration.*

697 *f* 20a Minuchihr receiving news of the affair of Zal and Rudaba.

Upper edge shallow double-stepped.

8.2 × 19.7 cm.

698 *f* 23b Baby Rustam in his cradle with his mother, a maid and an old nurse in attendance.

Upper edge single-stepped. Note brickwork.

8.9 × 19.7 cm. *See illustration.*

699 *f* 26b Rustam mourning the death of Suhrab.

His tiger-skin is deep blue.

7.6 × 19.7 cm.

700 *f* 30b Rustam pulling off the ears of the herdsman.

Central group badly smudged and rubbed.

7.6 × 19.7 cm.

682 Yusuf sold as a slave. Mashhad, 1550

685 Yusuf standing before Zulaykha. Mashhad, 1550

688 Two youths in a landscape. Qazwin, *c* 1580

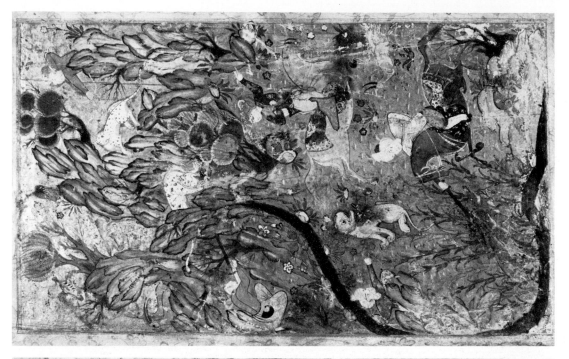

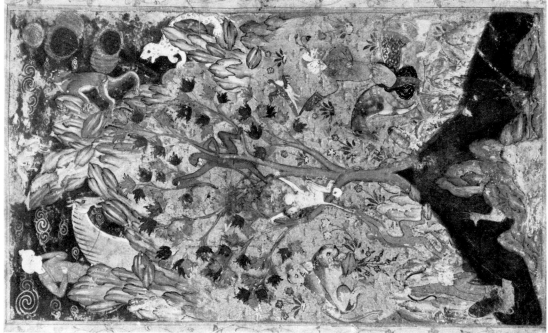

687 A princely hunt. Qazwin, c 1580

693 Duwalrani reading a love-letter. Provincial. 1581

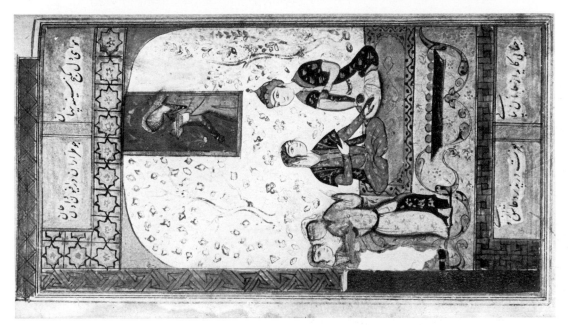

691 Duwalrani and Khizr Khan seated together. Provincial.
1581

694 Meeting of Iraj and his brothers. Provincial, late 16th century

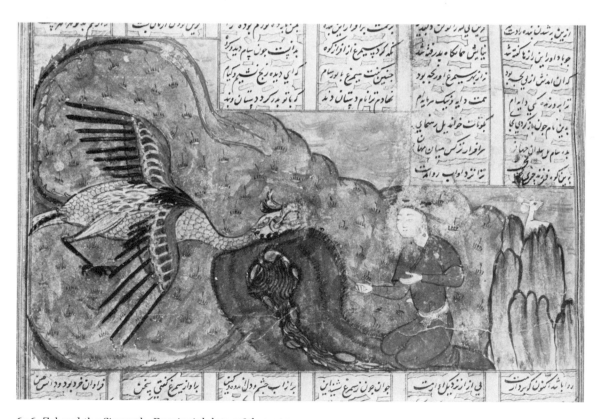

696 Zal and the Simurgh. Provincial, late 16th century

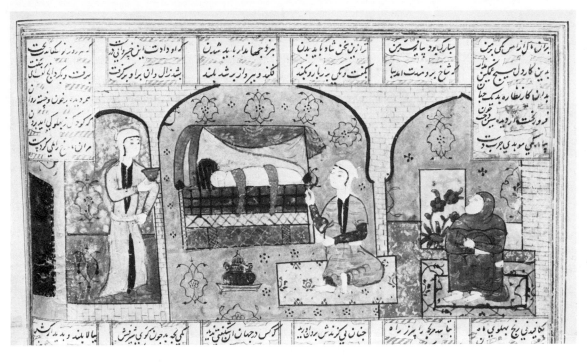

698 Baby Rustam in his cradle. Provincial, late 16th century

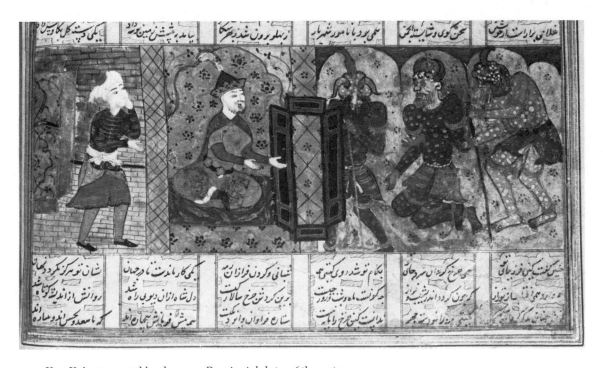

702 Kay Ka'us tempted by demons. Provincial, late 16th century

701 *f* 31b Rustam and the White Demon: Awlad tied to the tree.
Rubbed. 7.6 × 19.7 cm.

702 *f* 34b Demons tempting Kay Ka'us with the idea of a flying-machine.

Note architecture.
7.6 × 19.7 cm. *See illustration.*

703 *f* 46a Sending of the letter of Siyawush to Kay Ka'us.
Upper edge double-stepped.
8.2 × 19.7 cm.

704 *f* 48b Siyawush before Afrasiyab, while a grey-beard makes to kiss the latter's foot.
An incident just before Siyawush plays polo with Afrasiyab.

Note architecture.
Faces damaged and retouched.
7.6 × 19.7 cm.

705 *f* 52a Garsiwaz enquiring after the affairs of Siyawush.
Upper edge double-stepped. Note architecture and brickwork.
7.9 × 19.7 cm. *See illustration.*

706 *f* 53b Capture of Siyawush by Afrasiyab's men.
Rubbed. 7.6 × 19.7 cm.

707 *f* 57a Pilsam speared by Rustam.
The latter's tiger-skin cuirass is coloured bright blue with black and gold stripes. Pilsam's helmet is dome-shaped.
7.6 × 19.7 cm.

708 *f* 61a Firangis, Kay Khusraw, and Giw crossing the Jihun.
7.6 × 19.7 cm.

709 *f* 63a Kay Khusraw hunting [just after his accession].
7.9 × 19.7 cm. *See illustration.*

710 *f* 66a Interview of Farud with a Persian envoy.
Upper edge triple-stepped to the left.
9.5 × 19.7 cm. *See illustration.*

711 *f* 68a Persians carrying loot from Farud's castle.
7.6 × 19.7 cm.

712 *f* 70b Battle between the troops of Gudarz and Piran.
Rubbed and principal face damaged.
7.6 × 19.7 cm.

713 *f* 73b Preliminaries to the combat between Tus and Arzhang the Turk.
The Turanians wear curious high-domed helmets.
7.6 × 19.7 cm.

714 *f* 76a Grey-bearded messenger delivering news of the Persian army to Kay Khusraw under an awning.
7.6 × 19.7 cm. *See illustration.*

715 *f* 78a Rustam shoots Ashkabus.
His tiger-skin here is bright orange.
7.3 × 12.7 cm.

716 *f* 81a Afrasiyab's council of war with Shangul.
Single shallow step in upper edge. Note architecture.
6 × 19.7 cm.

717 *f* 83a The captive Khaqan of Chin before Rustam.
Rustam's tiger-skin is deep blue.
4.1 × 19.7 cm.

718 *f* 86a Rustam and Puladwand.
Seals 2 and 3 (see above, p 111). Rustam's groom wears a very tall-domed blue cap with ear (or back) flap, and the hero's tiger-skin is yellow.
8.2 × 19.7 cm.

719 *f* 91a Rustam talking to Bizhan after rescuing him from the pit.
Seal 2. Two small patches of brown paper. Rustam's tiger-skin bright orange.
7.6 × 19.7 cm.

720 *f* 95a Human urging Piran to fight.
Interior scene with a sort of arcade in the background. Note architecture and brickwork.
7.6 × 19.7 cm.

721 *f* 97a Combat of Human and Bizhan.
Single shallow step in upper edge. Bizhan wears a domed helmet.
7.6 × 19.7 cm.

722 *f* 100a Gudarz sends a reply to Piran's letter.
Double-stepped to middle of top edge. Note architecture.
8.6 × 19.7 cm.

705 Garsiwaz enquiring about Siyawush. Provincial, late 16th century

709 Kay Khusraw hunting. Provincial, late 16th century

710 Farud parleying with a Persian envoy. Provincial, late 16th century

714 Kay Khusraw receives news of his army. Provincial, late 16th century

723 ƒ107b Kay Khusraw, enthroned beneath an extraordinary structure, receiving envoys from Afrasiyab.
Single deepish step in upper edge.
Central figure badly smudged and an ugly black patch on the left of the miniature.
10.2 × 19.7 cm.

724 ƒ112b Hum informing Kay Khusraw of his capture of Afrasiyab.
Rocky landscape (slightly Mughal).
8.6 × 19.7 cm.

725 ƒ115b The Persians petitioning Kay Khusraw.
Shallow double-stepping at upper edge. Note architecture.
7.6 × 19.7 cm.

726 ƒ118b Gushtasp in the blacksmith's shop in Rum.
Single shallow step at upper edge. Note architecture.
7.6 × 19.7 cm.

727 ƒ119b Gushtasp killing the wolf.
7.6 × 19.7 cm.

728 ƒ120b Gushtasp killing the dragon.
7.9 × 19.7 cm.

729 ƒ126a Parley between Isfandiyar and Bidarafsh.
7.6 × 19.7 cm.

730 ƒ130b Isfandiyar killing the lions.
7.6 × 19.7 cm.

731 ƒ131a Isfandiyar killing the dragon.
7.6 × 19.7 cm.

732 ƒ132b Isfandiyar's view of the Brazen Hold (?).
(Youth and girl in a building) Seal 3. Note architecture.
7.6 × 19.7 cm.

733 ƒ134b Isfandiyar fighting the Turanians.
Single deep step on left of upper edge.
9.5 × 19.7 cm.

734 ƒ137a Rustam and the rock rolled on him by Bahman.
Single deep step on left of upper edge.
9.5 × 19.7 cm.

735 ƒ139b Interview between Rustam and Isfandiyar.
Upper edge double-stepped. Note architecture. Rustam's tiger-skin is bright orange.
9.2 × 19.7 cm.

736 ƒ143b Rustam (on foot) shoots Isfandiyar (mounted) in the eyes.
Rustam wears a blue tiger-skin.
9.2 × 19.7 cm.

737 ƒ146a The death of Rustam.
Seals 2 and 3. Very large flowers, and two small sections of text intrude on the lower half of the miniature.
Rubbed, and the figure of Shaghad scrubbed out.
10.8 × 19.7 cm.

738 ƒ149a Darab in converse with Rashnawad.
A bit smudged. 7.6 × 19.7 cm.

739 ƒ152b Battle between Dara and Iskandar.
Seals 2, 3. Domed helmets.
7.6 × 19.7 cm.

740 ƒ156a Fur slain by Iskandar.
Seals 2, 3. 7.6 × 19.7 cm.

741 ƒ159b Iskandar passing through the Land of Darkness.
The artist has peopled it in a very lively manner with multicoloured scorpions, worms, and creeping things of various kinds. Single step on left of upper edge. Seal 2 (twice).
10.2 × 19.7 cm. *See illustration.*

742 ƒ160b Local inhabitant (face badly damaged) tells Iskandar about the Talking Tree.
Single step on left of upper edge.
10.2 × 19.7 cm.

743 ƒ164a Quarrel of Ardashir and the sons of Ardawan.
7.6 × 19.7 cm.

744 ƒ167a Ardashir and one of his warriors (faces damaged) reconnoitring the fortress of Haftawad.
Note brickwork.
9.5 × 19.7 cm.

745 ƒ171b Defeat of the Romans by Shapur.
Rubbed. 7.6 × 19.7 cm.

746 *f* 177a Bahram Gur riding in Arabia.
8.6 × 19.7 cm.

747 *f* 178b Yazdagird, mounted on the magic horse, rides into the Lake of Su.
Three warriors express consternation on the shore. Very large flowers in what appears to be blue sky.
7.6 × 19.7 cm.

748 *f* 181b Encounter of Bahram and Baraham the Jew.
Domed helmets. 7.6 × 19.7 cm.

749 *f* 184a Bahram Gur enthroned with attendants and musicians.
A very creditable exercise in the Inju style, possibly by the painter of the majority of the miniatures. Single shallow step.
9.5 × 19.7 cm. *See illustration.*

750 *f* 188a Bahram Gur returns to his palace.
6.7 × 19.7 cm.

751 *f* 191b Bahram Gur wrestling with an Indian champion before King Shangul.
Another Inju pastiche.
Rubbed near outer edge.
3.2 × 19.7 cm. *See illustration.*

752 *f* 196a Enthronement of Balash.
The third and last of the Inju style miniatures in this manuscript.
Some surface damage, and the king rather rubbed. Single shallow step in upper edge.
7.6 × 19.7 cm. *See illustration.*

753 *f* 200b Mundhir seeking Nushirwan's help against Caesar.
Double-stepping in upper edge.
8.2 × 19.7 cm.

754 *f* 204b Ram Barzin approaching the stronghold of Nushzad, the rebel prince.
Domed helmets.
7.6 × 19.7 cm.

755 *f* 207a Encounter of Gaw with Talhand on his elephant.
Lower left-hand corner damaged and repaired.
7.6 × 19.7 cm.

756 *f* 211a Nushirwan inspects his horses.
Rubbed and bottom edge damaged and repaired. Single

shallow step on left of top edge.
8.2 × 19.7 cm.

757 *f* 215b Nushirwan's fifth session with Buzurj-mihr in a pleasant landscape.
Figure of Buzurjmihr very slightly smudged.
7.9 × 19.7 cm. *See illustration.*

758 *f* 219b Buzurjmihr before Nushirwan on his throne.
Double-stepping in upper edge. Note architecture.
8.2 × 19.7 cm.

759 *f* 223a Nushirwan and his adviser discussing the state of the world.
Double step. Note architecture and colouring.
9.2 × 19.7 cm.

760 *f* 227b Battle between Bahram Chubina and Sawa Shah.
Lower right-hand corner damaged and repaired.
7.6 × 19.7 cm.

761 *f* 232a Encounter of three warriors in a land-scape, one on foot and the others mounted.
The story of Bahram Chubina – just before accession of Khusraw. Double-stepped.
8.2 × 19.7 cm.

762 *f* 235b Battle between Khusraw and Bahram Chubina.
Just before the former flees to Rum.
Faces damaged. Rubbed in lower right-hand corner.
8.9 × 19.7 cm.

763 *f* 238b Khusraw fighting Manuyan (?) in Rum.
Surface damage and repair. Single shallow step.
7.6 × 19.7 cm.

764 *f* 242b Battle between Khusraw and Bahram Chubina. The latter's men have domed helmets.
8.2 × 19.7 cm.

765 *f* 246a Bahram Chubina shooting the Lion-Ape (shown as a pink dragon) from behind rocks.
7.6 × 19.7 cm. *See illustration.*

766 *f* 247b Khusraw receiving the answer to his letter to the Khaqan of Chin about Bahram Chubina.
Faces flaked. Note architecture.
8.2 × 19.7 cm.

767 *f* 252 Encounter of a warrior (Khusraw?) and

741 Iskandar in the Land of Darkness. Provincial, late 16th century

749 Bahram Gur enthroned (Inju imitation). Provincial, late 16th century

751 Bahram Gur wrestling (Inju imitation). Provincial, late 16th century

752 Enthronement of Balash (Inju imitation). Provincial, late 16th century

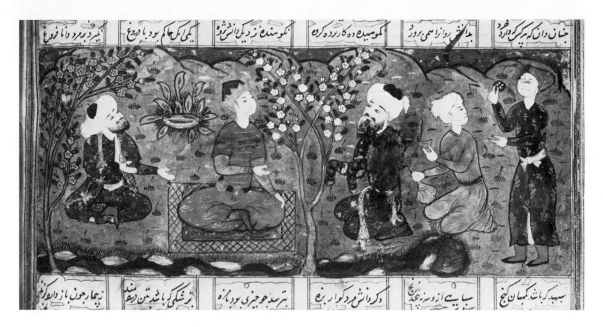

757 Nushirwan and his vizier Buzurjmihr. Provincial, late 16th century

765 Bahram Chubina shooting the Lion-Ape. Provincial, late 16th century

two youths by a stream in a landscape.
Early in the story of Khusraw and Shirin. Deep step on the left.
10.2 × 19.7 cm.

768 ƒ261b Combat of Rustam (clad as his name-sake the hero) with Sa'd b. Waqqas at the battle of Qadisiyya.
Rubbed across faces. 9.2 × 19.7 cm.

Some of the architectural features, anomalies of colouring and other non-Persian details, such as the domed helmets, to which attention has been drawn above, may suggest that the proper place for these miniatures is with the Indian group on p 275. But a final decision on this problem is still some way off.

Firdawsi: Shahnama (769-800)
Ryl Pers 910 (see above, Nos **481-549**)
For observations on the painters and their styles, see above, p 119-20.

769 ƒ262b The Court of Luhrasp.
This is by painter D (see above, p 119), and appears to date from c 1570-80.
19 × 20.2 cm. *See illustration.*

770 ƒ288b Isfandiyar and the witch.
A small but excellent miniature by painter E, who may perhaps be the 'young Isfahani' of the British Museum *Garshasp Nama* (see *VAM 1967* No 48). Lady's headdress c 1580: she is very like the drawing attributed to Mir *Muṣawwir* in the Keir Collection (*Keir* III.233). 9.5 × 15.8 cm. *See illustration.*

771 ƒ289b Isfandiyar and the Simurgh.
Bold design and execution. Admirable. Painter E.
12.7 × 15.2 cm. *See colour pl XII.*

772 ƒ334b Iskandar supporting the dying Dara.
Large flowers and prominent clouds. Painter E.
19 × 19.7 cm. *See illustration.*

773 ƒ361a The spinning maidens and the Worm of Kerman.
Painter D. 10.2 × 15.2 cm.

774 ƒ391a The cobbler riding the King's lion.
Human-faced golden sun in top left-hand corner. Painter D.
13.3 × 15.2 cm. *See illustration.*

775 ƒ419a Piruz and his men falling into the pits

prepared for them by Khush-nawaz.
Painter D. 10.8 × 15.2 cm.

776 ƒ423a Sufaray slain in battle by Qubad.
Painter D. 12.7 × 15.2 cm.

777 ƒ426a The execution of Mazdak.
Painter D. 12.1 × 15.2 cm.

778 ƒ426b Enthronement of Nushirwan.
The design of animals etc. on the white wall behind the throne is of amazing fineness. The artist has sketched a little face in the lower margin. Painter D.
10.2 × 15.2 cm. *See illustration.*

779 ƒ433b Nushirwan, riding with his followers, encounters villagers, one with a tambourine.
Painter D. 12.7 × 15.2 cm.

780 ƒ438a Nushirwan punishes his erring wife and her paramour.
Painter D. 10.8 × 15.2 cm.

781 ƒ459b Battle of Gaw and Talhand (the origin of chess).
Painter D. 12.1 × 15.2 cm.

782 ƒ486b Parmuda, son of Sawa Shah, put in bonds by Bahram Chubina.
The wall of the prison is almost as exquisitely decorated as that of Nushirwan's palace in No **778**. Painter D.
11.4 × 15.2 cm.

783 ƒ489a Although the heading says 'Bahram Gur sees a woman magician' this must be Bahram Chubina. He is here shown in pursuit of game and attended by a groom. Painter D.
10.2 × 15.2 cm.

784 ƒ493b The murder of Ayin Gashasp.
Painter D. 11.4 × 15.2 cm.

785 ƒ497a Meeting of Khusraw and Bahram Chubina with attendants under a tree.
Painter D. 12.7 × 15.2 cm.

786 ƒ500b Defeat of Khusraw by Bahram Chubina.
Painter D. 12.1 × 15.2 cm.

787 ƒ501b Murder of King Hurmuzd by Bandwi and Gustaham.
Rather rough execution. Painter D.
11.4 × 15.2 cm.

769 The court of Luhrasp. Qazwin, late 16th century

800 Shirin clasping the tomb of Khusraw. Qazwin, late 16th century

788 *f* 505a Bahram, son of Siyawush, playing polo: Bahram Chubina with a drawn sword about to slay him.
Painter D. 10.8 × 15.2 cm.

789 *f* 510a Caesar and his court discussing the making of a talisman.
Faces retouched. Painter D.
10.8 × 15.2 cm.

790 *f* 513b Kut the Roman slain by Bahram Chubina.
A neat little miniature. Painter D.
8.9 × 15.2 cm.

791 *f* 516a Battle of Khusraw with Bahram Chubina.
Painter D. 12.1 × 15.2 cm.

792 *f* 517a Bahram Chubina given refreshments by an old woman.
Painter D. 10.8 × 15.2 cm.

793 *f* 520b The Lion-Ape swallowing a maiden, watched by three others on the horizon.
Their head-dresses appear to be a trifle later than that in No **770**. A curiously shaped discolouration has come through from the Lion-Ape on the following folio. Painter D.
10.8 × 15.2 cm.

794 *f* 521b Bahram Chubina attacking the Lion-Ape.
The creature is depicted in both miniatures as a spotted yellow two-legged dragon, with a branching horn, red muzzle, and gold streamers. Painter D.
12.1 × 15.2 cm.

795 *f* 524b Bahram Chubina on his death-bed.
An attendant with refreshments: two armed warriors, one of whom appears to kick a bare-headed grey-beard – the murderer Qulun – who kneels before Bahram with hands bound behind his back. Painter D.
11.4 × 15.2 cm.

796 *f* 533a Khusraw on a hawking expedition just before his meeting with Shirin.
His face is a little damaged. Painter D.
12.7 × 15.2 cm.

797 *f* 535b Barbad in a tree playing music to Khusraw in the garden.
Painter D. 14 × 15.2 cm (plus tip of cypress in upper margin)

798 *f* 540b Enthronement of Shirwi, son of Khusraw.
Barbad the lute-player in the foreground. Painter D.
12.1 × 15.2 cm.

799 *f* 545b Murder of Khusraw.
He is surrounded by sleeping maids and burning candles.
The faces of Khusraw and two of the maids repainted. Painter D.
12.7 × 15.2 cm.

800 *f* 547b Shirin clasping the tomb of Khusraw.
Landscape with figures. An old man has a baton turban. Painter D.
12.7 × 15.2 cm. *See illustration.*

[Below the colophon (*f* 562a) is a fairly crude Indian eighteenth- or early nineteenth-century miniature of a landscape with animals and a sportsman with a gun.]

The Khurasan Style

Painting at Mashhad, the administrative capital of the great province of Khurasan under the Safawids, has already been noticed (above p 242). The present section is devoted to a style that seems to have flourished in the eastern part of that province, in the neighbourhood of Herat and Bakharz, for a comparatively short period during the second half of the sixteenth century. It has something in common with the Commercial Turkman style of the previous century in that it was a deliberately simplified version of a court style, and from the large number of manuscripts in which examples of it are found it seems highly probable that it was used to illustrate volumes produced commercially for patrons of comparatively modest means.

Stylistically, it may be permissible to trace its origins to the painter Muhammadi, reputedly a son of Sultan Muhammad, and a native of Herat (according to Iskandar Munshi and to the painter Riza's inscription on a copy he made of one of Muhammadi's works; see *VAM 1967* No 67). The figure-drawing and the faces of many miniatures in the present group bear a striking similarity to authenticated works of Muhammadi, such as the Boston 'Lovers' (*Robinson PD*, pl 46) or the India Office 'Young Dervish' (*Robinson IO*, pl v). But we know so little of Muhammadi that it does not seem possible at present to press this suggestion.

The style itself is characterized by firm, competent figure drawing, extreme economy of surface detail, bubble-like rock formations on the horizon, and a predilection for ground of olive green or pale blue.

Of the examples in the present collection, the first, though its miniatures are somewhat marred by European-style repainting, is interesting for its early date. The second (No **804**) evidently came from a *Shahnama* manuscript of impressive proportions and high quality. *Shahnama* illustrations of Khurasan type are rare, though there is a copy of the epic in the Chester Beatty Library which contains fifty-nine miniatures in this style (MS 295; *VAM 1967*, No 173, pl 50, 51).

For the Khurasan group, see especially *Robinson B* p 151, where twenty of the manuscripts are listed; of these, three are stated in their colophons to have been copied in the district (*wilayat*) of Bakharz, and three at Herat, while scribes of Bakharz and Herat copied two of the others. See also *Robinson IO*, p 44 and Nos 214-225. For Muhammadi, see A. Welch in *Studies on Isfahan*, Part 11, pp 466-470 (but his attribution of the miniatures in Topkapi MS H.777 to Muhammadi may perhaps be questioned).

Hilali: Layla and Majnun (801-803)

Ryl Pers 907 (ex Clarke, Fox, de Sacy (?))

Oriental binding of reddish leather (worn and re-backed) with stamped gilt medallions, pendants, frame-panels and corner-pieces, probably eighteenth-century. On the front fly-leaf in Persian and English is written: 'The highly valued property of Gholam Hussin Khan', and on the back doublure is pasted an extract from Dr Clarke's catalogue, reading, in part, 'My Father bought it at the sale of the late Mr C. Fox of Bristol, whose elegant MS translations into blank verse are in my possession'. It may be noted that MS 43 (p 241) also came from Mr Fox's collection, and was restored to its proper order by Dr Clarke.

23.8 × 15.2 cm. 78 ff, the margins of various colours. The pencil numbering of the folios unaccountably omits *f* 1, and so ends on 77; nevertheless, to save renumbering throughout, it has been followed in the list of miniatures below. Fine *nasta'liq* in 2 columns of 12 lines to the page. W.S., gold sprinkled, 14.3 × 6.7 cm. A smallish, but extremely fine illuminated heading at the beginning of the text.

Colophon on *f* 77a (78a) signed by Muhammad *al-katib* Raza and dated Rabi' I 969/November 1561. The middle digit was read as a 4 by Dr Clarke in his catalogue, followed by Kerney in his handlist of the Bibliotheca Lindesiana oriental manuscripts.

There are three miniatures, interesting and comparatively early examples of the Khurasan style. As is well-known, Persian miniatures frequently expand beyond the confines of the written surface, whose bounding lines are interrupted to accommodate this exuberance. Here, however, though the painting spreads far into the margins, the rulings remain.

The European-style repainting of faces in this manuscript is clearly by the same hand as that in MS 43. The common denominator is Mr C. Fox of Bristol. Perhaps he obtained both MSS from a dealer

801 Layla and Majnun at school. Khurasan, 1561

who fancied himself as a 'restorer', or – and this possibility cannot be ruled out – he tried his hand at it himself. In either case, some fine and interesting work has been seriously impaired.

801 *f* 13b Layla and Majnun at school.
Above, a young man in night attire attempting to recapture an escaping falcon.
The face and turban of an old man in the lower right-hand corner have been repainted in the European manner.
18.7 × 9.5 cm. *See illustration.*

802 *f* 66b The battle of the clans.
Tents, camels, and flocks above; in the centre a young warrior (face obliterated) with a veiled lady riding pillion, cleaves a dismounted foeman; lower right, a crowned prince (Nawfal?) and his bodyguard.
A bearded spearman, lower left, has had his face and turban Europeanized.
20.2 × 13.3 cm. *See illustration.*

803 *f* 70b The tribal council.
The upper part of the miniature is occupied by a camp scene, with a large tent, various animals, a woodcutter, a woman milking, etc. Below, the council of four bearded elders beside another tent.
The faces of the elders and of one or two of the other figures have been repainted in European style.
20.2 × 11.2 cm. *See illustration.*

Album (804)
Ryl Indian Drawings 18

804 *f* 32a Miniature from a large manuscript of the *Shahnama c* 1580. Gushtasp slays the rhinoceros.
He is in the act of beheading the monster (realistically represented), his wounded horse in the foreground. Plain hillside of pale blue with sparse plants; the sky is pale olive-green. A striking and effective miniature. Slight flaking in places.
28.6 × 17.8 cm. *See colour pl XIII.*

Safawid Painting in Western India

It seems clear that even after the establishment of the Mughal Empire in India, manuscripts were produced there with illustrations more or less directly derived from Persian models, and quite uninfluenced by the Mughal court style. Such volumes are the India Office Library *Sindbad Nama* (Ethé 1236) and the Dunimarle *Anwar i Suhayli* now in the Victoria and Albert Museum (*Stchoukine MS*, No 199, p 138). A further most interesting example has recently come to light: a copy of the first part of Nizami's *Iskandar Nama* dedicated to Nusrat Shah of Bengal and dated 938/1532 (*Colnaghi 1978*, pp 133-152, where it is fully described and illustrated by Mr Robert Skelton). As with Indian miniatures of the Timurid period, accurate dating and location are usually impossible; colophons, where they exist, are completely unin-formative (the *Iskandar Nama* above being a prominent exception). But an approximate date can generally be deduced from comparable Persian work. It seems likely that manuscripts of this kind were produced under Muslim patronage in parts of India as yet independent of, or remote from, Mughal rule.

The John Rylands Hatifi (Nos **805-819**) is an interesting example from the mid sixteenth century, whilst in one of the LIbrary's *Shahnamas* (Nos **694-768**) we may perhaps have a set of Indian miniatures of a generation later. Many of the criteria already adduced by Fraad and Ettinghausen for Indian painting of the Timurid period still apply (see above, p 95), and will be found noted in the descriptions that follow. But examples are much rarer than in the fifteenth century.

Hatifi: Layla wa Majnun (805-819)

Ryl Pers 28 (ex Bland)

Late oriental binding of black morocco (re-cornered and re-backed) with remains of gilt paper inlay.

19 × 12.7 cm. 97 *ff*, the margins gold-flecked. Good *nasta'liq* in two columns of 11 lines to the page. W.S. powdered with gold, 12.1 × 6.7 cm. Remains of fine illuminated heading at the beginning of the text (central panel lost and replaced later in a rather rough style) and intercolumnar band of fine illumination. Persian foliation in ink, corrected in pencil (*f* 1 omitted from numbering). Damaged colophon on *f* 97a giving the copyist's name as Yusuf. Verse jottings on *f* 97b.

The manuscript contains 16 miniatures in a provincial style, probably of the mid sixteenth century. These miniatures are of no more than second-rate quality, but are of some stylistic interest. Noteworthy features are:

1 the form of turban worn by male characters.
2 the prominence given to tigers in the animal scenes.
3 fondness for mauve and yellow, and the orange vermilion of *f* No **814**.
4 non-Persian forms of throne (No **805**), crown (passim), sword (No **815**), interior architecture (No **809**), tent (No **811**), sun, moon and sky (*passim*). The spindly trees are also characteristic and without parallel in sixteenth-century Persian painting. The rather weak drawing with uncertain spindly lines is also noticeable, and the pale landscapes with faintly stippled backgrounds are a persistent feature.

All these considerations seem to point to somewhere in non-Mughal India in the middle years of the sixteenth century. The spindly drawing and the slight traces of Shiraz influence are reminiscent of the dispersed *Shahnama* of a century earlier, now generally accepted as Indian (see *VAM 1967*, No 113, FE, c.17). Compare also the India Office *Sindbad Nama* (Ethé 1236) and the Victoria and Albert Museum *Anwar i Suhayli*, two other sixteenth-century non-Mughal Indian illustrated manuscripts.

805 *f* 15a Outdoor court scene with building, left. The poet presents his work to the prince-patron. The throne is of charpoy type, without a back, though with steps, and the turbans have red *kullas* of truncated conical shape. The women's headdresses are of sixteenth-century type with small aigrette and gold frontlet. Circular gold sun and small snaky white clouds.
Damaged (rotting green) at outside edge.
9.5 × 9.5 cm.

805a *f* 20b Birth of Majnun.
He is being bathed by four ladies seated in front of a decorated wall. The architectural features and brick-work are not of Persian type.
7.6 × 7 cm.

806 *ƒ* 22b Festive gathering on a carpet under an awning in honour of the child Majnun, who sits on his father's lap.
A trifle rubbed, and a small repair.
7.6 × 6.7 cm.

807 *ƒ* 23b Layla and Majnun at school.
She sits behind the schoolmaster, Majnun and two other boys before him. Books on shelves in two alcoves above. Mauve brickwork again.
7.6 × 6.7 cm.

808 *ƒ* 26a Six ladies in a landscape, the sun (with a face) *and* the moon in the sky.
Three wear the white headcloth with frontlet, one a plumed crown, and the other two rounded caps with pointed gold finials. All carry gold tablets similar to, though rather larger and more elaborate than, the learning-tablets held by the pupils in the previous miniature.
9.5 × 6.7 cm. *See illustration.*

809 *ƒ* 27b Layla and two of her maids in an interior surrounded by mauve brickwork and with a shaft of the same dividing the back wall in two.
One very small repair.
6.7 × 6.7 cm.

810 *ƒ* 35a An elderly man with a staff takes Majnun by the hand in the wilderness.
The only animals shown are two tigers. The sky, of a rather darker blue than in previous miniatures, again contains both the sun and moon and a number of little white clouds touched with pink.
A repair.
9.5 × 6.7 cm.

811 *ƒ* 46a Prince seated in a tent, his sword-bearer in attendance; two young men seated before him on a carpet under an awning; and a standing attendant with a dish.
The dome of the tent rises to a gold onion-shaped finial, and is coloured a strange olive-brown.
11.4 × 6.7 cm.

812 *ƒ* 49a Outdoor scene, with two bearded men seated on a carpet on a low dais of mauve brickwork, attended by a cup-bearer, while the young Majnun caresses a dog.
11.4 × 6.7 cm.

813 *ƒ* 55a Greybeard seated in an *iwan* holding a rosary, an attendant seated behind him.
Before him is Majnun seated on a carpet, with a bearded man standing with a staff. Brightly coloured building with the characteristic mauve brickwork. Green landscape.
9.2 × 6.7 cm. *See illustration.*

814 *ƒ* 60b Layla's maid, bearing a letter, visits Majnun in the wilderness; a tiger in the centre.
The background hill is of a rather startling orange vermilion.
A number of small repairs on left-hand side.
8.6 × 6.7 cm.

815 *ƒ* 72b A man prostrating himself before Majnun outside a building.
His drawn sword (the hilt of distinctly un-Persian type) lies on the ground between them. A maid is in the doorway and Layla (?), her face obliterated, appears at a window. Green landscape.
Some damage and discolouration.
11.4 × 6.7 cm.

816 *ƒ* 76a The battle of the clans, set against a lush green landscape.
The warriors wear tall helmets with large pennons, and the two leading horses are fully caparisoned: wicker-work shields with metal bosses: on either side a chief wearing a crown: long-shafted gold maces, and a standard of unusual form (without flag). Two footmen engage in the foreground.
Rubbing and a small repair.
10.8 × 11.4 cm. *See illustration.*

817 *ƒ* 79b Majnun offers fruit to a man about to saw down a tree.
Faces damaged, and parts of tree lost (rotting green).
11.4 × 6.7 cm.

818 *ƒ* 88a Layla's funeral cortège.
Small repairs.
11.4 × 6.7 cm.

819 *ƒ* 94a Two men at the tomb, which rests on a platform of the usual mauve brickwork.
Small tear and repair.
7.6 × 6.7 cm.

813 Majnun before a holy man. W. India, mid 16th century

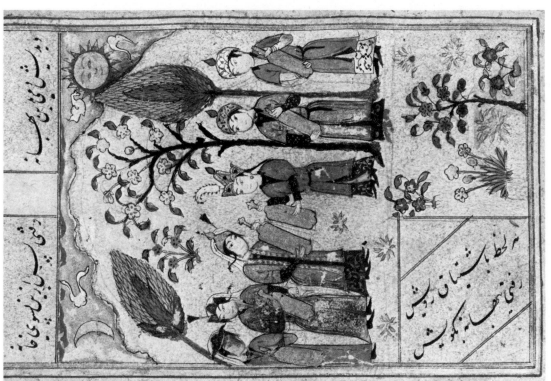

808 Six ladies with gold tablets. W. India, mid 16th century

816 The battle of the clans. W. India, mid 16th century

The Isfahan Style

The Isfahan style is clearly recognizable, and has been fully documented and described in many previous books on Persian painting (see especially *Stchoukine SA*, *BWG* chapter VI, and *Welch AS*); little of an introductory nature is therefore called for here. We note the increasingly calligraphic character of the drawing; the filling-out of the figures; the modified colour-scheme with its prominent yellows, browns and purples; and the generally sensuous and rather decadent tone.

The transition from the preceding court style of Qazwin and Mashhad can most readily be seen in the magnificent but fragmentary Chester Beatty *Shahnama* (MS 277), most probably commissioned by Shah 'Abbas shortly after his accession, about 1590. In it appear side-by-side the finest work of the old-established master Sadiqi, and of his young pupil Riza, founder of the new style.

The John Rylands Library has a small group of drawings (Nos **820**, **822**, **1580**) illustrating the style in its early form, though they may well be Indian copies of Persian originals. Its maturity is well exemplified in the Qazwini of 1632 (Nos **1126-1480**) and the *Shahnama* of 1650 (Nos **1481-1579**). The Italianizing style that transformed Safawid painting in its latter years can be seen in a small but exquisite watercolour by 'Ali Quli (No **1582**).

Album (820, 821)
Ryl Indian Drawings 12

820 ƒ11a Tinted drawing.
Two warriors of Shah 'Abbas, treated in caricature fashion, one holding a matchlock gun, and the other testing an arrow.
The drawing may originally have been Persian work of the end of the sixteenth century, but the ground and various details of colour were apparently added in India. It is indeed quite possible that the whole is by an Indian artist, imitating the Persian style. The Moorish form of the sword carried by the man on the right is noteworthy. These figures remind one of the slightly earlier drawings alleged by Martin to have been warriors of Timur (*Martin* II, pl 55)
Drawing 19.7 × 12.1 cm; W.S. 39.4 × 27.9 cm. *See illustration.*

821 ƒ24a Tinted drawing.
Young prince hawking.
Despite almost complete Indian repainting, vestiges survive of a good Persian drawing of perhaps 1590-1600. In the lower left-hand corner is part of a signature (lower part cut off) which was apparently *mashshaqahu Riza-i 'Abbasi*.
In the present state of the drawing it is not possible to express an opinion on its authenticity or otherwise.
12.1 × 17.8 cm.

Album (822)
Ryl Indian Drawings 13

822 ƒ8a Tinted drawing.
A young huntsman, his face in profile, seated, adjusting his shoe.
His turban (loosely wound round a fur-edged cap) and short gun are on the ground. Underneath, on the mount, is written 'Tahmasp, *wazir* of Nadir Shah'. This is a drawing of excellent quality, but the shading of the face (cf. No **1580**), the drawing of the ear and the gold plants in the background make it difficult to accept this drawing as a Persian original. It is probably an Indian copy after an early work of Riza, *c* 1600.
11.4 × 8.9 cm. *See illustration.*

Qazwini: 'Aja' ib al-Makhluqat (823-1125)
Ryl Pers 2 (ex Bland, Lloyd)
Eighteenth-century European binding of plain suede leather inscribed in ink on the spine 'AJAYB AL MAKHLOOKAT'. The manuscript was owned by Herbert Lloyd in 1781.
24.7 × 17.2 cm. 221 ff Cursive *nasta'liq*, 19 lines to the page. W.S. 17.8 × 10.2 cm. Illuminated heading on ƒ1b in a rough broad style, the central medallion inscribed 'Herbt. Lloyd' by the former owner, whose name also appears stamped in several places in the MS. The colophon (ƒ221a) gives the date 5 Muharram

1029/12 December 1619 and the copyist's name as Riza son of 'Abd Muhammad Dizfuli.
There are 300 miniatures and diagrams in a rather rough provincial (Asbarabad?) version of the contemporary Isfahan style, with strong colouring.

823 ƒ 9b Female Siamese twins
(joined at the waist) against a background of blue sky. 7.6 × 10.2 cm.

824 ƒ 10b Constellation of the Horse.
With part of a gold and silver disc: plain blue background. 8.2 × 10.2 cm.

825 ƒ 11b An orange and silver disc with gold centre, on plain blue background, representing the Heavens. 6.3 × 10.2 cm.

826 ƒ 12a The Milky Way.
Represented as a variegated orange-red diagonal band between two gold discs (Sun and Moon). 4.4 × 10.2 cm.

827 ƒ 12b Seated youth, crowned, on background of blue sky (the Moon). 7 × 10.2 cm.

828 ƒ 14a Orange disc with silver border and gold semicircle at the top (Mercury). 6.3 × 10.2 cm.

829 ƒ 14a Seated youth in turban on blue sky background (Mars?). 5.7 × 6.3 cm.

830 ƒ 14b The Lion, with Sun behind. 6.3 × 6.3 cm.

831 ƒ 15a Venus, a girl playing a harp. 5.7 × 10.2 cm.

832 ƒ 15a A disc of concentric bands, silver, orange, gold. 5.7 × 10.2 cm.

833 ƒ 15b Virtually the same as No 827. 7.6 × 10.2 cm.

834 ƒ 16b Very similar to No 826, but the Sun has rays. 6.3 × 10.2 cm.

835 ƒ 17a Jupiter.
A seated crowned youth with a silver-bordered orange disc. 5 × 10.2 cm.

836 ƒ 19b The constellation Boötes.
Represented as a standing youth with a staff. 8.2 × 10.2 cm.

837 ƒ 20a The constellation Andromeda.
Represented as a youth running. 7 × 10.2 cm.

838 ƒ 20b The constellation Perseus.
Represented as a youth holding a demon's head and standing on one leg. 9.5 × 10.2 cm.

839 ƒ 21a The constellation Ophiuchus.
Represented as a youth holding a snake. 8.2 × 10.2 cm.

840 ƒ 21b The constellation of Pegasus.
The forepart only shown. 5.7 × 10.2 cm.

841 ƒ 22a Zodiacal Sign of the Ram. 5 × 10.2 cm.

842 ƒ 22b The Bull (forepart only)
7.6 × 10.2 cm. *See illustration.*

843 ƒ 23a The Twins
A two-headed spread-eagled youth. 5.7 × 10.2 cm.

844 ƒ 23a The Crab.
Its shell a large smiling face: background of water. 5.7 × 10.2 cm.

845 ƒ 23b The Lion (and Sun, with human eyes).
5.7 × 10.2 cm. *See illustration.*

846 ƒ 23b The Virgin.
A seated girl. 5.7 × 10.2 cm. *See illustration.*

847 ƒ 24a The Scales.
Crowned youth, seated, holding balance. 5 × 10.2 cm.

848 ƒ 24a The Scorpion.
Plain black. 4.4 × 10.2 cm.

849 ƒ 24b The Archer.
From the waist down he becomes a dragon, at whose head he aims an arrow. 4.4 × 10.2 cm.

850 ƒ 24b The Goat.
More like an ibex. 3.8 × 10.2 cm.

851 ƒ 25a Miniature divided vertically into (right) the Water-carrier and (left) the Fishes (water background). 6.3 × 10.2 cm.

820 Two soldiers of Shah 'Abbas. Isfahan/India, late 16th century

852 *ƒ*25b The constellation of Orion.
A standing youth with staff. 6.3 × 10.2 cm.

853 *ƒ*26a The constellation of Canis Major.
4.4 × 10.2 cm.

854 *ƒ*27a The constellation Centaurus.
Holding a human head and a pair of antlers.
5.7 × 10.2 cm.

855 *ƒ*31a Very similar to No **825**, but with larger
centre. 6.3 × 10 cm.

856 *ƒ*32a The Four Angels of God's Throne.
5.7 × 10.2 cm.

857 *ƒ*32b The angel al-Ruh, with four wings.
7.6 × 10.2 cm.

858 *ƒ*33a The angel Israfil. 7.6 × 10.2 cm.

858 *ƒ*33a The archangel Gabriel (Jibra'il).
6.3 × 10.2 cm.

859 *ƒ*33b The archangel Michael (Mika'il).
5.7 × 10.2 cm.

860 *ƒ*34a The angel 'Azra'il. 6.3 × 10.2 cm.

861 *ƒ*35a Winged bull. 5 × 10.2 cm.

862 *ƒ*35a Two birds on pink ground.
3.8 × 10.2 cm.

863 *ƒ*35a Winged horse. 4.4 × 10.2 cm.

864 *ƒ*35b Two angels. 4.4 × 10.2 cm.

865 *ƒ*35b The angel al-Haqzana offering a gold
dish. 7.6 × 10.2 cm.

866 *ƒ*36a The angels Harut and Marut suspended
head downwards in darkness
Faces damaged. 7 × 10.2 cm.

867 *ƒ*45a A veiled, haloed young prophet (Khizr)
discoursing with another man in a black enclosed
space. 7 × 10.2 cm.

868 *ƒ*49a The rainbow. 5.7 × 10.2 cm.

869 *ƒ*52b Naked inhabitant of one of the islands in
the China Sea, by a river. 6.3 × 10.2 cm.

870 *ƒ*53a Winged female inhabitant of the same.
7.6 × 10.2 cm.

871 *ƒ*53b Inhabitants of the island of Rami.
One large and pink, the other two smaller and white.
5.7 × 10.2 cm.

872 *ƒ*53b The Queen of the island of Waq-waq and
her court. 5 × 10.2 cm.

873 *ƒ*54a Inhabitants of the island al-Bana.
One pink and the other white. 6.3 × 10.2 cm.

874 *ƒ*54b Three monstrous demon-like inhabitants
of the island al-Hawaran (Atwaran?). 5.7 × 10.2 cm.
See illustration.

875 *ƒ*54b Three black men by a stream.
5 × 10.2 cm. *See illustration.*

876 *ƒ*55a Two horned deer-like beasts in a river.
4.4 × 10.2 cm.

877 *ƒ*55b Large pink fish with tusks. 6.3 × 10.2 cm.

878 *ƒ*55b Black fish with egg-shaped head.
3.2 × 10.2 cm.

879 *ƒ*56b Three inhabitants (white, pink and
brown) of the island Barta'il in the Indian Ocean.
5.7 × 10.2 cm.

880 *ƒ*57b Four fire-breathing, dog-headed monsters
by a domed silver building (the island of the Castle).
6.3 × 10.8 cm.

881 *ƒ*58a Dragon swallowing an ox (the Island of
Tinnin). 5.7 × 10.8 cm.

882 *ƒ*58b Human-headed pink fish and forepart of
large white fish. 5.7 × 6.3 cm.

883 *ƒ*58b Green fish with egg-shaped head.
5.7 × 4.4 cm.

884 *ƒ*60b White fish with pair of tusks. 5 × 6.3 cm.
See illustration.

885 *ƒ*60b Green fish with curving flat-ended tusks.
7 × 4.4 cm. *See illustration.*

886 *ƒ*60b White spotted fish something like a ray.
With an orange horn on its back. *See illustration.*

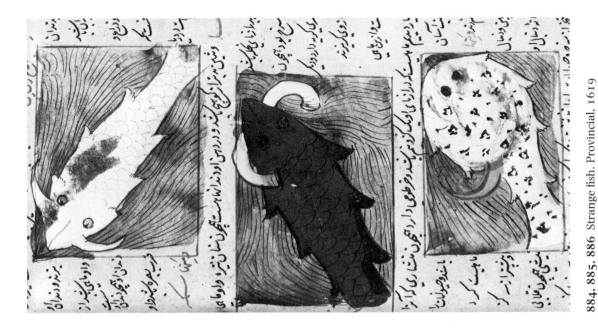

884, 885, 886 Strange fish. Provincial. 1619

874, 875 Outlandish islanders. Provincial. 1619

[285]

922 *f* 76b A representation of the World, or the Seven Climates.
In the form of a rectangle with a central black hexagon from whose angles water channels radiate, dividing the remaining field into six differently coloured rhomboidal sections.
8.2 × 7 cm.

923 *f* 79a Shirin enthroned, with her maidens, illustrating the section on Mount Bisitun.
8.9 × 10.2 cm. *See illustration.*

924 *f* 81b 'The People of the Cave'
Thirteen recumbent figures with bags over their heads illustrating the Section on Mount Raqim.
9.5 × 10.2 cm.

925 *f* 82a Waterfalls on Mount Sawa.
8.2 × 10.2 cm.

926 *f* 85a The magic figures of an ox and a fish on Mount Nahawand. 7 × 10.8 cm. *See illustration.*

927 *f* 85a The Fountain of Lions on Mount Hamand. 5 × 10.2 cm. *See illustration.*

928 *f* 85b The petrified shepherd, his flock and milkmaid, on Mount Yala Yasham.
No sign of petrifaction! 7.6 × 10.2 cm.

929 *f* 89a The river Nile, with a tortoise, two snakes and a white fish.
5 × 9.5 cm.

930 *f* 108b The orange tree. 10.8 × 10.2 cm.

931 *f* 109a The plum tree. 5.7 × 10.2 cm.

932 *f* 109b The cypress. 8.9 × 10.2 cm.

933 *f* 110a The turpentine tree. 7 × 10.2 cm.

934 *f* 110a The balsam tree. 7.6 × 10.2 cm.

935 *f* 110b The oak tree. 8.2 × 10.2 cm.

936 *f* 111a The apple tree. 7 × 10.2 cm.

937 *f* 111b The fir tree. 5.7 × 10.2 cm.

938 *f* 111b The mulberry tree. 6.3 × 10.2 cm.

939 *f* 112a The fig tree. 10.2 × 10.2 cm.

940 *f* 112b The nut tree. 6.3 × 10.2 cm.

941 *f* 113a Palma Christi. 7.6 × 10.2 cm.

942 *f* 113b The willow. 8.9 × 10.2 cm.

943 *f* 114a The elm tree. 8.9 × 10.2 cm.

944 *f* 114b The plane tree. 10.8 × 10.2 cm.

945 *f* 115a The pomegranate. 9.5 × 10.2 cm.

946 *f* 116a The olive tree. 8.9 × 10.2 cm.

947 *f* 116b The cypress. 9.5 × 10.2 cm.

948 *f* 117a The quince. 10.8 × 10.2 cm.

949 *f* 117b The sumac. 8.9 × 10.2 cm.

950 *f* 118a The cherry tree. 5.7 × 10.2 cm.

951 *f* 118a The chestnut. 6.3 × 10.2 cm.

952 *f* 118b The fir tree. 5 × 10.2 cm.

953 *f* 118b The tamarisk. 5 × 10.2 cm.

954 *f* 119a The juniper. 8.9 × 10.2 cm.

955 *f* 119b The jujube tree. 10.2 × 10.2 cm.

956 *f* 120a The ambergris tree. 9.5 × 10.2 cm.

957 *f* 120b *Fāwāniyā*, wood on which fire makes no impression.
7 × 10.2 cm.

958 *f* 120b The pepper tree. 6.3 × 10.2 cm.

959 *f* 121a The pistachio. 8.9 × 10.2 cm.

960 *f* 121b The filbert nut. 9.5 × 10.2 cm.

961 *f* 122b The vine. 9.5 × 10.2 cm.

962 *f* 123b Unidentified (*kamthari*). 7.6 × 5.7 cm.

971, 972 Automata. Provincial. 1619

926, 927 Mountain phenomena. Provincial. 1619

963 ƒ124a The lemon tree. 5.7 × 10.2 cm.

964 ƒ124 Youth warming his hands at a fire, while a snake emerges from its hole.
Illustration of an anecdote about the lemon tree which is supposed to be an antidote to snake-bite.
10.2 × 10.2 cm.

965 ƒ168b Man on a tower. 7.6 × 10.2 cm.

966 ƒ169a Man entering a building in which there is a crown. 6.3 × 10.2 cm.

967 ƒ169b Building with a closed gate.
3.8 × 10.2 cm.

968 ƒ170a Noah, his family and animals in the Ark. 10.2 × 10.2 cm.

969 ƒ170a Diagrammatic design of uncertain import. 4.4 × 10.2 cm.

970 ƒ170b Automaton of a lancer on a dome.
7.6 × 10.2 cm.

971 ƒ171a Two youths (an automaton), one kneeling on one knee with six straight lines radiating from his body. 7 × 10.2 cm. *See illustration.*

972 ƒ171a Automaton sitting on a wheel and holding a candle. 5 × 10.2 cm. *See illustration.*

973 ƒ171b Automaton with four lutes.
7.6 × 10.2 cm.

974 ƒ183b The Sun. 5.7 × 5 cm.

975 ƒ183b Bow, on silver ground. 3.8 × 4.4 cm.

976 ƒ183b Crowned youth seated. 4.4 × 5 cm.

977 ƒ184a Diagram of concentric circles.
5.7 × 5 cm.

978 ƒ184a Wide vertical silver stripe on blue ground. 3.2 × 5.7 cm.

979 ƒ184b Magic square. 5 × 3.8 cm.

980 ƒ185a Magic square. 5.7 × 5 cm.

981 ƒ185a Magic square.
Numbers not written in. 5 × 5 cm.

982 ƒ185a Magic square. 3.8 × 3.8 cm.

983 ƒ186a Magic square.
Numbers not written in. 7 × 3.8 cm.

984 ƒ186a Magic square.
Numbers not written in. 4.4 × 4.4 cm.

985 ƒ186b Polycrates taking the ring from the corpse in the horse.
A face has been crudely drawn, later, on the corpse's face-cloth.
7 × 5.7 cm.

986 ƒ187a Head of large white fish with a pearl in its mouth. 3.8 × 5 cm.

987 ƒ187a Man and child. 7.6 × 4.4 cm.

988 ƒ187b Youth on throne (talismans of Jupiter).
6.3 × 5 cm.

989 ƒ187b Naked man and woman (talismans of Mars). 5.7 × 5 cm.

990 ƒ188a Youth with shield (talismans of the Sun). 5 × 6.3 cm.

991 ƒ188a Naked woman and child, the latter carrying a sword (talismans of Venus). 7.6 × 5 cm.

992 ƒ188b Man with a cock's-comb holding up a bottle and a cock (talismans of Mercury). 5.7 × 5 cm.

993 ƒ188b Youth and two cows (talismans of the Moon). 6.3 × 5 cm.

994 ƒ189a A peacock. 3.8 × 5 cm.

995 ƒ189b Three bowls of fire. 3.8 × 3.8 cm.

996 ƒ189b Ochre surface, nothing painted on it.
3.8 × 3.8 cm.

997 ƒ190a Sleeping man robbed (?) by another.
5 × 4.4 cm.

998 ƒ190b Man on donkey and another leading a captive. 5.7 × 10.2 cm.

999 ƒ191a Three men approaching a woman.
7.6 × 10.2 cm.

1000 ƒ191b Two men and a woman in a building. 6.3 × 10.2 cm.

1001 ƒ191b Man and woman seated in a building. 5 × 10.2 cm.

1002 ƒ192a Pair of lovers, and man outside. 7.6 × 10.2 cm.

1003 ƒƒ192b A woman and her bound husband in a house: a robber is making off with loot. 7.6 × 10.2 cm. *See illustration.*

1004 ƒ193a Three women in gold head-cloths riding through a crowd of demons. 7.6 × 10.2 cm.

1005 ƒ193b Greybeard copulating with a young woman. A bit discoloured and rubbed, as are several of the miniatures from here onwards. 5 × 10.2 cm.

1006 ƒ194a Five men seated in converse. 5 × 10.2 cm.

1007 ƒ194a Man chopping a tree, addressed by another. 5 × 10.2 cm.

1008 ƒ194b Man kneeling upon and striking another on the ground. 5 × 10.2 cm.

1009 ƒ195a Man on the ground struggling with a demon. 5 × 10.2 cm.

1010 ƒ195a Seated demon addressing two men, (these two quite badly damaged). 5.7 × 10.2 cm.

1011 ƒ195b A black and a yellow demon. 8.2 × 10.2 cm.

1012 ƒ196a A purple demon running. 5.7 × 10.2 cm.

1013 ƒ196a A yellow demon running. 5.7 × 10.2 cm.

1014 ƒ196b Orange monkey riding an ostrich. 5.7 × 10.2 cm.

1015 ƒ196b Grey monkey running. 5 × 10.2 cm.

1016 ƒ197a Solomon enthroned with angel and demons. 5.7 × 10.3 cm.

1017 ƒ197b Solomon approached by two mounted demons. 5.7 × 10.2 cm.

1018 ƒ197b Yellow and orange wolves (?) joined along their backs. 5.7 × 10.2 cm.

1019 ƒ198a Solomon entertained by a cow-headed demon playing the lute. 5.7 × 10.2 cm.

1020 ƒ198b The horse. 5 × 10.2 cm.

1021 ƒ198b The mule. 3.8 × 10.2 cm.

1022 ƒ199a The ass. 5 × 10.2 cm.

1023 ƒ199a The wild ass. 5.7 × 10.2 cm.

1024 ƒ199b Fire-breathing dragon about to swallow a snake. 3.8 × 10.2 cm.

1025 ƒ199b A snake. 3.8 × 10.2 cm.

1026 ƒ200a Snake swallowing a bird. 3.8 × 5 cm.

1027 ƒ200a A bee (?) (*zabāb*, 'mole'). 3.2 × 2.5 cm.

1028 ƒ200a Unidentified (*durūḥ*). 3.8 × 2.5 cm.

1029 ƒ200b A wasp. 3.8 × 3.2 cm.

1030 ƒ200b A venomous lizard (*sāmmi abraṣ*). 3.8 × 5 cm.

1031 ƒ200b A tortoise. 3.2 × 3.8 cm.

1032 ƒ201a *Sannāja*, a huge bull-like creature. 6.3 × 10.2 cm.

1033 ƒ201a A lizard (weasel? – *sana'a*, apparently not the name of any creature). 3.8 × 10.2 cm.

1034 ƒ201b Orange cat (*ṭarfan*). 3.8 × 10.2 cm.

(Space left for *'utabal* (?), not filled in)

1035 ƒ202a A jackal. 4.4 × 5 cm.

1036 ƒ202a A polecat. 2.5 × 3.8 cm.

1037 ƒ202b A hare. 5 × 5 cm.

1038 ƒ202b A lion. 5 × 6.3 cm.

1039 ƒ203a A tiger. 6.3 × 10.2 cm.

1040   ƒ 203a A fox (?) (*niqab*). 3.8 × 5 cm.

1041   ƒ 203a Unidentified (*qūs*). 2.5 × 2.5 cm.

1042   ƒ 203b A wild boar. 5.7 × 10.2 cm.

1043   ƒ 203b A bear. 5 × 10.2 cm.

1044   ƒ 204a A wolf (*dhib*). 4.4 × 5 cm.
Cf. No **1051**.

1045   ƒ 204a Rhinoceros giving birth. 5 × 10.2 cm.

1046   ƒ 204b Rat-like creature with prominent gold eyes. 2.5 × 5.7 cm.

1047   ƒ 204b Striped grey beast seated. 3.8 × 5 cm.

1048   ƒ 204b Striped red-brown beast seated.
5 × 3.8 cm.

1049   ƒ 205a A laughing hyena (?). 3.8 × 5 cm.

1050   ƒ 205a A unicorn. 5 × 5.7 cm.

1051   ƒ 205b A wolf. 5 × 10.2 cm. Cf. No **1044**
See illustration.

1052   ƒ 205b Grey cat with gold eye.
3.8 × 5 cm.

1053   ƒ 205b A cheetah. 5 × 5 cm.

1054   ƒ 206a An elephant. 8.9 × 10.8 cm.

1055   ƒ 206a Another kind of cheetah.
3.8 × 5.7 cm.

1056   ƒ 206b The heron. 3.8 × 4.4 cm.

1057   ƒ 206b The pheasant (?). 2 × 5 cm.

1058   ƒ 206b Two ducks. 3.8 × 5 cm.

1059   ƒ 206b An eagle. 3.2 × 5 cm.

1060   ƒ 207a A pigeon. 3.2 × 4.4 cm.

1061   ƒ 207a A parrot. 3.8 × 5 cm.

1062   ƒ 207a A nightingale. 3.8 × 4.4 cm.

1063   ƒ 207b An owl. 5 × 4.4 cm.

1064   ƒ 207b A pheasant (more like a cock).
3.8 × 5.7 cm.

1065   ƒ 207b Reading uncertain: a red and gold bird standing in water. 3.2 × 5 cm.

1066   ƒ 207b A kite. 2.5 × 5 cm.

1067   ƒ 208a A pigeon. 3.8 × 2.5 cm.

1068   ƒ 208a A swallow. 3.8 × 2.5 cm.

1069   ƒ 208a A bat (very bird-like). 4.4 × 2.5 cm.

1070   ƒ 208b Francolin (a pair). 3.8 × 4.4 cm.

1071   ƒ 208b A cock. 5 × 4.4 cm.

1072   ƒ 208b A hen. 3.8 × 4.4 cm.

1073   ƒ 209a A vulture. 5 × 3.2 cm.

1074   ƒ 209a A crow. 3.8 × 3.8 cm.

1075   ƒ 209a A starling (coloured yellow).
3.8 × 4.4 cm.

1076   ƒ 209b A falcon. 3.8 × 4.4 cm.

1077   ƒ 209b *Shiqāq* ('quarrelsome'). 3.8 × 5 cm.

1078   ƒ 209b Green bird hanging upside down (*safir*). 3.2 × 5 cm.

1079   ƒ 209b A hawk. 3.2 × 4.4 cm.

1080   ƒ 210a A peacock. 5 × 4.4 cm.

1081   ƒ 210a A sparrow. 3.2 × 3.8 cm.

1082   ƒ 210a An eagle. 3.2 × 4.4 cm.

1083   ƒ 210a A wagtail. 3.8 × 5 cm.

1084   ƒ 210b The *simurgh* or '*anqa*. 7.6 × 10.2 cm.

1085   ƒ 211a A raven. 3.8 × 3.8 cm.

1086   ƒ 211a Kind of duck. 3.8 × 4.4 cm.

1087   ƒ 211a A diver (illustration is of a large fish).
3.8 × 3.8 cm.

1032, 1033 The monster *ṣannāja*, and a lizard.
Provincial. 1619

1003 The conniving wife, and the burglar. Provincial. 1619

1129 The planet Mercury. Isfahan, 1632

1049, 1050, 1051 Hyena. unicorn, and wolf. Provincial, 1619

1088 *f* 211b A ring-dove. 3.8 × 4.4 cm.

1089 *f* 211b A partridge. 3.2 × 4.4 cm.

1090 *f* 211b A lark. 5 × 3.8 cm.

1091 *f* 212a A sand-grouse. 3.2 × 3.8 cm.

1092 *f* 212a A turtle-dove. 3.2 × 3.8 cm.

1093 *f* 212a A phoenix (black bird amid flames). 3.8 × 5 cm.

1094 *f* 212a A crane. 3.8 × 4.4 cm.

1095 *f* 212b A stork. 4.4 × 4.4 cm.

1096 *f* 212b A grebe. 3.2 × 4.4 cm.

1097 *f* 212b A macaw. 3.2 × 4.4 cm.

1098 *f* 212b A vulture. 3.2 × 4.4 cm.

1099 *f* 213a An ostrich. 5 × 4.4 cm.

1100 *f* 213a A hoopoe. 3.8 × 3.8 cm.

1101 *f* 213b A water-bird (unlabelled). 3.8 × 4.4 cm.

1102 *f* 213b A weevil. 3.8 × 3.2 cm.

1103 *f* 214a An asp? (*arz*). 3.8 × 3.8 cm.

1104 *f* 214a Tiger-like sea-serpent (unlabelled). 3.8 × 4.4 cm.

1105 *f* 214a A bat (*ḥawad?*). 3.2 × 3.2 cm.

1106 *f* 214b Bird with sun shining on it (*hirbā*, a chameleon!). 3.8 × 5 cm.

1107 *f* 214b A camel. 6.3 × 10.2 cm.

1108 *f* 215a A cow. 5.7 × 10.2 cm.

1109 *f* 215a A stag ('wild cow'). 5 × 7 cm.

1110 *f* 215b A water-buffalo. 8.2 × 10.2 cm.

1111 *f* 216a A giraffe (nothing like!) 7 × 10.2 cm.

1112 *f* 216a Two sheep-like animals. 5 × 10.2 cm.

1113 *f* 216b A sort of antelope. 5 × 10.2 cm.

1114 *f* 216b A sort of fawn. 3.8 × 5 cm.

1115 *f* 217a A wild goat. 5.7 × 10.2 cm.

1116 *f* 217a A kind of lizard. 3.2 × 4.4 cm.

1117 *f* 217b A scorpion. 3.8 × 3.8 cm.

1118 *f* 217b A spider. 3.2 × 3.2 cm.

1119 *f* 217b A rat (?). 3.2 × 3.8 cm.

1120 *f* 218a A moth. 3.2 × 3.2 cm.

1121 *f* 218a A porcupine. 3.8 × 5 cm.

1122 *f* 219a A kind of yellow worm or lizard (*lūnil*). 3.2 × 5 cm.

1123 *f* 219b Jerboa. 3.8 × 4.4 cm.

1124 *f* 220a Two footless men, one pink and the other orange. 5.7 × 5 cm.

1125 *f* 220a An elephant-headed man with wings. 5.7 × 5 cm.

Qazwini: 'Aja'ib al-Makhluqat (1126-1480)
Ryl Pers 3 (ex Bland, de Sacy)

Contemporary binding of black morocco (rebacked and repaired) with fine stamped gilt medallions (flowers) and pendants (rabbits). Doublures of crimson leather, with medallions and pendants of gold cut-out work on blue, green, and vermillion backgrounds. At the beginning are two Persian seals, with short librarians' entries: 1. Pitifāt ʿAlī Khān; 2. Muʿizz al-Dawla Bahādur Khān (?) dated 1162/1749; one of the inscriptions appears to record the gift of the manuscript from the first to the second.

34.2 × 17.8 cm. 256 *ff*; the pencil numbering includes three fly-leaves at the beginning, so that what should be *f* 1 is numbered 4. However to save renumbering throughout, this numbering has been followed in listing the miniatures. The colour of the *ff* varies from cream through coffee to several shades of green. Good calligraphic *nastaʿliq*, 21 lines to the page. W.S. 27 × 12.3 cm. An extremely fine illuminated heading at the beginning of the text, the central medallion left unpainted. The whole manuscript is in very good condition. Colophon on *f* 259a (256a), signed by Shamsa, and dated 12 Dhu'l-hijja 1041/30 June 1632.

The 355 miniatures, which admirably exemplify the mature Isfahan style, maintain a high standard of execution throughout.

Exhibited: Victoria and Albert Museum 1967. (*VAM 1967* No 72)

[ƒ 13*a* Blank space left for a miniature.]

1126 ƒ 14a The full moon, with a face, in a star-spangled sky. 10.2 × 12.7 cm.

1127 ƒ 14b Half-moon among stars. 6.3 × 12.7 cm.

1128 ƒ 15a The moon half eclipsed, among stars. 7.6 × 12.7 cm.

1129 ƒ 16b Bearded man seated writing, representing the planet Mercury; background of stars. 8.2 × 8.2 cm. *See illustration.*

1130 ƒ 17a Seated lady with sprays of flowers, representing the planet Venus; background of stars on green ground. 6.3 × 8.9 cm.

1131 ƒ 17b The sun in splendour. Cloudy background. 6.3 × 8.2 cm.

1132 ƒ 18a The sun without rays. Slight discolouration along inner edge. 3.8 × 8.2 cm.

1133 ƒ 19a Bare-headed warrior with shield and drawn sword, representing the planet Mars. 5 × 7 cm.

1134 ƒ 19b Youth wearing a skull-cap and carrying a shield and drawn sword, representing the planet Jupiter. 6.3 × 7 cm.

1135 ƒ 19b Dark-skinned, crowned, six-armed, bearded man seated on a mat, representing the planet Saturn.
In various hands he holds a sword, a mouse, a pick, a sieve (?), and a burning brazier. 7.6 × 7 cm.

[ƒ 20a. Blank space left for a miniature.]

All the following miniatures of constellations have starry backgrounds.

1136 ƒ 21a The constellation of the Great Bear. 5 × 8.2 cm.

1137 ƒ 21b The constellation of the Lesser Bear. 6.3 × 8.2 cm.

1138 ƒ 22a The constellation of Draco. 6.3 × 7.6 cm.

1139 ƒ 22b The constellation of Cepheus. 5 × 7.6 cm.

1140 ƒ 22b The constellation of Boötes. A man with a walking-stick. 6.3 × 7.6 cm.

1141 ƒ 23a The constellation of the Cup (*jāthī*). 4.8 × 12.7 cm.

1142 ƒ 23a The constellation of Andromeda. A kneeling youth with outstretched arms. 5 × 8.2 cm.

1143 ƒ 23a The constellation of the Hawk (*dajājat* 'hen'). On pink ground. 4.8 × 7.6 cm.

1144 ƒ 23b The constellation of Cygnus. A flying hawk. 5 × 8.2 cm.

1145 ƒ 23b The constellation of Cassiopeia. A lady sitting on a chair. 5.7 × 7.6 cm.

1146 ƒ 23b The constellation of Perseus. A youth carrying a severed head (placed sideways). 3.8 × 7.6 cm.

1147 ƒ 24a The constellation of a youth by a tent. White background. 24.1 × 7.6 cm.

1148 ƒ 24a The constellation of Ophiuchus. Youth holding snake. 5 × 7.6 cm.

1149 ƒ 24a The constellation of the Arrow. Pink background. 2.5 × 7.6 cm.

1150 ƒ 24b The constellation of the Eagle. 3.8 × 7.6 cm.

1151 ƒ 24b The constellation of the Dolphin. 2.5 × 7.9 cm.

1152 ƒ 24b The constellation of the Half-Horse (*qita 'al-faras*). 5 × 8.2 cm.

1153 ƒ 25a The constellation of Pegasus (*faras al-'azam*). Shown winged. 4.8 × 7.9 cm.

1154 *f* 25a The constellation of Andromeda. No chain shown. 5 × 8.2 cm.

1155 *f* 26b The constellation of the Horse. 3.8 × 12.1 cm.

1156 *f* 26b The constellation of the Crab. Should be the triangle, *muthallath*; green ground. 2.5 × 7.3 cm.

1157 *f* 26b The constellation of the Ram. 3.7 × 7.6 cm.

1158 *f* 26a The constellation of the Bull. Represented as a camel. 5 × 7.6 cm.

1160 *f* 26a The constellation of the Twins. One cleanshaven and fair, the other dark skinned with moustache. 5 × 8.2 cm.

1161 *f* 26b The constellation of the Crab, represented as a white mule. 3.8 × 7.6 cm.

1162 *f* 26b The constellation of the Lion. Mauve background. 6 × 8.6 cm.

1163 *f* 27a The constellation of the Virgin. 5 × 12.7 cm.

1164 *f* 27a The constellation of the Scales, also represented as a young woman. 3.8 × 12.7 cm.

1165 *f* 27a The constellation of the Scorpion. Mauve background. 3.8 × 8.9 cm.

1166 *f* 27b The constellation of Sagittarius, represented by a crane. 5 × 8.9 cm.

1167 *f* The constellation of Capricornus. 2.5 × 6.7 cm.

1168 *f* 27b The constellation of Aquarius, represented by a fish. 6.3 × 7.6 cm.

1169 *f* 28a The constellation of Pisces, represented by one fish. 2.5 × 8.9 cm.

1170 *f* 28a The constellation of Cetus, a fish. 2.5 × 6.3 cm.

1171 *f* 28b The constellation of the Bow. 5 × 8.2 cm.

1172 *f* 28b The constellation of the Hare, represented by a crane. 3.8 × 12.7 cm.

1173 *f* 29a The constellation of Canis Major. 2.5 × 8.2 cm.

1174 *f* 29a The constellation of Canis Minor. 2.5 × 8.2 cm.

1175 *f* 29b The constellation of Argo Navis. No suggestion of masts or oars: green background. 6.3 × 12.7 cm.

1176 *f* 30a The constellation of the Dove. 3.8 × 7 cm.

1177 *f* 30a An area of pink sky with stars. (Should be the Snake, *shiyā'*). 3.8 × 12.7 cm.

1178 *f* 30a A fish, representing the constellation of the Crow. 2.5 × 7.6 cm.

1179 *f* 30b The constellation of Centaurus. 3.8 × 12.7 cm.

1180 *f* 30b Patch of pink sky with stars, representing the constellation of the date-cluster (*shamārikh*). 2.5 × 4.1 cm.

1181 *f* 30b A white duck, representing the constellation Corona. 2.5 × 5.7 cm.

1182 *f* 30b The constellation of the Fish. 2.5 × 12.7 cm.

1183 *f* 37a The four angels who support God's throne. Their heads are as the symbols of the Evangelists, except that the bull (of St Luke) has become a leopard. 11.4 × 12.7 cm. *See illustration.*

1184 *f* 37b The angel Israfil blowing his horn. 10.2 × 12.7 cm. *See illustration.*

1185 *f* 38a The archangel Gabriel, crowned, with threefold wings. 10.2 × 12.7 cm.

1186 *f* 38b The archangel Michael, and the fallen angels in the outer darkness. 10.2 × 12.7 cm. *See illustration.*

1183 The four angels who support God's throne. Isfahan, 1632

1184 The angel Israfil. Isfahan, 1632

1187 ƒ39b The angel 'Azra'il seated opposite Solomon enthroned, both their faces veiled.
10.2 × 12.7 cm.

1188 ƒ40b The angels Harut and Marut suspended head-downwards in a pit.
Very slight smudging. 10.8 × 12.7 cm.

1189 ƒ53a The prophet Khizr, haloed, and an Israelite youth before an enthroned King Anuqat (?).
7.6 × 12.7 cm.

[ƒ 56b Blank space left for a miniature]

1190 ƒ57b A rainbow. 7.6 × 7.9 cm.

1191 ƒ61a Ships and fish in the great surrounding Ocean.
24.1 × 12.7 cm. *See colour pl XIV.*

1192 ƒ62a Two naked inhabitants of the islands of Zanj in the China Sea.
7.6 × 7.9 cm. *See illustration.*

1193 ƒ62a Two flying cats on the same island.
5 × 7.6 cm. *See illustration.*

1194 ƒ62a A lynx-like animal on the same island.
5 × 7.6 cm. *See illustration.*

1195 ƒ62b Three winged natives of the same island. Brightly coloured birds in the trees.
10.2 × 12.7 cm.

1196 ƒ63a Two naked inhabitants of the island of Amani.
The man brown-skinned, the woman light-skinned, offering him an apple.
6.3 × 8.9 cm. *See illustration.*

1197 ƒ63a The Queen of the island of Waq-waq enthroned with her naked women courtiers.
Their skins range from black to white.
10.2 × 12.7 cm. *See illustration.*

1198 ƒ63b Birds in a large tree on the island of Sala.
6.3 × 12.7 cm.

1186 The archangel Michael, and fallen angels. Isfahan, 1632

1199 ƒ63b A naked woman seated on a platform, fixed in the fork of a tree on the island of Bana(n). 8.9 × 8.9 cm.

1200 ƒ64a Men in a ship surprised by beast-headed men appearing in the sea off the island of Atwaran. 6.3 × 7.6 cm.

1201 ƒ64a Two men in the sea. 3.8 × 6.3 cm.

1202 ƒ64b Fauna of the islands.
A kind of deer-rhinoceros seated under a tree. 5 × 8.9 cm.

1203 ƒ64b Men hunting fish. 5 × 7.9 cm.

1204 ƒ64b Tortoises by a stream. 5 × 8.2 cm.

1205 ƒ64b Two large and two small fish.
The former with long pointed noses. 6.3 × 7.9 cm.

1206 ƒ65a Two serpents.
One coiled round a tree, and the other round a rock. 7.6 × 8.2 cm. *See illustration.*

1207 ƒ66a (The Indian Ocean).
Two naked inhabitants of the island of Barta'il reclining under a tree by a stream. 7.6 × 8.9 cm.

1208 ƒ66b Men in a boat off the island of the Castle, fighting off an attack by beast-headed, man-like creatures. 8.9 × 8.2 cm.

1209 ƒ67a Inhabitants of the island of Jaba amid the flames of their fiery mountain. 5 × 7.6 cm.

1210 ƒ67a Scene on the island of the Dragon (*tinnīn*).
On a mauve hilltop between two trees, a group of buildings of markedly European type. In the middle ground two oxen, and in the foreground a yellow dragon about to advance on them.
14 × 12.7 cm. *See illustration.*

1211 ƒ67b A yellow bear-like creature with a black horn between its eyes. 3.8 × 7 cm.

1212 ƒ67b Three pigeons and their eggs in a large nest. 5 × 7.6 cm.

1213 ƒ67b Two flying fish. 3.8 × 8.2 cm.

1214 ƒ68a A fish with a long neck and snake-like head. 3.8 × 7 cm.

1215 ƒ68a A ring-shaped fish with a spike. 5 × 7.9 cm.

1216 ƒ69b Various remarkable fish. 3.8 × 8.9 cm. *See illustration.*

1217 ƒ69b Various remarkable fish. 2.5 × 8.9 cm. *See illustration.*

1218 ƒ69b Various remarkable fish. 3.8 × 8.6 cm. *See illustration.*

1219 ƒ70b Man carried into the air above his boat, grasping the legs of a giant bird. 12.7 × 12.7 cm. *See illustration.*

1220 ƒ71b Men in a boat and a youth on shore by a hermit's cell in a forest on the island of Jasasa. 11.4 × 12.7 cm. *See illustration.*

1221 ƒ71b Owl-faced fish, and two small ones. 3.8 × 8.9 cm.

1222 ƒ72b Inhabitants of the island of Nas hunting birds. 6.3 × 12.7 cm.

1223 ƒ73a Two men seated before dishes of rice and bread, while a demon behind them empties fruit from a sack. 6.3 × 12.7 cm.

1224 ƒ73a Man crouching behind a tree on a river-bank while two demons approach. 8.9 × 12.7 cm.

1225 ƒ73b The Old Man of the Sea riding on a victim's shoulders. 7.6 × 8.9 cm. *See illustration.*

1226 ƒ73b A large fish and two small ones. 5 × 12.7 cm.

1227 ƒ74b The bronze figure on the stone tower in the forest on the island of Manara. 11.4 × 8.9 cm. *See illustration.*

1228 ƒ75a Two men in a small house, with a jackdaw (?) on the dome, approached by a man with a dish of fruit. 10.2 × 12.7 cm. *See illustration.*

1229 ƒ75b Young man squatting on the shell of a rabbit-eared turtle, a snake in front of him. 5 × 6.3 cm.

1192, 1193, 1194 Fauna of the island of Zanj. Isfahan, 1632

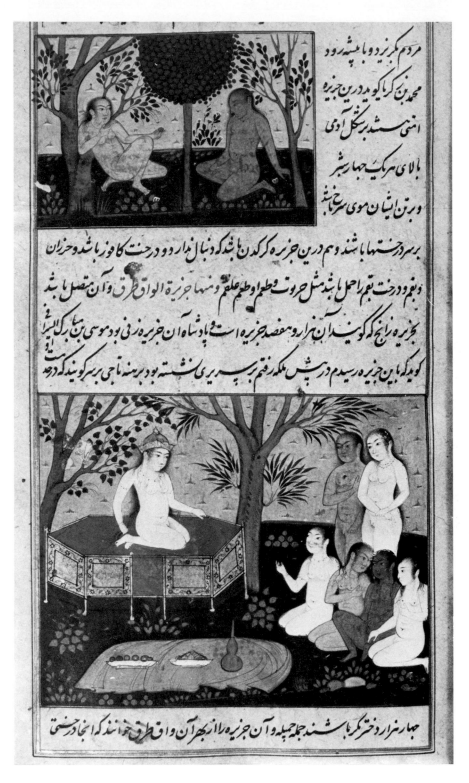

1196, 1197 Islanders of Amani, and the Queen of Waq-waq. Isfahan, 1632

1195 Winged islanders, and birds. Isfahan, 1632

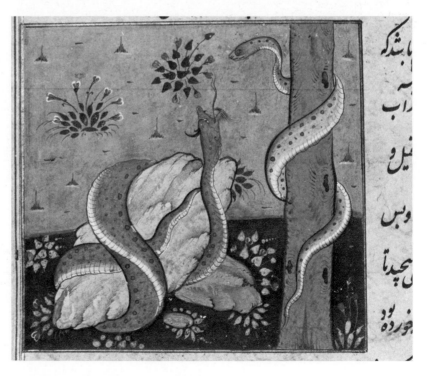

1206 Tree and rock serpents. Isfahan, 1632

1209, 1210 The Fiery Island and the island of the Dragon. Isfahan, 1632

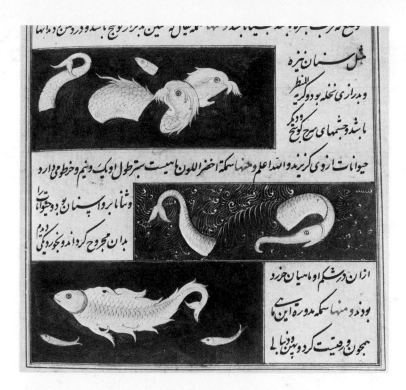

1216, 1217, 1218 Strange fish. Isfahan, 1632

1219 Man carried by the roc. Isfahan, 1632

1225 The Old Man of the Sea riding a victim. Isfahan, 1632

1220 Scene on the island of Jasasa. Isfahan, 1632

1228 Islanders at home. Isfahan, 1632

1227 The figure on the tower. Isfahan, 1632

1230 *f* 76a A human-headed, frog-bodied creature sitting in the sea among the fish.
6.3 × 7.6 cm. *See illustration.*

1231 *f* 76a Three fish. 3.8 × 7.6 cm.

1232 *f* 76b A fish.
Smudged and unfinished. 3.8 × 7 cm.

1233 *f* 76b A flying fish. 2.5 × 8.9 cm.

1234 *f* 77b A fish. 5 × 8.2 cm.

1235 *f* 78a Two young men, and a fat prince seated on a mat. 5 × 8.6 cm.

1236 *f* 78b A fish with rabbit's ears. 3.8 × 6.3 cm.

1237 *f* 78b A fish without a lower jaw.
3.8 × 7.6 cm.

1238 *f* 78b Two naked men, one on shore and the other in the water. 6.3 × 7.6 cm.

1239 *f* 79a White bullock grazing by a stream.
6.3 × 8.9 cm.

1240 *f* 79b The sea-monster *timsāh* (crocodile).
5 × 8.2 cm.

1241 *f* 80a The monster *tinnīn*.
A thick serpent-like creature with semi-human head, wings, and five smaller serpents growing from its neck.
5 × 12.7 cm. *See illustration.*

1242 *f* 80a An eel (*jirri*), represented as a fish with a snake's tail, on land. 3.8 × 7.6 cm.

1243 *f* 80b A dolphin, represented with wings.
3.8 × 7 cm.

1244 *f* 81a The crab, represented more like a large bug, crawling along the waterside. 5 × 7 cm.

1245 *f* 81b Creature called *sartān al-bahr*, represented as a smooth pale-grey scorpion.
2.5 × 7.6 cm.

1246 *f* 81b *Saqanqūr*, crocodile spawn, represented as a small lizard-like creature. 2.5 × 6.3 cm.

1247 *f* 83a Black horse galloping in a meadow.
3.8 × 6.7 cm.

1248 *f* 83b Stallion covering a mare. 6.3 × 7.9 cm.

1249 *f* 84a The beaver or sable (*qunduz*), represented like a white dachshund. 5 × 8.2 cm.

1250 *f* 84a This is apparently intended to represent the porcupine (*qunfud*); actually it is a fish-like creature with ears, a long nose, and snail-like shell on its back.
5 × 7.6 cm.

1251 *f* 84b The dog.
A small brown terrier, running. 3.8 × 6.3 cm.

1252 *f* 86b A hilly landscape with two young men, a small flock, and a village of rather western appearance behind.
10.2 × 12.7 cm. *See illustration.*

1253 *f* 88a The Mountain Abu Qays, with a waterfall. 7.6 × 8.2 cm.

1254 *f* 88a The double mountain of Ajawasalmi.
7.6 × 21.6 cm.

1255 *f* 88b Mount Asbara, with a rabbit at its base.
7.9 × 8.2 cm.

1256 *f* 89b Mount Bisutun, showing Farhad's sculpture (seated prince and dervish, and a standing youth). 7.6 × 8.6 cm.

1257 *f* 91a Mount Damawand with a smith at work in a panel on the mountain, and two men's heads; a rather European village below. 7.9 × 8.2 cm.

1258 *f* 91b Mount Razwi, with a small waterfall and two tall trees beside it. 8.9 × 12.7 cm.

1259 *f* 93a The mountains of Ceylon, coloured an angry red, with an exotic village behind, and trees in the foreground. 7.6 × 8.9 cm.

1260 *f* 94a The mountain of Tyre, a rabbit at the base, waterfall, and a building in the foreground.
7.6 × 9.5 cm.

1262 *f* 95b The mountain of Birds, with birds clustering round the hole near the summit.
6.3 × 7.6 cm.

1263 *f* 101a The River Nile, with a representation of the nilometer (*miqyās*). 6.3 × 7.6 cm.

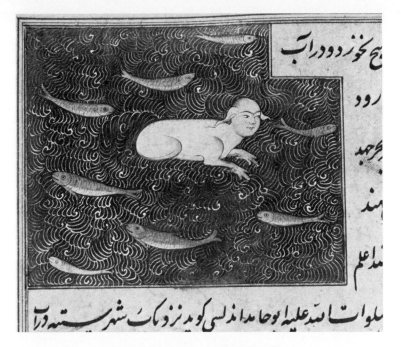

1230 Human-headed marine creature. Isfahan, 1632

1241 The great dragon *tinnīn*. Isfahan, 1632

(Trees)

1264 ƒ128b The ebony tree. 6.3 × 7.6 cm.

1265 ƒ128b The myrtle. 5 × 6.3 cm.

1266 ƒ128b The orange tree. 5 × 6.3 cm.
Cf. No **1294**.

1267 ƒ129a The plum tree. 6.3 × 7.6 cm.

1268 ƒ129b(a) The Egyptian thorn (*amughaylān*).
6.3 × 7.3 cm. Cf. No **1277**.

1269 ƒ129b(b) The myrobalam and turpentine tree.
7.6 × 7 cm.

1270 ƒ130a The balsam tree. 6.3 × 7.9 cm.

1271 ƒ130b The *tanūb*, 'a kind of fir tree'.
No resemblance in the miniature. 6 × 7.6 cm.

1272 ƒ131b The wild fig tree. 6.3 × 7.6 cm.

1273 ƒ132a Galingale (?) (*Khusraw-dār*).
3.6 × 5.7 cm.

1274 ƒ132b The laurel. 6.3 × 7.3 cm.

1275 ƒ133b The olive tree.
Slight discolouration. 5 × 7 cm.

1276 ƒ134b The sumach tree. 6.7 × 7 cm.

1277 ƒ134b The Egyptian thorn (?).
The manuscript has *sandaras*, which does not appear in
the dictionary as the name of a tree. But MS 37 has
samurat in the corresponding place. The miniature
certainly bears no resemblance to No **1268**.
6.3 × 6.3 cm.

1278 ƒ135a The cherry tree. 6.3 × 6.7 cm.

1279 ƒ135a The sandalwood tree. 5.3 × 5.7 cm.

1280 ƒ135b The tamarisk. 6.3 × 6.3 cm.

1281 ƒ135b The juniper tree. 6.7 × 6.3 cm.

1282 ƒ136a The aloes-wood tree. 5.3 × 7.3 cm.

1283 ƒ136a The ambergris tree. 6.7 × 6.3 cm.

1284 ƒ136b *Fāwāniyā*, a fire-proof tree. 5 × 6.3 cm.

1285 ƒ136b The pepper tree. 6.3 × 6.3 cm.

1286 ƒ137a The filbert (nut) tree.
Top right-hand corner discoloured. 5.3 × 6.7 cm.

1287 ƒ137a The box-thorn (*fid-haraj*, in error for
filzahra; cf. MS. 37 *fil-zahraj*). 6.3 × 6.3 cm.

1288 ƒ137b The clove tree. 5 × 7 cm.

1289 ƒ137b Reeds. 6.3 × 6.3 cm.

1290 ƒ138a The camphor tree. 5 × 5 cm.

1291 ƒ139a *Lāghiya* (so also in MS 37).
Not traced as the name of a tree. 6.3 × 6.3 cm.

1292 ƒ139b The frankincense tree. 5 × 7.6 cm.

1293 ƒ140b The banana tree. 6.3 × 6.3 cm.

1294 ƒ141a The orange tree (*nāranj*). 6.3 × 7.6 cm.
Cf. No **1266**.

1295 ƒ141a The coconut tree. 6.7 × 6.3 cm.

1296 ƒ141b The palm tree. 6.3 × 7 cm.

1297 ƒ181b Sculptured panel on a rock representing Kisra (Nushirwan) mounted. 7.9 × 8.2 cm.

1298 ƒ182b Prince having his hands washed from
a tank in Istanbul; attendants carrying incense-
burners.
10.4 × 12.7 cm. *See illustration.*

1299 ƒ183b (On the customs of the Turks).
Two parties of armed men facing each other: two other
men on the horizon.
7.6 × 9.2 cm. *See illustration.*

1300 ƒ183b Interior scene with two ladies seated,
and behind each two men, one with a drawn sword. A
black goat painted on the wall behind.
10.2 × 12.7 cm. *See illustration.*

1301 ƒ185a (Indian customs).
Young man worshipping an idol.
6.3 × 6.7 cm. *See illustration.*

1252 Exotic landscape with figures.
Isfahan, 1632

1298 Prince washing his hands.
Isfahan, 1632

1302 ƒ185a Dire results of gambling.
The loser has lost all his clothes and is now about to have his fingers cut off by the ruthless winner – a dark-skinned young man in a skull-cap.
8.9 × 12.7 cm. *See illustration.*

1303 ƒ185b Indian lovers copulating in a house.
On the terrace another Indian points them out to a young Persian visitor.
10.2 × 12.7 cm. *See illustration.*

1304 ƒ186a Corpse of an Indian on a blazing funeral pyre. 8.2 × 8.2 cm.

1305 ƒ192b Figure of a mounted man on the top of a dome at Baghdad. 10.4 × 21.6 cm.

1306 ƒ193b Five men at sea in a boat.
8.9 × 12.7 cm.

1307 ƒ193b A mechanical well. 7.9 × 8.2 cm.

1308 ƒ194a Mechanical contrivance for drawing water.
A mounted figure on the top of a building in which are a wheel and water falling into a dish. In the lower part of the building (divided from the upper by two lines of text) a young man kneels, watching water pouring into a bowl from above, and holding a jar in readiness.
21.6 × 12.7 cm. *See illustration.*

1309 ƒ194b Young prince seated under an awning with three armed men before him.
BJRL xxxiv (1951) p 79. 8.9 × 12.7 cm.

1310 ƒ194b Young prince seated on a throne, holding a lighted candle; a wheel below. 7.6 × 8.2 cm.

1311 ƒ195a Contrivance consisting of the figure of a young woman seated above a large brown pear-shaped vessel from whose mouth project two bottles (?) on shafts (*sandūq al-ma'ni*). 8.6 × 7.9 cm.

1312 ƒ207a Young man taking a reading with an astrolabe. 5 × 5 cm.

1313 ƒ207b Young man taking a reading with an astrolabe. 5.7 × 5.3 cm.

1314 ƒ207b Young man seated on a mat leans back to observe the sunrise; an attendant behind him.
6.3 × 5.7 cm.

1315 ƒ207b Young man taking an observation with an astrolabe. 6.3 × 4.8 cm.

[ff 208b, 209a 4 spaces left for miniatures]

1316 ƒ210a Three men under a tree preparing a talisman: a mixed flock grazes beside them.
7.6 × 12.7 cm.

1317 ƒ210b Five men in converse, with bottles and dishes of fruit before them.
Slight flaking at inner edge. 8.9 × 12.7 cm.

1318 ƒ211a Young man holding a bird and a fish and standing on a lizard, representing talismans connected with the planet Saturn. 7.9 × 5.7 cm.

1319 ƒ211a Young man riding on a large bird, representing talismans connected with the planet Jupiter.
7.6 × 7.6 cm.

1320 ƒ211b Naked bearded man with his arm round the neck of a young woman (clothed), representing talismans connected with the planet Mars.
Slight flaking. 6.3 × 5.3 cm.

1321 ƒ211b Man carrying a shield and a whip, and walking on a green dragon, representing talismans connected with the Sun.
7.6 × 7.6 cm.

1322 ƒ212a Naked girl followed by a small boy with a drawn sword, representing talismans connected with the planet Venus. 7.3 × 6.3 cm.

1323 ƒ212a Man with wings and a cock's-comb, holding up a jar in his left hand, a cock standing behind him.
His right hand was probably holding his *membrum virile*, but the latter has been erased. This represents talismans connected with the planet Mercury.
7.9 × 6 cm.

1324 ƒ212b Lady with a scalloped gold halo, holding a whip and standing between two bullocks, representing the Moon's talismans.
8.9 × 6.7 cm. *See illustration.*

1325 ƒ213a A certain bird connected with love spells. 4.1 × 5.7 cm.

1299, 1300 Customs of the Turks. Isfahan, 1632

1301, 1302 Idolatry and gambling in India. Isfahan, 1632

1308 Mechanical contrivance for drawing water. Isfahan, 1632

1324 Personification of the Moon. Isfahan, 1632

1303 Persian visitor shown Indian love-making. Isfahan, 1632

1326 *ƒ*213a Young man crouching over an incense-burner. 5 × 6.3 cm.

1327 *ƒ*213b A padlock lying in a meadow. 3.8 × 5.3 cm.

1328 *ƒ*214a Young man seated, holding a black purse (?), a standing girl looking back at him. Slight discolouration. 6.7 × 6 cm.

1329 *ƒ*214b Young man in a curious gold cap following another to whom he is attached by a cord round his neck. 6.3 × 7.6 cm.

1330 *ƒ*214b Two youths in converse in an interior. One of them, in a short coat, holds a purse (?) similar to that in No **1328** above. 7.6 × 7.9 cm.

1331 *ƒ*215a Young couple seated before the *qazi*. 7.6 × 8.9 cm.

1332 *ƒ*215a Young couple conversing in an interior. 7.6 × 8.2 cm. *See illustration.*

1333 *ƒ*215b Lady conversing with a slave in a landscape. 6.7 × 7.3 cm.

1334 *ƒ*215b Interior, with the slave repelling the ladies' advances, watched by another man in an attitude of surprise. 7.6 × 7.6 cm. *See illustration.*

1335 *ƒ*216a Arrest of a malefactor in the presence of a lady who clenches her fists. Slight discolouration. 7.9 × 8.2 cm.

1336 *ƒ*217a Greybeard seducing a young woman. 7.6 × 7.6 cm.

1337 *ƒ*217a The young woman in a swoon. 4.1 × 5.7 cm.

1338 *ƒ*217a The greybeard prostrating himself before a young man with a golden collar: two others behind. 5.7 × 7.6 cm.

1339 *ƒ*217b Three men seated before a holy man under a tree outside the latter's cell. 7.6 × 12.7 cm.

1340 *ƒ*218a Bareheaded man in a golden collar falls from a tree upon another man: a saw behind. 6.3 × 7.9 cm.

1341 *ƒ*218b Mourners round a corpse on a bier. 7.6 × 12.7 cm.

1342 *ƒ*219a A centaur. 6.3 × 6.3 cm.

1343 *ƒ*219a Reclining pink *jinn* under a tree. 4.1 × 12.7 cm.

1344 *ƒ*219a Blue *jinn* with his club seated under a tree. 7.6 × 7.6 cm.

1345 *ƒ*219b Blue *jinn* riding an ostrich. 7.6 × 7 cm.

1346 *ƒ*219b Brown *jinn* clubbing a man he has thrown to the ground. 5 × 6.7 cm.

1347 *ƒ*219b Interior, with a bearded man seated on a mat, in conversation with a youth. Slight flaking. 6.3 × 12.7 cm.

1348 *ƒ*220a Beast-headed *jinn* before Solomon. 8.9 × 12.7 cm.

1349 *ƒ*220b Brown *jinn* riding a winged black horse. 6.3 × 7 cm.

1350 *ƒ*220b White *jinn* playing the lute to a man seated on a mat. Slight discolouration. 6.3 × 8.9 cm.

1351 *ƒ*221a Bearded white *jinn* hastening from the presence of a veiled personage seated on a mat. Slight discolouration at edges. 6.3 × 7.6 cm.

1352 *ƒ*221a A grey *jinn* with a camel's head and elephant's body, walking like a bear. 6.3 × 7.6 cm.

1353 *ƒ*221a Solomon enthroned with a group of his subjects before him. 7.6 × 12.7 cm.

1354 *ƒ*221b Solomon at the upper window of a castle, observes a consultation of demons below. 8.9 × 12.7 cm. *See illustration.*

1355 *ƒ*222a Camels straying while a caravan rests. 17.8 × 12.7 cm. *See illustration.*

1356 *ƒ*222b Youth conversing with a holy man at the entrance to his cell. 6.3 × 7.6 cm.

1357 *ƒ*222b Youth conversing with an old woman at the foot of a precipitous purple mountain. 10.2 × 6 cm.

1331, 1332 Marriage customs. Isfahan, 1632

1334 Slave repelling a lady's advances. Isfahan, 1632

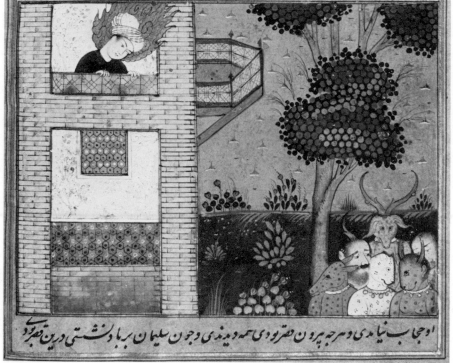

1354 Solomon observes demons in consultation. Isfahan, 1632

1355 Camels straying while caravan rests. Isfahan, 1632

1368, 1369, 1370 Three pairs of snakes. Isfahan, 1632

1358 ƒ233a Youth in discussion with four others, one of whom appears to be a Turk, all seated. 8.9 × 9.2 cm.

1359 ƒ223b Youth conversing with a young woman seated at the entrance to her tent. 7.9 × 8.9 cm.

1360 ƒ223b Wolf seizing a goat from the flock: head and shoulders of a young man below, right, 4.1 × 7.6 cm.

1361 ƒ223b Wise man dressed in white discussing poetry with four young men. 5 × 12.7 cm.

1362 ƒ224a Bearded man bringing a covered dish of food to a young man seated in a crypt or dungeon. 8.6 × 7.6 cm.

1363 ƒ224b The horse. 5 × 7.6 cm.

1364 ƒ225a The mule. 4.1 × 8.2 cm.

1365 ƒ225b The ass. 5 × 7 cm.

1366 ƒ225b Another representation of the ass. 5 × 7.6 cm.

1367 ƒ226a The snail. 5.3 × 6.3 cm.

1368 ƒ226b Pair of snakes. 5 × 10.2 cm.

1369 ƒ226b Pair of snakes. 3.8 × 7.6 cm.

1370 ƒ226b Pair of snakes. 4.1 × 12.7 cm. *See illustration.*

1371 ƒ227a Pair of snakes with reddish backs. 4.1 × 12.7 cm.

1372 ƒ227a Pair of earthworms. 5 × 7 cm.

1373 ƒ227b The black beetle. 3.2 × 3.8 cm.

1374 ƒ227b The caterpillar. 5 × 6.3 cm.

1375 ƒ228a The fly. 4.1 × 3.8 cm.

1376 ƒ228b Probably intended for cantharides, or Spanish fly (*dharārīh*; the text has *darūj* which, besides being out of alphabetical order, is not traceable as the name of any creature). The representation is of a pair of small worms, one red and the other brown. 2.5 × 3.8 cm.

1377 ƒ228b The tarantula. 3.8 × 4.4 cm.

1378 ƒ228b The wasp. 4.1 × 3.8 cm.

1379 ƒ228b *Sāmmi abras.* 'A large and venomous kind of lizard', but the creature represented resembles a centipede. 2.5 × 3.8 cm.

1380 ƒ229a The tortoise. 2.8 × 2.8 cm.

1381 ƒ229a The *ṣannāja*. A fabulous beast represented as something like a crocodile. 5 × 8.9 cm. *See illustration.*

1382 ƒ229a Small, white, grub-like insect. Its name has not been written in, but it may be intended to represent *ẓabb*, a kind of lizard, which follows *ṣanāja* in MS 37. 2.5 × 5 cm.

1383 ƒ229b A little green lizard called *tanab*. 2.8 × 6.3 cm.

1384 ƒ230a A feline called *ṭarfān*. 2.8 × 6.3 cm.

1385 ƒ230a A dog-like creature called *'atāba* running by a river in which are three fish. 6.3 × 7 cm.

1386 ƒ230b A running dog or fox-like creature called *ibn dil* ('son of the heart'). 4.1 × 7.6 cm.

1387 ƒ231a The polecat or weasel, represented as a sort of lizard. 3.8 × 6.3 cm.

1388 ƒ231b Pair of rabbits. 4.1 × 6 cm.

1389 ƒ231b The lion. 6 × 7.6 cm.

1390 ƒ232a The tiger. 4.1 × 6.7 cm.

1391 ƒ232b The fox, represented lying on its back. 2.8 × 5 cm.

1392 ƒ233a A kind of antelope with a single horn on its forehead, called *ḥūs*. 4.8 × 7.6 cm.

1393 ƒ233a The wild boar. 2.8 × 4.1 cm.

1394 ƒ233b The bear. 3.2 × 4.8 cm.

1395 ƒ233b Lion watching a man up a tree, the latter only visible below the waist. 5 × 7.9 cm.

1381 The *ṣannāja*. Isfahan, 1632

1409 Two monkeys. Isfahan, 1632

1396 *f* 234a The weasel, represented more like a small wolf. 2.8 × 4.8 cm.

1397 *f* 234a A running lupine animal called *dunb* ('a tail'). 4.8 × 6.3 cm.

1398 *f* 235a The elephant called *sinbad* giving birth. 5.3 × 7.6 cm.

1399 *f* 235a The ermine. 4.1 × 5.7 cm.

1400 *f* 235a The cat. 3.8 × 6 cm.

1401 *f* 235b The wild ('desert') cat. 2.8 × 5.7 cm.

1402 *f* 235b A fabulous beast called *sarash*. (*Sarānash* in MS 37 – No 333). It has holes in its snout by which it plays music. 5 × 7.9 cm.

1403 *f* 236a Another fabulous beast called *shādawār*.
Like an ibex, with musical horns. 6 × 4.1 cm.

1404 *f* 236a The hyena. 4.1 × 6.3 cm.

1405 *f* 236b The lynx. 2.8 × 5.3 cm.

1406 *f* 236b This would appear to be the crocodile; the name is written as *biyāṣ*, which is not in alphabetical order, and does not appear in the dictionary. 3.8 × 5.7 cm.

1407 *f* 237a The cheetah. 3.8 × 7 cm.

1408 *f* 237a The elephant, caparisoned. 7.6 × 8.2 cm.

1409 *f* 238a Two monkeys gathering and eating fruit from a tree.
6.3 × 7 cm. *See illustration.*

1410 *f* 238b The rhinoceros.
9.2 × 12.7 cm. *See illustration.*

1411 *f* 239a A brown and a white dog.
These are drawn in a very natural and lively manner. 3.6 × 5.7 cm. *See illustration.*

1412 *f* 239b The leopard (*namir*). 3.8 × 7 cm.

1413 *f* 240a An antelope with very long slender horns, called *naghiyūn* (?), drinking at a stream. 6 × 8.9 cm.

1414 *f* 240a Three small birds with long pointed beaks rather like humming-birds, called, apparently, *mush* (?). 3.6 × 5 cm.

1415 *f* 240a A pair of finch-like birds called *pir-nafas*. 2.5 × 4.1 cm.

1416 *f* 240b Aquatic birds (*urdak*), ducks and a swan (?). 3.8 × 5 cm.

1417 *f* 240b The falcon on its perch. 3.8 × 5 cm.

1418 *f* 241a The sparrow-hawk. 2.5 × 3.6 cm.

1419 *f* 241a Parrots. 3.8 × 4.8 cm.

1420 *f* 241a Pair of nightingales. 2.5 × 3.8 cm.

1421 *f* 241a Pair of plump little birds called *barbū'*. 3.2 × 3.8 cm.

1422 *f* 241b Pair of swallows flying in the sky.
They are given the name *tadharw* which is translated as 'cock pheasant' or 'jungle cock' in the dictionary. 3.8 × 5.7 cm.

1423 *f* 242a The bustard. 2.5 × 4.4 cm.

1424 *f* 242a The kite. 3.6 × 3.8 cm.

1425 *f* 242a Pair of pigeons. 3.6 × 4.1 cm.

1426 *f* 242b The swallow (*khuṭṭāf*).
But this little bird is not much like a swallow. 2.5 × 4.1 cm.

1427 *f* 243a A flying bat. 2.5 × 3.8 cm.

1428 *f* 243a The francolin. 3.6 × 4.1 cm.

1429 *f* 243b Two cocks squaring up to one another. 5 × 6.3 cm. *See illustration.*

1430 *f* 244a Pair of quails.
(*Dajāj* is written, which means cock or hen, but it is probably an error for *daj*, which can mean quail. 2.5 × 3.2 cm.

1431 *f* 244a A carrion-eating bird (*rakhma*) flying amid beautifully painted rocks.
5 × 5.3 cm. *See illustration.*

1432 *f* 244b The raven. 3.8 × 5 cm.

1410 The rhinoceros. Isfahan, 1632

1411 Two dogs. Isfahan, 1632

1431 Bird flying amid rocks. Isfahan, 1632

1429 Two cocks. Isfahan, 1632

1433 *f* 244b *Zarzad.*
A pinkish bird with a rather long red beak. Possibly intended for *zurzur*, the starling. 3.8 × 3.8 cm.

1434 *f* 245a The falcon.
Two are shown, on their perches. 5 × 5.7 cm.

1435 *f* 245a The royal white falcon (*shāhīn*).
2.5 × 2.5 cm.

1436 *f* 245a *Saqrāq.*
A small pink and grey bird. (*Saqrāq* normally means jug or pitcher.) 2.5 × 3.2 cm.

1437 *f* 245a Three white birds on a tree, two of them hanging upside down. 3.8 × 7.6 cm.

1438 *f* 245b Hawk.
Shown attacking the eyes of a deer. 3.8 × 4.4 cm.

1439 *f* 245b The peacock.
Two males shown, one with tail displayed.
6.3 × 6.3 cm. *See illustration.*

1440 *f* 246a The eagle. 3.8 × 4.4 cm.

1441 *f* 246b The magpie (?).
A small black, grey and white bird. 2.5 × 4.4 cm.

1442 *f* 246b The *'anqā*. A splendid phoenix-like bird perched on a tree-trunk in a landscape.
8.9 × 12.7 cm. *See illustration.*

1443 *f* 247a This is supposed to be the crow (*gharāb*), but is represented as a grey pigeon-like bird with white front, in flight. 2.5 × 4.4 cm.

1444 *f* 247b *Gharbīq* (?).
A pair of birds like cranes. 2.5 × 3.8 cm.

1445 *f* 247b Divers (*ghawās*).
Represented as ducks. 2.5 × 4.4 cm.

1446 *f* 247b Three ring-doves. 2.5 × 3.8 cm.

1447 *f* 248a Three partridges in a rocky landscape.
5 × 5.7 cm.

1448 *f* 248a Two larks in flight. 2.5 × 3.8 cm.

1449 *f* 248a Two sand-grouse. 3.8 × 3.8 cm.

1450 *f* 248b The turtle-dove (*qumri*). 3.8 × 3.8 cm.

1451 *f* 248b Phoenix (*quqnus*).
Two birds by a fire. 5 × 4.4 cm.

1452 *f* 248 The crane.
5 × 5.7 cm.

1453 *f* 249a The stork carrying off a snake.
5.7 × 6.3 cm.

1454 *f* 249a *Makā* ('macaw'), a duck-like bird with long beak. 3.2 × 5 cm.

1455 *f* 249a The vulture, but nothing like: the illustration is of a small grey bird defending its nest from a snake. 5 × 5 cm.

1456 *f* 249a Possibly intended for the vulture.
A brown bird with partly black wings and white underparts, in flight. 5 × 5.7 cm.

1457 *f* 249b The ostrich.
Feet are correct: otherwise like a crane. 6.3 × 8.2 cm.

1458 *f* 249b The hoopoe. 2.5 × 3.8 cm.

1459 *f* 250a The mountain swallow. 2.5 × 3.8 cm.

1460 *f* 250b The adjoining sections are *arazat* ('a worm which eats into ships') and *afa'ā* ('a large venomous serpent, viper, asp'). Both creatures here shown appear to be serpents. 3.8 × 8.9 cm.

1461 *f* 251b The dragon *tinnīn.*
Black with gold accessories, stalking through a rocky landscape, breathing fire.
6.3 × 12.1 cm. *See illustration.*

1462 *f* 252a The locust. 1.2 × 3.2 cm.

1463 *f* 252a *Ḥirbā* ('chameleon').
Represented as a gaily coloured bird displaying its wings to the sun. 2.5 × 2 cm.

1464 *f* 252a The camel.
Seated, two packs beside it. 8.9 × 5 cm.

1465 *f* 252b Black humped ox, with gold necklace.
3.8 × 6.3 cm.

1466 *f* 253b The wild ox.
Represented as a stag. 5 × 8.2 cm.

1467 *f* 253b *Jāwamīsh*, a grey ox. 7 × 6.3 cm.

1468 *f* 254a The giraffe.
White with a single horn. 5 × 12.1 cm.

1468a *f* 254a A pair of sheep. 3.8 × 5.7 cm.

1469 *f* 254b The goat. 5 × 5 cm.

1470 *f* 255a *Zabi.*
A kind of antelope. 3.8 × 5 cm.

1471 *f* 255a *Bayān.*
A golden lizard. 3.8 × 6.3 cm.

1472 *f* 255b The scorpion.
Pale green. 5 × 6.3 cm.

1473 *f* 255b The spider. 3.8 × 5 cm.

1474 *f* 255b Spider suspended from its web.
2.5 × 4.4 cm.

1475 *f* 255b Spider catching a fly. 3.8 × 3.8 cm.

1476 *f* 256b Another spider. 3.8 × 4.4 cm.

1477 *f* 256b The mouse. 2.5 × 3.8 cm.

1478 *f* 256b Three mice playing. 2.5 × 6.3 cm.

1479 *f* 256b The butterfly. 2.5 × 3.8 cm.

1480 *f* 256b The hedgehog. 3.8 × 5 cm.

1439 Two peacocks. Isfahan, 1632

1442 The *'anqā*. Isfahan, 1632

1461 The great dragon *tinnīn*. Isfahan, 1632

Firdawsi: Shahnama (1481-1579)

Ryl Pers 909 (ex de Sacy, Castellobranco, Clarke)
Sumptuous early nineteenth-century European binding of brown calf, tooled and gilt, and incorporating the
inlaid gilt medallions, pendants and corner-pieces
from the original covers. The doublures likewise
incorporate the cut-out work (gold on blue) of the
original, the pieces being inlaid in a panel of brown silk
set within a tooled and gilt leather frame. The date of
this elaborate binding may perhaps be deduced from
the 1808 watermark on the sheets of thin Whatman
paper bound into the volume to protect the miniatures.
The spine is lettered SHAHI NAMEH FIRDOOSY. On
the front fly-leaf is written (Dr Clarke's writing) 'This
fine copy of the Shah Nameh is embellished by about
one hundred paintings. Every page has been collated;
and the work is perfect', and underneath an entry from
a bookseller's or auctioneer's catalogue, describing the
manuscript, is mounted. Below this again is the name
of a former owner Le Ch. J. Ferrão de Castellobranco.
On the upper corner of the back fly-leaf is the small
trade label of *T. Kaye, Bookseller, Stationer, Printer and
Publisher of the Liverpool Courier, 42, Castle Street,
Liverpool*, who may perhaps have been responsible for
the present binding. Kerney's MS catalogue says that
Dr Clarke and Silvestre de Sacy were former owners.
40.7 × 25.5 cm. 493 *ff* of which five (*ff* 157, 208, 354,
355, 492) are modern replacements. The missing
originals carried miniatures. Fair *nasta'liq* in 4 columns
of 31 lines to the page. W.S. 28.6 × 15 cm. Illuminated
headings in a bold style, but of good quality, on *ff* 1b
(Baysunghuri preface) and 12b (beginning of text): in
both these openings margins and text are decorated.
Headings on large panels of floral scrolls in gold appear
on *ff* 75b ('Beginning of the story of Suhrab and
Rustam'), 87b ('Beginning of the story of Siyawush'),
and 177a ('Beginning of the story of the Barzu Nama').
The colophon on *f* 493a is dated Thursday, 23 Jumada
II, 1060/23 June 1650, by the copyist Yusuf b.
Mahmud Shah b. Yusuf.

The manuscript contains 99 miniatures of rather
less than first-rate quality, in typical mid seventeenth-
century Isfahan style: figures are on the large side and
execution tends to be summary. A noteworthy feature,
(also of the Trinity College, Dublin, *Shahnama* of 1650)
is the extensive use of silver, some of which has
remained untarnished. An inferior, but contemporary,
painter contributed a few miniatures towards the end.

[*Note*. In many cases the lateral measurements of the
miniatures in this manuscript must be regarded as no
more than approximate. Its very tight binding makes
accurate measurement impossible.]

1481 *f* 15a Hushang avenges his father Siyamak on
the demon: he lifts him by girdle and collar and is
about to fling him down.
Elephant and rhinoceros in the foreground.
10.2 × 15.2 cm.

1482 *f* 22a The tyrant Zahhak secured in his palace
by Faridun.
Kawa with his banner on the left, and Jamshid's sisters
behind.
14 × 19 cm.

1483 *f* 27a Murder of Iraj by his brothers Tur and
Salm.
The former attacks him with a stool or small throne.
10.2 × 17.8 cm.

1484 *f* 30b Tur slain by Minuchihr in revenge for
Iraj.
12.1 × 15.8 cm. (plus banners in upper margin).

1485 *f* 32a Salm slain by Minuchihr in revenge for
Iraj.
15.8 × 19 cm. (plus banners in the upper margin).

1486 *f* 36b Zal, enthroned, listens to a description of
Rudaba, his future bride.
11.4 × 15.2 cm.

1487 *f* 47a The birth of Rustam, Zal and the
Simurgh above. Slightly rubbed.
25.5 × 20.2 cm. *See illustration.*

1488 *f* 49a Rustam kills the mad elephant.
Small patches of discolouration.
16.5 × 20.2 cm. *See illustration.*

1489 *f* 57a Rustam catches his charger Rakhsh.
Slight damage.
15.2 × 20.2 cm. *See illustration.*

1490 *f* 59a Rustam lifts Afrasiyab from the saddle.
Since the last miniature the hero has grown a fine red
beard and moustache.
20.2 × 19 cm.

1491 *f* 60b Kay Ka'us beguiled by a demon in
disguise who persuades him to attack Mazandaran.
7 × 12.1 cm.

1492 *f* 63a Rustam asleep (though his eyes are
open) while Rakhsh slays a marauding lion.
12.1 × 12.7 cm.

1487 The birth of Rustam. Isfahan, 1650

1488 Rustam and the mad elephant. Isfahan, 1650

1489 Rustam catches his charger. Isfahan, 1650

1493 ƒ63b Rustam, aided by Rakhsh, slays the dragon.
8.9 × 21.6 cm.

1494 ƒ64a Rustam drinking with the witch.
7 × 11.4 cm.

1495 ƒ65a Rustam captures Awlad.
Slight patches of discolouration.
12.1 × 12.7 cm.

1496 ƒ65b Rustam in combat with the demon Arzhang.
Slight discolouration.
11.4 × 15.2 cm.

1497 ƒ66a Rustam slays the White Demon: Awlad tied to a large tree which occupies the left-hand margin.
Slight discolouration. 25.5 × 21.6 cm.

1498 ƒ71b Rustam lassoes the King of Hamawaran.
22.8 × 17.8 cm.

1499 ƒ84a Suhrab about to kill Rustam.
8.9 × 15.2 cm.

1500 ƒ85a Rustam bewails the dying Suhrab.
14 × 15.2 cm.

1501 ƒ99a Siyawush going to play polo before Afrasiyab.
Siyawush's face scrubbed out and clumsily redrawn.
21.6 × 17.8 cm.

1502 ƒ101a Siyawush entertained by his step-mother Sudaba in her apartment.
5 × 15.2 cm.

1503 ƒ107b The murder of Siyawush.
The text describes the dispute of Siyawush and Afrasiyab.
12.1 × 15.2 cm.

1504 ƒ109a The murder of Siyawush.
Again, this time in accordance with the text.
12.7 × 15.2 cm.

1505 ƒ113a Rustam directs the slaying of Surkha, son of Afrasiyab, in revenge for Siyawush.
Surkha's face badly flaked.
10.2 × 12.7 cm.

1506 ƒ130a Bizhan wounds Farud outside the latter's castle.
14 × 20.2 cm. *See illustration.*

1507 ƒ133b Kay Khusraw receives news of the Persian defeat from Tus.
15.2 × 15.2 cm.

1508 ƒ139a Combat of Tus with Human son of Wisa.
10.8 × 19 cm (plus banners in upper margin).

1509 ƒ147a Combat of Kamus, the Turanian champion, with Giw and Tus.
12.1 × 17.8 cm.

1510 ƒ149a Rustam shoots Ashkabus and his horse.
Rustam's figure is entirely in the margin, detached from the main miniature.
11.4 × 17.8 cm.

1511 ƒ150b Kamus lassoed by Rustam.
Rustam's face damaged.
12.1 × 17.8 cm.

1512 ƒ155b Rustam lifts Shangul from the saddle on his lance.
14.6 × 15.2 cm (plus banners in upper margin).

[ƒ 27 is a modern replacement; the original ƒ must have carried a miniature of Rustam and the Khaqan.]

1513 ƒ162b Combat of Rustam and Puladwand, here represented as a horned blue demon, and his mount a rhinoceros.
12.7 × 17.8 cm (plus banners in the upper margin).

1514 ƒ165a The demon Akwan lassoed by Rustam.
15.2 × 17.8 cm. *See illustration.*

1515 ƒ168a Captive Bizhan before Afrasiyab: Piran pleads for his life.
12.1 × 12.7 cm.

1516 ƒ177b Suhrab, drinking in a tent with Shahru, daughter of a village headman (*dihqān*), falls in love with her. (Beginning of the *Barzu Nama*.)
10.8 × 16.5 cm.

1517 ƒ185a Combat of Rustam with his grandson Barzu.
13.3 × 20.2 cm (plus banners in upper margin).

1506 Farud wounded by Bizhan. Isfahan, 1650

1514 The demon Akwan lassoed by Rustam. Isfahan, 1650

1518 *f* 193a Second combat of Rustam and Barzu. 15.2 × 21.6 cm (plus banners in upper margin).

1519 *f* 205a Combat of Rustam and Pilsam, the Slavonian (*saqlābī*). 18.4 × 21.6 cm.

[*f* 208 is a modern replacement; the original *f* probably carried a miniature of the second combat of Rustam and Pilsam.]

1520 *f* 211a Combat of Barzu and Afrasiyab. Slight damage. 9.5 × 17.8 cm.

1521 *f* 220a Combat of Bizhan and Human. 13.3 × 19 cm (plus banners in upper margin).

1522 *f* 226b Battle between the troops of Gudarz and Piran. Slight damage. 14 × 19 cm (plus banners in the upper margin).

1523 *f* 229a Combat of Fariburz and Kulbad. 14.6 × 20.2 cm (plus banners in upper margin).

1524 *f* 229b Combat of Giw and Gurwi. 8.2 × 15.2 cm.

1525 *f* 229b Combat of Guraza and Siyamak. 10.2 × 15.2 cm.

1526 *f* 230a Combat of Furuhil and Zangula. 8.9 × 21.6 cm.

1527 *f* 230a Combat of Ruhham and Barman. 7.6 × 19 cm.

1528 *f* 230b Combat of Bizhan and Ruin. 10.2 × 19 cm.

1529 *f* 230b Combat of Hajir and Sipahram. Discolouration. 10.2 × 20.2 cm.

1530 *f* 231a Combat of Zanga and Akhwast. 9.5 × 14.6 cm.

1531 *f* 231a Combat of Gurgin and Andariman. Discolouration. 7.6 × 11.4 cm.

1532 *f* 231b Combat of Barta and Kuhram. 11.4 × 19 cm.

1533 *f* 232a Combat of Gudarz and Piran, with javelins.

Discolouration, obliterating Piran's eyes. 15.2 × 19 cm.

1534 *f* 234b Lahhak and Farshidward slain by Gustaham. 12.1 × 16.5 cm.

1535 *f* 255a Execution of Afrasiyab by Kay Khusraw. Slight damage. 12.7 × 16.5 cm (plus the branches of two trees, which continue upwards between the columns of text, and burst out into leaf in the upper margin).

1536 *f* 263b Gushtasp asks the hand of Kitayun, daughter of Caesar, in marriage. 10.2 × 11.4 cm.

1537 *f* 265a Gushtasp shoots the wolf (here shown as a benignly smiling dog-like beast); his wounded horse on its back in the middle. 10.2 × 20.2 cm.

1538 *f* 266b Gushtasp slays the dragon. The artist has confused this incident with the later dragon-slaying by Gushtasp's son Isfandiyar, having represented the spiked armoured car used by the latter in the middle of the composition. Curiously enough, none of Isfandiyar's Seven Stages is illustrated in this manuscript. 15.2 × 20.2 cm. *See illustration.*

1539 *f* 298a Combat of Isfandiyar and Arjasp. 20.9 × 19 cm.

1540 *f* 289b Arjasp seized by Isfandiyar. 12.7 × 17.8 cm.

1541 *f* 290a Execution of Arjasp's followers. Damage. 12.7 × 11.4 cm.

1542 *f* 296a Rustam entertained by Isfandiyar. 14 × 11.4 cm.

1543 *f* 300a Rustam and Isfandiyar wrestling on horseback. Slight discolouration. 15.5 × 20.2 cm (plus banners in the upper margin).

1544 *f* 300b The slaying of Nush-azar and Mihr-i-nush, sons of Isfandiyar. Slight discolouration. 12.7 × 15.2 cm.

1545 *f* 301a Beginning of the combat between Rustam and Isfandiyar. 12.7 × 20.2 cm.

1538 Gushtasp and the dragon. Isfahan, 1650

1546 Wounded Rustam cured by the *Simurgh*. Isfahan, 1650

1546 *f* 302b The wounded Rustam supported by his father Zal, while the *Simurgh* plucks the arrows from his body; Rakhsh, also wounded with arrows, in the foreground, together with the fire in which Zal burned the *Simurgh's* feather to summon her assistance.
Very slight damage. 15.2 × 15.2 cm. *See illustration.*

1547 *f* 303b Rustam shoots Isfandiyar in the eyes with the magic arrow.
10.2 × 15.2 cm.

1548 *f* 307b Rustam, supporting himself in the pit in which he and Rakhsh are impaled, shoots his treacherous brother through the tree.
The latter, whose face has been scrubbed out and clumsily redrawn, is entirely in the margin, separated from the main miniature by a column of text.
26.7 × 21.6 cm. *See illustration.*

1549 *f* 310a Execution of Faramurz by Bahman.
16.5 × 11.4 cm.

1550 *f* 316a Defeat of Dara by Iskandar.
10.2 × 22.8 cm (plus banner in upper margin).

1551 *f* 317b Iskandar comforts the dying Dara, whose murderers are brought in captive.
17.8 × 19 cm (plus banner in upper margin).

1552 *f* 319b Wedding feast of Iskandar and Dara's daughter Rushanak.
17.2 × 17.8 cm.

1553 *f* 323b Battle between the armies of Iskandar and Fur.
26 × 16.5 cm.

1554 *f* 324a Fur slain by Iskandar in single combat.
Slight discolouration.
15.8 × 20.2 cm (plus banners in upper margin).

[*ff* 354, 355 are modern replacements; the original *ff* seem to have carried two miniatures, probably representing early exploits of Bahram Gur.]

1555 *f* 359a Bahram Gur wins the crown from between the two lions
Cf. Riza's 'Khusraw and the lion' in the Victoria and Albert Museum (*VAM 1967*, pl 30).
16.5 × 17.8 cm. *See illustration.*

1556 *f* 361b Bahram Gur hunting lions.
20.2 × 20.2 cm.

1557 *f* 365a Bahram Gur killing the dragon.
12.1 × 22.2 cm.

1558 *f* 367a Bahram Gur shooting lions.
15.2 × 21.6 cm.

1559 *f* 370b Bahram Gur hunting lion and wild ass.
13.3 × 15.8 cm.

1560 *f* 376b Bahram Gur kills a rhinoceros in India.
As in Nos **1553**, **1554**, **1562**, and **1563** Mughal Indian turbans are carefully represented.
14 × 19 cm.

1561 *f* 377a Bahram Gur kills a dragon in India; he uses a battle-axe – an unusual touch. 9.5 × 19.7 cm.

1562 *f* 409a The introduction of chess from India at the Court of Nushirwan.
12.7 × 16.5 cm.

1563 *f* 410a The sage Buzurjmihr introducing backgammon to the Indian court. 17.8 × 15.2 cm.

1564 *f* 431b Defeat of Sawa Shah by Bahram Chubina.
10.8 × 17.8 (plus banner in upper margin).

1565 *f* 432a Sawa Shah slain by Bahram Chubina.
10.8 × 16.5 cm.

1566 *f* 445a Battle between Bahram Chubina and Khusraw Parwiz.
Slight discolouration.
17.2 × 19 cm (plus banners in upper margin).

1567 *f* 455b Second battle of Khusraw and Bahram Chubina. 14 × 20.2 cm.

1568 *f* 448b Bahram Chubina is presented with a testimonial by the Persians. 12.7 × 16.5 cm.

1569 *f* 455b Kut the Roman slain by Bahram Chubina.
15.2 × 20.2 cm (plus banners in the upper margin).

1570 *f* 456a This appears to be the same subject as the preceding miniature, but is the work of an inferior and careless hand.
16.5 × 20.2 cm (plus banners in upper margin).

1571 *f* 456b Bahram Chubina fights on, on foot.
The same inferior artist as the preceding.
13.3 × 19 cm (plus banners in upper margin).

1548 The death of Rustam. Isfahan, 1650

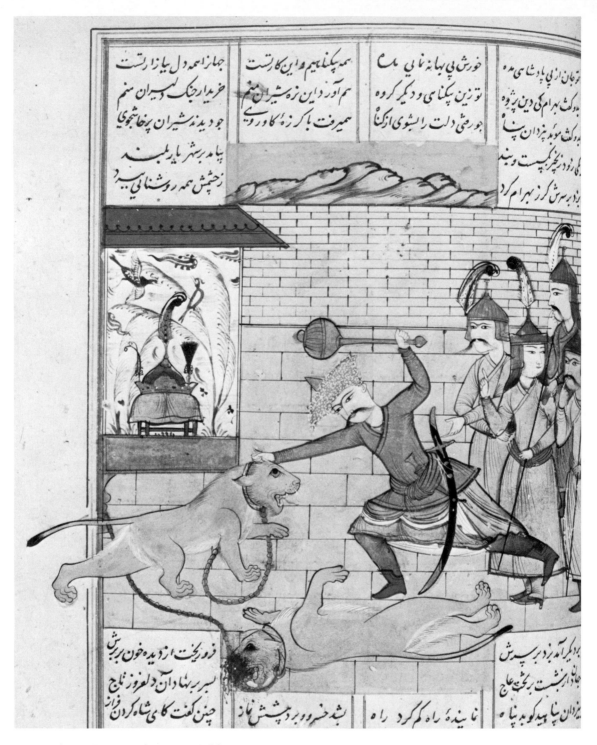

1555 Bahram Gur wins the crown. Isfahan, 1650

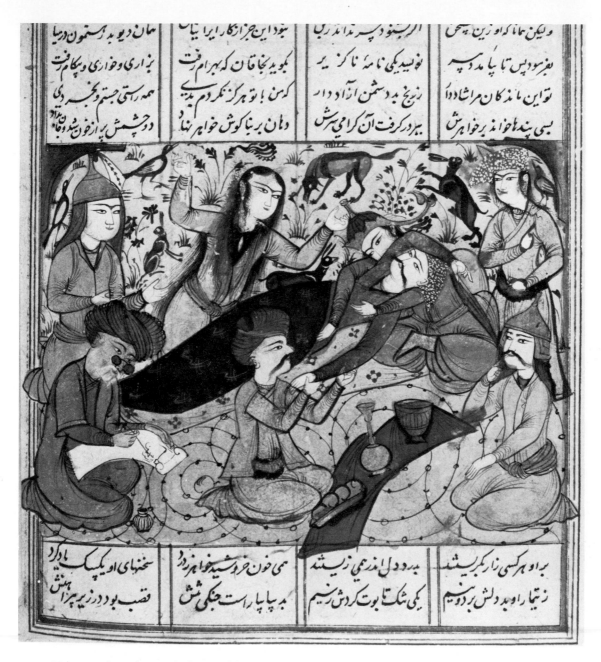

1574 Mourning for Bahram Chubina. Isfahan, 1650

1575 Gurdiya displaying her prowess. Isfahan, 1650

1576 Khusraw hunting. Isfahan, 1650

1580 Standing youth. Isfahan/India, 17th c

1572 ƒ458b A captive led away after Khusraw's defeat of Bahram Chubina.
13.3 × 19.7 cm (plus banners in upper iargin).

1573 ƒ462a Bahram Chubina at the court of the Khaqan.
Inferior artist again. 15.8 × 15.8 cm.

1574 ƒ464b Mourning for Bahram Chubina, murdered by Qulun.
Note the *munshi* on the left, wearing spectacles.
11.4 × 15.8 cm. *See illustration.*

1575 ƒ468a Gurdiya, sister of Bahram Chubina, displaying her military accomplishments before Khusraw and his queen.
The latter's face slightly smudged.
18.4 × 17.8 cm. *See illustration.*

1576 ƒ471b Khusraw hunting.
16.5 × 15.8 cm. *See illustration.*

1577 ƒ482a The court of Ardashir III.
12.1 × 16.5 cm.

1578 ƒ483a Piruz, son of Khusraw, dragged at the horse's tail, Queen Purandukht watching from the horizon.
12.7 × 19.7 cm.

1579 ƒ486a The Persian general Rustam slain by the Arab leader Sa'd b. Waqqas at the battle of Qadisiyya.
No attempt has been made to differentiate the Arab's costume or arms.
14 × 20.2 cm (plus banners in upper margin).

[ƒ 492 is a modern replacement, and the original ƒ probably carried a miniature of the death of Mahwi and his sons.]

Album (1580, 1581)
Ryl Indian Drawings 12

1580 ƒ1b Tinted drawing.
Standing youth with bottle and cup.
He wears a turban loosely tied round a floppy fur-lined cap; an overcoat and a voluminous magenta scarf are thrown about his shoulders. The drawing and, in places, the finish (e.g. the ear) are not up to Riza's standard, and this may well be an Indian copy (perhaps mid seventeenth century) of an original by Riza or a close follower.
15.8 × 7.6 cm. *See illustration.*

1581 ƒ9a Shah 'Abbas, the Mughal ambassador Khan 'Alam, and a page.
Signed, *raqam i kamina Riza-i 'Abbasi.*
This miniature, whose authenticity is doubtful, was published and discussed by the present writer in *Burlington*, February 1972, pp 58-63. The face of the page almost suggests Afzal al-Husayni.
20.2 × 14.6 cm. *See colour Pl XV.*

Album (1582)
Ryl Indian Drawings 6

1582 No 15 Small circular watercolour of very fine quality after a European original of the penitent Magdalene, illuminated by a ray of light from above.
Signed, *raqam 'Ali Quli.*
Diameter 4.4 cm. *See colour pl XVI.*

The Post-Safawid Period

The Qajar Style

Only two examples of this style, typical, though not quite of first-rate quality, are to be found in the John Rylands Library, on the covers of MS 946, and a lengthy account of it would therefore be out of place here.

As already noted, a Europeanizing style founded on Flemish models became fashionable during the last half-century of Safawid rule, its leading exponents being Shafi' 'Abbasi, Muhammad Zaman, and 'Ali Quli Jabbadar (No **1582**). During the eighteenth century the relics of this style were combined with western European (probably Dutch and English) elements under the patronage of Nadir Shah (1736-47) and of Karim Khan Zand at Shiraz (1750-79). Muhammad Sadiq, whose work covers the second half of the century, seems to have been the master who successfully combined these elements into what became the court style of the early Qajar period. Miniature painting and the illustration of manuscripts gave way to a great extent to large portraits and other paintings in oils, and the meticulous decoration of small objects – pen-boxes, mirror-cases, and caskets – of papier-mâché, painted on a surface of fine gesso and covered with transparent lacquer or varnish. This technique had been used for book-covers from early Safawid times (see above, p 242). In the early Qajar period many of the best examples are the work of Najaf 'Ali and his school at Isfahan, to which the present examples appear to be related.

Hafiz: Diwan (1583-1584)
Ryl Pers 946
Unillustrated *nasta'liq* text on gold-sprinkled paper, in 2 columns of 11 lines to the page:
13.3 × 7.9 cm. W.S. 8.9 × 4.4 cm. Illuminated heading of rather poor quality on *f* 1b. No colophon, but probably second half of the seventeenth century.

The painted lacquer covers warrant the inclusion of this manuscript in the catalogue. They probably date from *c* 1825, and appear to be Isfahan work in the style of Najaf 'Ali. Plain red doublures.

1583 Front cover.
An elderly dervish, perhaps intended for the poet Sa'di, seated on a tiger skin holding a book; beside him is a young and beautiful dervish with crutch and begging-bowl. Landscape and buildings behind; a stream with ducks in the foreground.
See illustration.

1584 Back cover.
A younger dervish, probably representing Hafiz, seated, supported by his crutch and holding a rosary. His youthful attendant dervish appears to be addressing him respectfully. Background etc. exactly as front cover. Small chips.
See illustration.

1583 Sa'di and a young dervish. Isfahan, c 1825

Appendix: The 'Aja'ib al-Makhluqat of Qazwini

As there are three Persian copies of this work, all fully illustrated, in the Library, a note on the work and its author, with a comparative table showing the incidence of illustrations in its various parts and aligning the John Rylands copies with notable Qazwini manuscripts in other collections, may be usefully appended.

Professor E. G. Browne wrote (*A Literary History of Persia*, London 1906, Vol II, p 482):

Another geographer and cosmographer of a less scientific type [sc. than Yaqut] is Zakariyya b. Muhammad b. Mahmud al-Qazwini, the author of two works (both published by Wüstenfeld in 1848-49). One of these is entitled *'Aja'ibu'l-Makhluqat* ('The Marvels of Creation', or, rather 'of created things'), and treats of the solar system, the stars and other heavenly bodies, and the animal, vegetable and mineral kingdoms, and also contains a section on monsters and bogies of various kinds. [There follow a few lines on Qazwini's other work, the *Athar al-Bilad*, or *Monuments of the Lands*] The former of these two books is by far the most popular in the East, and manuscripts, often with miniatures, both of the original [Arabic] and still more of the Persian translation, are common. The latter, however, is in reality by far the more important and interesting, for not only does it contain a great deal of useful geographical information, but also much valuable biographical material, including, under the towns to which they belonged, a great number of the Persian poets. . . . The geographical information, too, though inferior in point of accuracy to that given by Yaqut and the earlier geographers, is full of interesting and entertaining matter. It is rather curious that though there is no mention made of England, the account of the Sixth Clime includes an article on Ireland, with some account of whale-fishing, while a long notice is devoted to Rome. Under the Seventh Clime we find accounts of the ordeals by fire, by water, and by battle in vogue amongst the Franks; of witchcraft, witch-finding, and witch-burning; and of the Varangian Fiord. Indeed, I know few more readable and entertaining works in Arabic than this. . . . The first edition was written in A.D. 1263, and the second, considerably enlarged and modified, in A.D. 1276. The author was born at Qazwin, in Persia, in A.D. 1203, lived for a while at Damascus about A.D. 1232, was Qadi (Judge) of Wasit and Hilla under the last Caliph al-Musta'sim, and died in A.D. 1283. His *'Aja'ibu'l-Makhluqat* is dedicated to 'Ata Malik-i-Juwayni, the author of the *Ta'rikh-i-Jahan-gusha*.

No apology is required for quoting at length, on a literary subject, from the greatest Persian scholar England has produced.

The manuscripts compared below are as follows; the numbers assigned to them (in chronological order) will be used in the comparative tables of miniatures.

1 John Rylands Library Pers MS 37 (*c* 1440; see above, Nos **1-404**).

2 British Library, MS Add 235644.

453 miniatures, many damaged and defaced, in the Shiraz-Timurid style. Dated 845/1441. *Robinson B*, p 24; *Titley*, No 238, p 87.

3 Royal Asiatic Society, MS 178.

150 miniatures in the Commercial Turkman style, attributed in the colophon to 'Abd al-Karim. Copyist, Muhammad b. Muhammad called Baqqal ('the Grocer'). Undated; *c* 1475. *VAM 1965*, pl 7, 8; *VAM 1967*, No 128, p 96; B. W. Robinson, 'R.A.S. MS 178: an unrecorded Persian painter' in *JRAS* 1970, pp 203-209.

4 Bodleian Library, MS Laud Or.132 (Ethé 399).

349 miniatures in the Commercial Turkman style. Undated (defective at beginning and end); *c* 1480-90. *Robinson B*, Nos 146-497, pp 32-47.

5 Chester Beatty Library, MS 212.

530 miniatures in Shiraz-Safawid style. Copyist, Murshid *al-kātib* al-Shirazi called 'Attar ('the Druggist'). Dated 25 Jumada I 952/4 August 1545. *CB*, Vol II, No 212, p 75; *BWG*, No 176, pl XCVI, XCVII; *VAM 1967*, No 144, p 102.

6 Cambridge University Library, MS Nn 3.74.

147 miniatures in Qazwin style. Dated 16 Jumada II 974/29 December 1566. *BWG*, No 204; *VAM 1951*, No 76; *VAM 1952*, pl 22.

7 John Rylands Library, Pers MS 2 (1619; see above, Nos **823-1125**).

8 John Rylands Library, Pers MS 3 (1632; see above, Nos **1126-1480**).

Contents of the work

Incidence of miniatures in the eight manuscripts listed above, according to the adjoining list of contents:

Contents	MS	1	2	3	4	5	6	7	8
A *Prefatory Matter*									
1 Praise of God and the Prophet.	A 1-3	17	3	1	1	1	–	4	–
2 The Author.									
3 Four Prefaces.									
a On Marvels.									
b On Classification.									
c On Significances.									
d On various Beings.									
B *Things Above*									
1 The Planets (including Sun and Moon).	B 1	7	5	–	9	5	–	12	10
2 The Stars (Fixed Stars, Constellations, the Zodiac).	2	33	39	21	21	72	–	20	46
3 Angels.	3	–	5	8	11	9	5	12	6
4 Time and Chronology.	4	1	–	–	–	–	–	1	1
C *Things Below*									
1 The Elements and Celestial Phenomena (*Fire, Air*).	C 1	6	1	–	1	1	2	1	1
2 *Water*: The Encircling Ocean and the Seven Seas, their Islands and Fauna.	2	36	56	18	96	58	6	63	61
a The China Sea.									
b The Indian Ocean.									
c The Persian Gulf.									
d The Red Sea.									
e The Sea of Zanzibar.									
f The Western Sea.									
g The Sea of Jaraz.									
3 *Earth*: The Seven Climates.	3	1	1	–	–	1	–	1	–
a Earthquakes and Subsidences.	a	–	–	–	–	–	–	–	–
b Mountains.	b	5	12	4	14	8	–	6	10
c Rivers and Springs.	c	–	4	–	1	6	–	1	1
d Pits and Chasms.	d	1	1	–	–	–	–	–	–
e Minerals.	e	–	–	–	–	–	–	–	–
4 *The Vegetable Kingdom*									
a Trees (arranged alphabetically).	4 a	64	55	28	30	63	–	35	33
b Plants and Herbs (arranged alphabetically).	b	131	128	–	17	115	–	–	–
5 *The Animal Kingdom.*									
a Man: racial qualities and customs, with anecdotes; the human soul; the human anatomy; man-made wonders, trades and manufactures, automata, talismans, magic and *jinn*.	5 a	4	13	18	36	42	13	48	66
b Beasts (arranged alphabetically).	b	38	41	23	37	41	42	45	42
c Birds (arranged alphabetically).	c	53	54	25	53	54	52	46	46
d Reptiles and Insects (arranged alphabetically).	d	8	17	–	25	34	24	13	30
e Strange beings from remote parts, hybrids, and monstrosities.	e	–	20	1	–	18	3	2	–

The above should only be taken as a general guide; manuscripts and versions vary considerably in their contents and arrangement, and Qazwini's elaborate subdividing has been simplified and abridged. But it should provide a broad idea of the work with special reference to illustrated copies.

Index of authors

Index of painters
and calligraphers

Index of subjects

Concordance of manuscripts

Library number followed by catalogue numbers

Ryl Pers 2   823-1125
Ryl Pers 3   1126-1480
Ryl Pers 6   550-554
Ryl Pers 8   613-631
Ryl Pers 9   431-474
Ryl Pers 12   661-667
Ryl Pers 18   687-690
Ryl Pers 20   562-566
Ryl Pers 23   681-685
Ryl Pers 24   425-430
Ryl Pers 28   805-819
Ryl Pers 29   686
Ryl Pers 31   673-676
Ryl Pers 35   668-670
Ryl Pers 36   405-423
Ryl Pers 37   1-404
Ryl Pers 43   677-680
Ryl Pers 45   555-561, 632-635
Ryl Pers 49   691-693

Ryl Pers 55   567-574
Ryl Pers 856   636-651
Ryl Pers 868   660
Ryl Pers 907   801-803
Ryl Pers 908   671, 672
Ryl Pers 909   1481-1579
Ryl Pers 910   481-549, 769-800
Ryl Pers 932   575-612
Ryl Pers 933   475-478, 694-768
Ryl Pers 945   652-655
Ryl Pers 946   1583, 1584
Ryl Turk 3   479, 480
Robinson Pers. 1   656-659
Indian Drawings: Album 6   1582
Indian Drawings: Album 12   820, 1580, 1581
Indian Drawings: Album 13   822
Indian Drawings: Album 16   424
Indian Drawings: Album 18   804